THE STORYBOOK ADVENTURES OF MARY MILLER

MONTANA WOMEN TRUE FAITH TRUE DEVOTION ONE GENERATION AT A TIME

Charity Lovshin

ARCHWAY
PUBLISHING

Archway Publishing books may be ordered through booksellers or by contacting:

Archway Publishing
1663 Liberty Drive
Bloomington, IN 47403
www.archwaypublishing.com
844-669-3957

Interior Image Credit: My Grandmother

ISBN: 978-1-6657-1686-4 (sc)
ISBN: 978-1-6657-1854-7 (hc)
ISBN: 978-1-6657-1687-1 (e)

Library of Congress Control Number: 2021925665

Print information available on the last page.

Archway Publishing rev. date: 01/29/2022

GENERATIONS OF WOMEN IN MONTANA
IN THE BEGINNING

Five Generations: From Back—Left to Right
Mary, Caroline, Montana, Linda, Bertha

CONTENTS

PREFACE

William McClurg and Caroline Grady McClurg

EACH generation of my women in my family—beginning with my great-great-grandmother, Caroline Grady, increased in knowledge of truth and was the means in helping the next generation learn how to make their life better, how to be wiser, and how to put knowledge into action.

My great-great-grandmother, my great-grandmother, my grand-mother, my mother, myself, and my daughters, each have learned from the last generation how to bring an increase of goodness and knowledge to our individual lives and to the world. We learn valuable and useable knowledge as we study the lives of our ancestors, and we learn how to put that knowledge into action by becoming stronger and more courageous as we live life.

My dad asked me when I began compiling this book about my grandma, Mary Miller Roggia, "Why did you start writing this book about your grandmother?"

As a child growing up, I heard my grandma tell stories about her growing up in Butte, Montana, and as I listened to her stories, I began to be interested in Butte and Montana History. My grandmother's mother was even named after the State of Montana.

I also loved that my grandfather, Bruno Roggia, was Italian and that he was a prisoner of war stationed in Montana. The country and people of Italy always remind me of romance, and I am a hopeless romantic.

I was fascinated by my grandmother's stories and wondered how she could still love her father when he did so many awful things to her family. This is what fascinated me, her love for even those that could have caused her to be an angry individual.

Really, her father did not know any better how to live his life than the way he lived it, because he did not have anyone to teach him anything different than what he knew and experienced his entire life. He just kept acting on the bad traditions of many generations before him. My grandmother knew this and held no hate in her heart towards him. This is the amazing thing about my grandmother; she is full of love, no matter what trials and tests she has faced in this life, love always won.

This novel is an example of how love can be exhibited in every circumstance, especially, through adversity and trial. My grandmother's story shows that having love in your heart leads to true happiness and joy.

Another quality that I love about my grandmother's life, is the story of her mother. Her mother was courageous and strong, and because of knowing her story, I too desire to be courageous and strong. I knew that if I wrote this book and learned about the history of the amazing women in my eternal family, these learned lessons would mold me into the woman I am meant to become.

This book is a gift. A gift to my grandmother from her Heavenly Father, and I was merely an instrument in my Heavenly Fathers hands at bringing her magical story to life.

My grandmother grew up in meager circumstances, but this did not stop her from generously giving to her family, her friends, and even strangers. She is still giving at ninety-four. She has given to her family a special and important kind of love that cannot be duplicated.

Although my grandmother's childhood years were full of continual struggle and indigency, her conquerable spirit came through triumphantly.

I desire to give my grandmother something she can read about her life, because she loves to read; and maybe, one day make her life's story into a motion picture, because she loves to watch movies.

Sometimes, in life we don't get the recognition from those we give to, and to my grandmother recognition didn't matter, because she gave out of the pure love in her enormous heart.

Many of us travel through mortality, not always receiving the proper thanks we deserve, but there's only one being we ultimately need to please, and that's God—our Heavenly Father.

This book is a thank you from Heavenly Father to my grandmother, and I know He's saying to her, "Well done, my good and faithful servant, well done! Thank you, My wonderful daughter, Mary, for fulfilling all the work I sent out for you to do on this mortal earth. You have been a valiant daughter and have accomplished My work, and here is My gift to you. I love you dearly."

I also love my grandmother dearly. Her example has been a framework for me to follow all my life. Her courage and kindness will always live in my heart. She is selfless and has always been there for me when I have needed her in any way. She is my example of courage, strength, obedience, and perseverance. I love you Grandma and am glad I was used as Heavenly Father's instrument in giving you this gift regarding your life.

Love
Charity Lovshin

ACKNOWLEDGMENTS

I want to thank my parents, Linda and Louis Lovshin, for giving me the courage to follow my dreams and for their emotional and financial support in the process.

I want to thank my grandma, Mary Miller Roggia, for telling me her stories and for being a strong influence in my life.

I would like to thank my professors at Montana Tech of the University of Montana for taking a chance on me, for believing in me, for letting me express myself without restriction, and for helping me develop talents I didn't even know I had. I love you all!

Henrietta Shirk
Glen Southergill
Pat Munday
Tim Kober
Nick Hawthorne
Jim Tracy
Chad Okrusch
Kay Eccleston

INTRODUCTION

WRITING this book has taught me who I want to be and who I can become; and I believe, whoever reads it, will find that same strength and courage which can, if they allow themselves to feel that strength and courage, will naturally bring them to a more peaceful place in their lives—developing a lasting strength that can only bring them forward in a positive direction.

When individuals develop the kind of strength, courage, and love that can be found in the pages of this book and then pass it on to their children, generations can be changed for the better.

When individuals understand how to be actively engaged in changing generations to build a better world, a better world will exist. God wants my posterity to see, as they read this book, that we can make it through anything with a little bit of faith, devotion, determination, strength, courage, and most importantly—lots of love.

We live in a world that wants the easy way. This story shows how one woman can change the world one generation at a time, and that there is no easy way to get through this life, except through having strength and faith.

We must speak. We learn when others speak, and I know that I need to speak about my grandmother's life, because her life will make an important impact and difference in the world.

My grandmother is not embarrassed about her life, she is proud of the way she came out of it. It is not fun to remember hard and difficult experiences, but if we have learned the lessons that we were supposed to learn from those experiences and challenges, that is when we rejoice in our troubles and trials and feel good about sharing them with others.

Through our individual stories, we can help others be better and know better. If we do not know better than previous generations, if we do not act better than previous generations, we cannot be better. If we did not learn about how we can be better than we will never be better. We will still be making the same mistakes.

This book will inspire many people. My grandmother's life was not the only life lived this way. She lived during a time of struggle and poverty and best of all, building. Writing this book will change the way people look at life, and it might even give someone else courage to get up and do something more which is why I am so passionate about publishing this book.

CHAPTER 1

My Journey Begins

I was born in Renton, King County, Washington, on the twentieth of May 1928. My life's adventure story begins with my birth; that's how we all come into this world, right? We aren't given the option to choose which families we come to before we are born—or maybe, we are. Maybe, there is a counsel in heaven before our birth and we are given various choices, and maybe, just maybe, there's a reason we choose a particular family combined with specific time and place. Yes, I'm sure we have an active voice in the choosing process. As I recall my childhood, I dare say, I might just figure out the reason I chose this one.

After entering the third year of my already adventurous life, Mom beautifully explained to me the story of my birth as we sat on the broken-down steps of our almost burnt down house, "Mary, you were born on a magical day. The crimson cherry blossoms were as pink as pinched cheeks and were blooming like popcorn popping in a hot, orange-red blazing fire. The exceptionally wide emerald leaves seemed to be bursting full of life and vigor as the warm, lemony sun illuminated their dewy petals, and just as lively and vigorous as they were on that mystical day, is just as you turned out to be."

The day Mom told me this, is my initial memory, which preceded my second memory of me getting into trouble. I'm not saying, I was an unpleasant child, but mom was fully aware of me being full of life and vigor at a very young age; whether she truly appreciated my unprecedented spunk is another story, but I'm not being asked to write that story.

It is 2002. I'm seventy-four years old, and my curious granddaughter, Charity, is asking me, "Grandma, what is your first memory?"

Charity is sitting here in my kitchen recording me with my old, black 1974 cassette tape recorder, asking inquiring questions concerning my early childhood.

Charity is beautiful at twenty-seven years old and reminds me a bit of myself in those very same years--petite, with dark-brown hair flowing down against the lower-middle of her slim back as she stands with poise at five-foot-four.

A good story is what I love, and Charity loves to write a good story, so I intentionally and happily engage in her probing questions.

"The earliest recollection of my young life beginning is living in Renton, King County, Washington," I tell her.

AS my mind gradually and happily wanders back to the beginning of my life—as far back as I can remember—I'm three years old, living near the deep-blue, cool ocean. The vast openness of the large ocean fascinates me as the salty air and billowing waves crash into the sharp, beaten down, silver, smooth rocks like rolling thunder. The calculating tide rises and lowers, presenting its powerful influence against the sands of the beach circulating them back into the ocean floor and onto the beach again, and I ponder if the tide preplans its journeyings.

I wonder where the ever-changing tide travels to each day, and as I do, I imagine being like the rolling tide and exploring the unknown. I'm destined to be an adventurer, exploring the world like a free-spirited pirate with no obstacles able to possibly obstruct my path.

No one gets in the way of pirates! No one!

As I ponder the intentions of the tide while building my magical sandcastle village, my tiny, pale feet purposefully sink deeper into the sandy grayish-white beach, and the coarse, yet, soft sand, slowly covers the tips of my disappearing, crinkly, water-filled toes.

Life is generally that way, isn't it? There is so much coarseness, but if we inadvertently focus on the visible coarseness, and we consciously choose not to come to the sandy beach because of it, we will never get to experience the unforeseen softness.

All I feel is the unforeseen softness as my happy toes slip deeper into the inviting sand. Life is a special, precious God-given gift. A precious gift full of exciting, unexpected, and some expected surprises and magical wonder if we allow ourselves to dream and believe.

The sandy village I'm excitedly building purposefully surrounds a real life rusty-brown, cedar wood, bruised rowboat. In my imagination, the jagged, baseball-sized hole in the bow of the boat was brought into existence when the boat ricocheted off pointed rocks while traveling in the angry riptide. The lovely couple who traveled in the boat before it crashed were caught in the riptide's fury, but this riptide pulled them into the shore instead of pulling them out to sea.

It's deliberate fate, I say.

The magical village of whitish-grey sand is being created by me because of the couple who I imagine crash landed onto this waiting, welcoming shore in this rowboat of destined love.

The lovely couple shared this fated boat because the fancy cruise ship they were traveling on surprisingly sunk deep into the uninviting, mysterious ocean on that harsh, dark night after violently crashing into an unseen iceberg almost completely hidden under the oceans top surface, and while waiting for rescuers, the couple's boat drifted rapidly into the spine-chilling emptiness as the frustrated wind picked up its pace sending the ocean waters in a hurry to escape the present destruction.

They were perfect strangers when they coincidentally arrived on their life-saving boat that cold, cruel night, and because no one immediately came to their rescue after miraculously arriving on the deserted beach, together; they had no choice but to build a village of their own.

In the lengthy process of building, love was inevitable. The couple's only option and hope was to build this soft, sandy city out of selfless love. I am going to build something out of love someday. I'm not sure what is in my immediate building out of love future, but I feel the magical and destined building process being intertwined into my very sinews and bones.

My siblings and I, and our friends, often play on this magnificent beach for hours surrounding this old, mystical, broken boat, pretending we are explorative pirates sailing the curious and endless sea.

Our modest-sized family pirate ship, with our red, white, and blue striped family flag flying high on the bow of the ship, always crash lands on this lonely, deserted island at the end of our journey.

The slow swelling, moderate storm that turns unexpectedly violent in the cold, dark night brings us purposefully toward the island, overtaking our every attempt at convincing the stubborn wind to pull our sturdy ship back out to sea. The piercing edges of the razer-like rocks beyond the far shore leave us no hope of water not inevitably slipping into the waiting, laughing hull.

Human life as we presently know it, doesn't exist on the lonely, isolated island, except for a tribe of islanders that speak an unknown foreign language. The islanders don't want undesirable intruders on their now-conquered island, so expected war becomes unavoidable.

We fight the dark-skinned, scantily dressed islanders for the land.

Of course, we are obviously always the victors, but we are a kind family of traveling pirates, so we justly divide the valuable land between us. Not one precious soul dies in the battle, because we settle on peace before immediate death is inevitable.

My young, imaginative mind is my sole outlet to experience worldly adventures. I become so lost and swept away in my wanted fantasies and wonderous dreams that I lose complete track of earthly time, and after I come back to my unwanted reality, I notice by the placement of the lemony-orange sun setting in the West, mom will be angrily curious as to my whereabouts.

Finally, after being fully engaged in my fascinating adventure on the deserted, sandy beach, I eventually arrive back to my humble home. Mom is obviously upset with me, and I'm not initially quite sure why. To say that I am ultimately surprised is another matter entirely; although, I might not be completely surprised that her increasing anger has something to do with the placement of the dying, crimson sun and its association with my arrival home.

I speedily run to my small, modest bed to conceal myself underneath it. Mom clearly knows where I am, because underneath my small broken-down bed is a place I hide often when I'm in apparent trouble. I'm only three years old, but already underneath my bed is a well-known place of false security.

Mom is swinging her heavy crutches carelessly under the fragile, single bed, attempting to intentionally coax me out from underneath it. I feel a complete sense of intimidation and over-anxiety as the silver crutches closely approach the right side of my tiny hip.

Before the crutches accomplish their intended design, to straight away free me from my now obvious hiding place, my short forehead unexpectedly affixes itself to a loose three-inch copper mattress spring. The razor-sharp edge of the broken spring creeps itself—slowly it seems—into my tender, pale, three-year-old flesh.

I instantly hear a slight ripping sound as I pull my torn forehead away from the culprit spring too quickly, and deep, crimson blood swiftly drips down my now-swollen face from my bruised forehead to my nose until it finally reaches my thin, pink hued lips, instantly staining my already torn worn-out purple shirt a deep red.

∽

MY mom, Montana Irene Fogleman, was born November 19, 1902. She is named after the state she was born in; although, people always call her Monta.

Mom's parents, Bertha McClurg and Nixon Fogleman, came from Iowa to homestead in Montana. Many people from all over the States were migrating to homestead in Montana in those years. Land was extremely cheap, and there was plenty of it to choose from. Grandma and Grandpa thought Montana was such a beautiful state, so they decided to call Mom, Montana.

Mom unexpectedly contracted a devastating, irreversible disease sweeping through the nation in 1908. Polio. She was almost six years old when the new, deforming disease swept through Red Lodge like an angry, dusty whirlwind on the dry, unexpected plains.

Mom initially grew up in Red Lodge, Montana. Other parts of Montana were infected with polio too. Polio seemed to viciously attack at least one intended child in every family. Doctors were seemingly bewildered on how to treat the numbing disease. It was eventually discovered that contaminated water and food might have been a leading cause in contracting polio.

Mom became deathly sick the year polio came to deliberately alter her life forever, and as a result, the right side of her body become forever numb, never destined to recover. Although, Mom eventually regained the use of her right arm and hand, from her hip down, feeling was no longer present.

Mom had to be carefully carried around like a small child for a few years while she learned how to be completely independent. Her doctor, Dr. Adams, gave her a set of sturdy crutches, and as she learned how to use the helpful crutches, independence slowly came to pass. Dr. Adams described her as being unstoppable afterwards.

Mom began attending the first grade when she was nine. Since she was six years old, she always had crutches, and her slow recovery, after contracting polio; prevented her from attending school for three years.

Mom graduated from the eighth grade in 1919. There was even an article in the Billings Gazette on Saturday, July 5, 1919, that said—

DIPLOMAS ARE GIVEN TO CARBON COUNTY PUPILS

Number is larger than before, tribute to teachers
Red Lodge July 4, 1919

County superintendent, Asgerd Haaland, and Deputy Superintendent, Idella Ray, are mailing out today to 71 children of the County diplomas certifying that they have completed eighth grade work and are eligible for admission to high school next fall. This is the largest number of eighth grade diplomas ever awarded at any one time and does not include the children who have completed the eighth grade in the city schools, says the **Picket – Journal**.

Ms. Haaland said yesterday that she was more than pleased with the results of the work in the schools of the County during the season just closed. In addition to the diplomas being mailed out, she said, "There will be a few more awarded later when the grades of several students are transferred from other counties.

Those who will receive diplomas this week are from **Joliet County:**

Willa Anderson, Ivor Cheney, Ray Jensen, Audrey Seright, Eugene Lindsay, France Christopherson, William White, Merritt Dell, Agnes Zimerman, **Montana Fogleman**, Margaret Bell, and **Frances Fogleman**.

Because Mom was obliged to attend first grade at nine, she graduated with her older sister Frances.

I'm so extremely proud of Mom graduating from 8th grade, considering her stricken state back then. It must have required considerable efforts and significant determination to attend school with cumbersome crutches, and school kids can be so intentionally cruel. Awkward crutches, however, never prevent Mom from fulfilling what needs to be accomplished. She is exceptionally strong and courageous.

BACK to underneath my bed and my now crimson, bloody face and floor.

After hearing my frenzied cries from the horrified sight of quickly dripping blood, and Mom finding out that my, now scarlet forehead had a considerable slice of open flesh missing, she felt instant compassion on me, helped me from underneath the bed, and quickly drove me to the doctor in our old beat-up black Ford.

After eventually arriving to the small-town doctor's office and him giving us his non-fatal diagnosis, he carefully sews my ½ inch wound tightly up with about nine stiff, itchy stiches, and says, "Mary, you will always have a permanent scar, and since you have been such an excellent patient, I'm going to give you a dime."

Then, the greatest event happened so far in my entire young life, the good doctor gently, and ever so slowly it seemed, cupped his right hand directly under my petite left hand, and with his free hand placed in it, a shiny, round, silver dime.

As I quickly embraced the circular, magnificent, sparkling dime—afraid that he might take it back—holding it with admiration in the open air, making sure it was indeed genuine; the sun's shiny amber rays—purposefully it seemed—shone brilliantly through the open window as a small breeze filled up the twenty-by-twenty-foot room, finding the small silver circle, creating sparkles like diamonds on a gold band while sending marvelous, deep rainbow prisms across the entire now larger than life room.

Okay, possibly, my imagination is getting the best of me today, and I'm still feeling sort of romantic about the couple who fell in love on the sandy beach. Afterall, it is 1931, and my family's circumstance are indigent, so receiving a shiny, obviously new dime is like getting an insignificant fortune.

This first, or rather second, devastating turned magical memory is when I remember my life starting.

I unintentionally understand more about real life than that of the common well-to-do average three-year-old, not by choice, I grant you, but by living my unique set of circumstances called life.

CHAPTER 2

The Old Man

MY young, indigent life's rollercoaster adventure ride really begins when my family leaves Renton, so I must inform you of the calamitous reason we are inadvertently leaving and moving for the multiple time in my adolescence.

My irresponsible father.

Before you immediately judge me in being overly harsh towards my father, you must understand my compelling story.

My father was an integral developer in the wonderful process of bringing me into this world, and for that, I am exceptionally grateful, but he wasn't much of an involved and present father figure in trying to shape a naïve, vital, inexperienced woman as myself into the most productive individual that would lead her to her greatest possible future.

My father, The Old Man, who I have always referred to him as, was born in Yugoslavia. Yugoslavia is well known for its population of over 2,000,000 people and land size of 21,851 square miles.

The Old Man's real name is Marko Ribicic, but when he came to America, he changed it to Joseph Miller. After his low-life father left his mother, The Old Man, his brother, his sister, and his mother, left Yugoslavia and moved to Bremen, Germany.

"Living in Bremen was more ideal and practical for our small family," says The Old Man. "After my father left us, Mom needed to move to a smaller town to survive."

The Old Man continues explaining to me that Bremen, compared to Yugoslavia, was a significantly smaller city consisting of a moderate population of over 200,000 people which covered 216 square miles of productive land.

He says, "Bremen is known for its production of dark, rich, brown coffee, sticky-white rice, sweet-cream corn, and stiff-grassy wheat."

He continues, "I always had plenty to eat in Bremen, because we lived on a modest farm. We grew our own herbs, vegetables, fruits, and wheat. When Mama made wheat bread, she would make enough to last two weeks.

I would spend many afternoons watching her prepare and make bread. She would swiftly whisk the dark yellow, slimy egg till it was firm and a foamy cream color, adding just a tidbit of water to the egg wash before smoothly brushin' the very top of the pale brown, floury bread with it. Then she'd place the yeasty bread in the old, shiny, hot copper oven.

While the much-anticipated wheat bread was bakin', Mama finely mashed a few cloves of fresh, steamed, white garlic; eventually adding them to warm, yellow butter which was slowly simmering on the warm stove.

While the yellow cream butter and pungent garlic simmered, she added fresh, finely chopped, green herbs from our 60 X 60-foot blustering garden.

After the golden, warm bread emerged from the hot copper oven, Mama placed two buttery dipping sauces and four thick fluffy pieces of wheat bread on two shiny, silver bent plates, bringing them to where we were anxiously waiting; sitting on rusty, bronze metal chairs under a four-by-four foot faded crimson table.

The outside of the bread was always a crispy, golden brown and the immediate inside, soft and malleable. It didn't take John and me long before we finished our first helping that we were beggin' for another delightful servin'.

That warm, buttery bread was so darn tasty, and we ate so much of it that when we were done eatin', we would both swell up like oversize circus balloons."

The Old Man goes on to tell me about the town of Bremen, saying, "During the weekdays, at harvest time, I would travel to town to get dry, red wine and bitter, pale olive oil for Mama while she milked the cow and prepared the mutton.

Sometimes, Mama would smoke the mutton, but most the time she prepared a brine, chopping the greenish-white cabbage real fine before placing it in the brine. Then, she layered the mutton with white, heavy salt, leaving it to ferment for a few days. Finally, she would cook the sour kraut brine and mutton together. This delicious meal would last us a few days which helped feed us during cold, bitter winter months.

We ate three times a day and drank sweet, red-and-white aged wine with lunch and supper."

His smile slowly widens as he continues saying, "There were all kinds of dances and fun for young people to do in Bremen. Many of the older, richer folks liked to spend time at the ancient museums and other famous places with ancient artifacts, but not me, John, and the other youth.

Mama generously gave me and John, my twin brother, money to see the curious animals, the fantastic real-life plays, and the bustling people in the crowded city; while Georgia, my helpful younger sister of three years stayed home faithfully helping Mama keep well our humble home.

John inherited our father's name. Ivan Ribicic was my old man's Yugoslavian name, but John was his nickname. John was born first, and I came a brief, two-minutes after. Father was not with our small family long before he and Mama divorced, and Father moved to tropical South America shortly after Georgia turned the tender age of three."

The Old Man proceeds to tell me the story of him and his old mule, saying, "In my youth, I was a bit of a troublemaker, Mary. When I was a spunky, curious lad of about eleven years, Mama asked me and John to finish our chores. We needed our trusted ol' mule's help to plow the hardened, winter garden ground, and on this particular day, the stubborn mule wouldn't budge from his resting place. He lazily laid there on the dusty, ol', faded, dirt ground chewing the already drying up left-over, crunchy, faded green hay from the previous day.

In attempts to encourage the ol' mule, John and I loaded its worn, brown double-sided leather satchel up on each side with food and water hoping the ol' mule would understand that we wanted him to get up and go to aid us in cleaving the surface of the dried-up soil. But the stubborn, ol' mule wouldn't budge."

John says to me, "What we gonna do now Joe, he doesn't want to go?"

"I'm gonna make him go John, come here."

I hurriedly sprint to the barn to find some dried up ol' firewood and some dry stick matches, and John speedily comes running after me. After collecting the firewood in our overflowing arms and finding some matches in father's ol', brown, tool splintered hutch, we come back to where the ol' mule is layin'.

The brownish-black ol' mule was nine years old, and his once shiny coat was now full of highlights of white and grey peekin' through. From a young'un, he was always willing to work and dedicate himself to our growing family, but his spirit seemed to be slowly dying on this particular day.

You see, I thought that if I built a small, but strong, sunset, blazing fire right underneath the now stubborn ol' mule, he would have no other option but to get up and go.

Ha-ha, I tell ya what, he swiftly left his cozy layin' spot and ran like the dickens when those blazin' flames began reachin' the backside of his ... well, you know.

The ultimate problem though was that he ran into the wide-open mountain range. John and I quickly rushed to catch him before he stranded too far, but we couldn't catch up with him.

After all this commotion, we see Mama come out if the chicken house, and after hearing the commotion coming from the yelping mule and two screaming dumb boys, Mama questions us, "What you gone and done to him?"

I says to her, "I built a fire underneath the lazy ol' mule to make him get up and go."

She says to us, "Don't worry, it'll be back. It'll just be up there a little while."

Well, the crazy confused ol' mule surely came back alright; but it was a couple lengthy days later, and he had a damaged leg. We guessed he was runnin' so fast that he gone and hurt himself, breakin' his leg in the process.

Bright, crimson blood came oozing out of an open slice of tender flesh in his upper right thigh. He was gone for so long that some of the blood had already hardened and dried like deer jerky, making it harder to patch him up.

I got a nasty, good licken' that night behind the faded red chicken coop with Father's tan-aged leather horse strap."

The Old Man says, "It was normal kid stuff, you know."

The Old Man continues, saying, "One day—in the humid, rainy spring—I went to talk to Mama about wanting to see the entire world."

I tell her, "I want to see the magnificent world Mama, so John and I decided we would begin by traveling to South America and live with Dad."

She didn't want us to go.

She said, "No, you're not going to go."

"But six months after I talked to Mama, she gave us boys her blessing."

"Go ahead," she tells us.

So, we did.

John and I left Germany on the ship Manifest SS Fredrich Der Grosse, which was heading to the port of entry in New York, New York, on May 28, 1913. From New York we made our journey to South America.

Shortly after John and I arrived in South America, we left. We couldn't get along with father."

I says to John, "John, let's go to North America to live."

"Joe, how you going to go to North America without any money."

"I'm goin' down to the dock, goin' to get a me a job and a good sailing boat, and then I'm goin' to go."

"The big boss at the smelly ol' fishin' dock, says all the jobs are filled up," says John.

"I told the big boss I would like to go to North America," I says to John.

The boss says to me, "Wait a minute Joe, I'll talk to the cook."

The fishery cook tells the boss that I can peel those brown russet potatoes if I want some work, so that is what we do.

John and I endlessly peeled those rusty ol' potatoes, and six months later, we are in Baltimore, Maryland with a whopping $450.00 apiece.

We traveled to Milwaukee, Wisconsin after quickly and sadly discovering there was no good work in Baltimore. We stayed with our sister, Georgia, for six months while we worked in a cast iron metal foundry. Georgia moved to America before we did. She met a strapping, young, blond American who was stationed in Germany for six short months, and they quickly and unexpectedly fell deeply in love. She moved to America after he completed his active duty.

Georgia has wavy, golden hair that hangs down to the middle of her back. She stands about 5" 2' and weighs a whopping 120 pounds. Her husband, Dan, was gifted with strong, wide, two-foot shoulders and stands an entire 6" 2'. They seem to make the perfect off centered match in both personality and size.

At the foundry, we produced metal castings. In a foundry, 'Metals are cast into shapes by melting them into a liquid, pouring the metal into a mold, and removing the mold material after the metal has solidified as it cools. The most common metals processed are aluminum and cast iron.'" (Wikipedia-Foundry)

After six months working at the skin staining, foul smellin' foundry, I say to Georgia, "Me and John are going to South Milwaukee to learn to be motormen. Motormen drive streetcars, and the rich people pay a lot of money."

Georgia is beyond happy to see us go. She had a couple energetic youngsters of her own, and we were a not so wanted burden.

After not finding work in South Milwaukee, me and John decided to travel to Montana.

We leave Milwaukee and move to Belt, Montana.

At the beginning of November, in 1915, me and John enlist in the Army. There were encouraging fliers hanging on every size tree in Belt, talking about men being needed for the worthwhile world war going on, saying there would be a valuable future and present benefits to joinin'.

Germany was, and still is, trying to take over the world. It's a good thing we left when we did, or we would be in the midst of ol' Hitler and his propaganda.

On May 23, 1915, Italy declared war on Austria-Hungary. On April 6, 1917, the United States declared war on Germany, and on June 24, 1917, American forces arrived in France.

John was sent to France in June for that tour of duty, and after being enlisted in the Army for only a meager 18 months, I was sent a sorrowful dispatch: 'John Miller, killed in France—served with honors.'

John's already faded Army tags were sent to me shortly after his expected death.

After serving in the army full term, I eventually traveled to Red Lodge, Montana. There were rich coal mines in Red Lodge, and pitch-black, dusty coal is essential for cookin' and in keeping houses warm in the below zero, cold winter months. Coal still is the most plentiful fuel today. It's a real money maker for the big wigs who own the elaborate coal mines.

I was living in Red Lodge for one year working in the coal mine, and one day, Bruce, a friend who was livin' in the all-male boarding house about just as long as I was, says to me, 'Joe, you should leave this boarding house and go live in that cozy, rich boarding house a quarter mile up the way.'"

I says, "What I goin' to do that for? I hear that snobbish boarding house costs double as much as this one."

Bruce says, "The moderate, well to do house is full of fancy, proper speakin' women. The boarders have four handsome, brown-haired, shapely daughters that reside there. I've seen them, and they are considerably handsome. You could snag yourself a good-to-do wife."

I was searchin' for a wife, so I made a definite decision in that instant to talk to the head of household about the possibility of living in the handsome lady boarding house and walked the lengthy quarter mile to your mother's house.

Your grandma Bertha answers the door, "What are you looking for?" She questions me.

"I'm lookin' for a new boarding house to occupy my livin' space."

After discussing the matter, she agreed to let me board there. There was one vacant room downstairs."

Your grandparents had four hardworkin', dedicated daughters, and one of their handsome daughters was your beautiful mother, Monta. Monta had instant eyes for me.

Monta always kicked my shins when I spoke broken English, and I would say, "Monta, what you gone and done that for?"

And she would say, "Your speaking broken English, and I want to tell you about it."

I would tell her, "I know I'm speakin' broken English. You don't have to keep kickin' me every time I do."

She says, "If I don't kick you, then you won't stop speaking it."

I suppose she made a valid point.

I knew Monta for an entire three years before we were married on May 21, 1921, in Red Lodge, Montana, and without the proper consent of Monta's parents mind you. Monta knew if she told her parents she wanted to marry me, they would instantly attempt to halt the whole shindig.

Monta's parents consider me a poor, low-class, uneducated bum. They didn't much take a likin' to me, and maybe, I was exactly what they thought me to be. I wasn't made of riches, and I received no formal education in Yugoslavia or Germany. School wasn't on my first agenda growin' up, ya know.

Mary, I do love your mama. I wanted to marry her because I loved her. You know. I mean, as much as I know how to love. I know I don't' always take the proper, decent actions, but I really do want to. I just don't know how to sometimes. I hope one glorious, blessed day, ya'll will see me in a different light.

Well, your mother left your grandmother and grandfather a message on the fancy, smooth parchment in the boarding house den, saying, "I'm going to marry Joe Miller today."

The day she took my hand was a golden, sunny day in May. The flowers were burstin' with sweet smelling blossoms like rainbow fireworks on the fourth of July, and possibilities of growth and future options seemed endless to us.

I found the preacher early in the mornin'.

He was plantin' in his garden when I asked him, "Will you marry Monta and me?"

The eager preacher agreed to marry us alright. He quickly cleaned up and drove in front of us to the modest church.

There was a small, compact Christian church on the out-skirts of town. The little, white, and pale blue stucco church was a humble and modest structure. The doors of the church—made of sweet-smelling cedar wood—were peeling and crimson red was attempting to exit through as the obvious first color. After walking through the cream-colored doors, we see a narrow hallway leading to the chapel.

Sixteen, separated, cherry wooden benches, with eight benches on each side, create a short and narrow middle isle. The good preacher's modest four-foot by two-foot crimson aspen pulpit is placed in the center of the stage with a modern, wooden, cherry piano just on the quick right.

The preacher welcomes us to the pulpit as Monta's uncle and aunt take their respective positions as the best man and lovely maid of honor.

Monta and I, leisurely walk in a step by step even rhythm toward the pulpit, and as the church's capable pianist plays comin' to the chapel, a feeling of approval from the good heaven instantly sweeps over my damaged soul.

After some I do's, I eagerly kiss my handsome, young bride. I'll never forget the satisfied smile that spread so easily across her porcelain face as dark hazel wisps of her heavy hair hung closely to her soft, smooth neck.

Monta's parents discovered our whereabouts shortly after the ceremony—finding us at the church. By the time they arrived at the church, grey, smokey clouds began to release their angry tears. The sun was suddenly disappearing as if the night was anxiously waiting to come upon us.

Nixon says, "Monta, what are you doing with that good for nothing bum?"

Monta says, "He's my husband now."

Nixon says, pointing to his two quarter-horse drawn, black covered wagon, "Monta, you climb in that wagon this instant and immediately come home with me."

Monta says to Nixon, "If Jo don't go—I don't go either."

CHAPTER 3

My Family Comes
Into The World

IN the latter part of 1922, our family began to grow into more than just a husband and a wife, and Mom and The Old Man's first child was born. My brother, Martin Boyd Miller, was a healthy eight-pound boy when he decided to enter the world on October 7, 1922, in Red Lodge, Carbon County, Montana. Everyone came to call him Mart for short.

Shortly after Martin was born, my family moved to Bozeman, Montana, where my sister, a more petite six-and-a-half-pound girl named Felicia Irene was born on September 25, 1924. Everyone called her Irene. My family did not reside in Bozeman long before they moved to Butte, Montana, which is where I spend most of my young life.

Butte, Montana is where my brother, a seven-pound, bouncing baby boy named William Wallace was born on May 5, 1926. Everyone called him Bill.

My presence had not quite set foot into the world yet at this pivotal point in history.

I must inform you that my old man never learned how to read and write. He always signed his name with an X. Even though he never learned how to read and write, he always managed his way around the world pretty good.

I can't honestly say I love or hate The Old Man. Most of the time, I try not to give my thoughts about him too much of my valuable time. I believe, if I admire anything about him, it is his twinkling, blue, pale eyes, his light, stiff, brown hair, and his pale, silky-smooth skin.

Oftentimes, The Old Man would purposefully place me gently on his short lap and kindly sing to me, telling me as he sweetly sang that I resemble his own beautiful mother, Mary Ribicic. He would also call me Mamishka, which means my little Mary.

I learned later in life that Mamishka is also a special doll. Mamishka dolls are also referred to as Nesting Dolls. You see, the dolls are made of malleable wood, most often coming from linden trees, and are said to symbolize motherhood and fertility.

There are several hallow dolls included with the Mamishka, and each doll varies in size but are the same shape. They represent generations, you see. The most fascinating detail about these unique dolls is that they fit inside one other.

The dolls originated from Russia, which is a land very far away from here. I do so hope to visit it one day though. I am not born yet, but my spirit looking down upon my growing family wishes to travel with them around this vast and miraculous world that they are residing in.

Other than The Old Man singing sweet, loving songs to me, I can't think of anything else that is desirable about him. He could have been exceptionally brilliant if he would have used his God given mind properly. I mean, we come into this world from a real God, so we must have somewhat of a Godlike mind I would imagine. Don't you think?

Because he is clever and sharp-witted, he could have accomplished a great many wonderful tasks and probably built many amazing and productive inventions adding discovery and production to this great world. The great problem is that he uses his God-given, intelligent brain to continually build trifling schemes that are almost never foolproof.

Schemes to obtain easy money.

Shortly after Bill was born, my not quite complete family proceeded to move to Renton, King County, Washington. The Old Man had a deceitful scheme brewing in his quirky mind, but I must explain to you why this particular stratagem appeared in his destructive thoughts.

A short time prior to my family moving to Renton, my Aunt Ruth was staying with my family in Butte. Ruth was seven years old at this time and was born in Red Lodge, Carbon County, Montana, December 18, 1918. She was my mother's youngest sister.

After my grandparents finalized their very public and lengthy divorce, Ruth had to reside with various relatives during the warm summer months because of where her mother, my grandmother, worked. Grandmother worked at the Brophry's in Red Lodge, Montana.

The Brophry's had no desire to have Ruth residing at their residence during the short summer months. She would be an added hungry mouth and large body to provide for and would be in the way of Grandmother effectively taking care of the Brophry family's needs when Mrs. Brophry's children and friends were home for the Summer, so Ruth was required to take turns staying with her sister's families. My mom was Ruth's oldest sister.

The unfortunate accident which occurred at the beginning of summer in 1926, proceeding my family's move to Washington, is what led to The Old Man's next maneuverous plot. My family very nearly lost their very lives on this dreadful night.

The Old Man purchased our first house in Butte, Montana, and he also obtained secondhand furniture to fill up the empty, meager house, attempting to make it a bona-fide home. Our address was 2162 South Montana Street, and The Old Man was working in the Black Rock Mine, located in Butte, at the time of the dreadful accident.

One cloudy, thunderous, frightful night, a terrible electrical storm came to visit the bustling city of Butte. Sharp electrical lights from angry, frustrated clouds filled the grim sky threatening to destroy and abolish anything in their immediate path. The vicious sparks of light purposefully struck the already scanty house causing a vast blaze of red-orange flames almost immediately within the home. My family's newly purchased home was ablaze with wild and savage flames immediately ascending to the low rooftop.

The hot, menacing fire spread quickly throughout the now deteriorating house which caused everyone to scramble desperately toward the outside clean air. Mom was having trouble escaping because of the obstruction of her opposing crutches, so The Old Man, as soon as he witnessed her dilemma, instantly broke the living room window and instinctively tossed Mom out of it like he was a catapult, and she was the ammunition.

Ruth, instinctively, lovingly, but quickly gathered Mart and Irene—leading them to safety across the cold, hard street. After making sure of Mart and Irene's safety, Ruth realized that my bother Bill was still in the house laying patiently in his crib, as you could not hear a cry from him.

Ruth, without hesitation, went bravely back into the red-black billowing flames, found him, and speedily snatched him from the tiny crib—quickly bringing him outside with the rest of the family. My precious brother Bill was just an innocent newborn, not knowing that his tiny life was in interment danger of death.

Just as soon as everyone escaped to safety, the flaring flames and billowing smoke-filled house fell with a terrible uproar that caused a crash as loud as the thunder that curtailed the lightening. The red, roaring fire engines could save nothing.

The only other immediate possessions belonging to my family

was our old black Ford, and the only clothes they possessed were attached to their bodies. Nothing was left, and despair seemed to be as thick as ice on a frozen lake.

Kind neighbors took my saddened and stricken family in for the immediate night and in the immediate days following. The caring community lovingly and heroically came to their much-required rescue as clothes and needed survival supplies were donated.

A few days after the fire, and after Grandma Fogleman found out about the destruction, she instantly wired Mom and The Old Man money. With the money Grandmother sent, my family was able to buy needed food.

A week after the fire had ample time to cool down, my stricken family went back to the burnt house to see if anything could be salvaged, but they found that everything that was in the house had melted.

The Old Man—in the aftermath of the fire—soon found a broken-down, small, ancient house to rent temporarily for a few weeks, and in this time, the insurance adjusters came to settle the $1,000.00 insurance claim that The Old Man had taken out on the house.

My poor, afflicted family had nowhere to live after the rent ran out on the house we were temporally renting, and the Old Man did not want to keep renting, so he decided to travel to different relatives' residents for the warm summer months, staying with them on an interim basis while contemplating what steps to take next in finding a new home. They stayed with Mom's relatives all Summer, and sometimes they camped underneath the star's bright lights.

First, my family visited and stayed at our cousin Lula's with her growing family of five, but because of the overwhelming circumstances, they resided there only a short while and had to move on as their stay was seriously straining the already large, rumbunctious family. My siblings enjoyed spending time with their cousins though, and Bill was growing into a cute toddler which created a welcomed distraction.

Next, they visited with my mom's Aunt and Uncle Bower, who lived by Hardin, Montana. Uncle had a big, spacious, well-to-do ranch and farm. My now, happier family, ate well and food was plentiful in their stay there, but just as before with Aunt Lula's family, they soon had to leave as they also became a burden.

After leaving Uncle Bower's, my family stayed with Grandmother and Grandfather McClurg for a short while—until Summer was ended.

After a summer filled with family adventure and intrigue, in the Fall of 1926, The Old Man eventually found another modest house on 3230 Sanders Street back in Butte. This is where they lived for a short while before they made their way to Washington.

Towards the ending months in Fall of 1927, The Old Man decided to move to Washington, so my family moved to Renton, King County, Washington, which is where I was born.

I arrived in this wonderful world on May 20, 1928, which leads me back to my original story about The Old Man and his inventive, deliberate scheme. After receiving such a large sum of cash from the dreadful and destructive lightening fire in Butte, he contemplated another evil, and not so thought-out plan of destruction. Yes, he thought he might attempt to gather another lump sum of insurance money on a house fire.

The year is now 1929, and I am now a cute active one year old with light blonde, wispy hair, and small frame. So far, I was the smallest child born into the family. After turning one, my family moved to Buckley, Washington.

When my family arrived in Buckley, The Old Man bought an old, blue farm-like house located in town. It was placed on a modest acre of hard, dusty land.

We were happily raising calves on the dry land which possessed the rickety, farmhouse. Even though the compact house was old and continually falling apart, with my imagination running wild as it did most of the time, I found that in my dreams, I was really on a rich, plentiful dairy farm laid with emerald, green, stiff grass for miles around, with all the milk and butter there was to consume after we milked the ever so giving white and black spotted cows.

The Old Man promised us that we could keep the wonderful baby calves, and as you can very well suppose and guess, he quickly broke his promise. You will come to understand that The Old Man is a pathological liar. Sometimes, I think he even lies about where he originated from.

As I grew up, I'd heard through a continuous grapevine of gossip that my old man changed his original Yugoslavian name to that of a dead American man, because he was blackballed from the mines.

Blackballed means that he can never work in the mines again. Everywhere he lives, he gets into insurmountable trouble, then not a single decent mine will hire him if they know his name. Working in the mines is how many able men make their living. The money is usually decent, although the work is extremely dangerous.

So, as we now know, "Miller" is not my real last name?

As you might assume, The Old Man took the adorable baby calves to the butcher shop which was the end of the calves on my imagined farm. I attempted many times to encourage and sway my imagination to imagine those precious calves back to my fantasy farm, but it was utterly impossible.

"Mary, sometimes promises are required to be broken," says The Old Man.

Since I've been born, I don't remember my old man keeping even one promise he made to me.

In Buckley, many beautiful and abounding fruit trees cumbered the lovely, small town, sending fruity aroma throughout the busy streets and booming businesses. You could walk anywhere around town and witness the magical, sweet-smelling trees spreading their joy and happiness to the welcoming residents as they showed off their colors and intoxicating aromas of cherries, plums, and pears just waiting to be picked and eaten. We also had a cherry tree in our small backyard.

Yes, we expectedly moved from the quaint blue farmhouse to another simple, damaged house located directly in the middle of the modest city.

One sunny summer day, The Old Man quickly packed us and our few belongings and said, "We are moving to town, so I can be a bartender."

This new-old house is not as exceptionally pretty as the blue farmhouse, but it is shelter.

As soon as we moved into the city house, The Old Man filled the broken-down house with furniture. He also bought insurance on the house. He used part of the money he received from the house fire in 1926 to purchase the house.

The year is 1931, I am three years old, and it is the beginning of Summer.

CHAPTER 4

My First Adventure

WHILE residing in Buckley, which contains about 4,000 residents, our neighbors assume that my old man and mom are brother and sister, and not because they naturally take a common resemblance to one another mind you. Now, why would they think that you might wonder to yourself? Because that's what my old man told everyone in town!

My old man quickly informed our welcoming neighbors that he was indeed taking care of his poor, pregnant sister, and her troubled kids.

Yes, Mom is pregnant again, so I am not the last of the lot to come into this world. Mom's recent newfound condition came as a surprise to us all. I attempt to understand why Mom, back in her delicate youth decided to marry the deranged old man, but as much as I attempt to rack my adolescent mind around any good and rational reasons, I can't seem to understand why she chose him.

My old man is currently managing an "all men" drunken saloon located in the center of Buckley. He has created quite a good business for himself workin' in that saloon. Nothing all that good last forever though, and he has intentionally gone and crossed some now angry employees that work for him. He is currently into a bit of complicated trouble because the employees have taken his money and ditched him, placing him in a difficult and strenuous predicament which is why he instantly, without hesitation, put into place another one of his schemes.

As we scurry outdoors to our only safety, the sparkly fireflies light up the immensely, dark night, and the songs of creeping crickets fill the warm night air welcoming in the coming summer months. The year is 1931, and again, the unknown darkness of the night is our immediate safety from immediate harm as we realize the smokey distress beginning to bellow inside our current home.

"Get out of bed quickly!" my old man exclaims in a seemingly expected and fake panic. "Go outside!"

We are all curiously wonderin' why he suddenly is encouragin' us to take such animate, rapid actions after the late-midnight hour.

Well, our curious questions are immediately answered as the fire-lit house begins to ample up with dark grey, suffocatin' smoke.

Mom exclaims in a panic, "The house is on fire, everybody out quick."

The hot flames are beginning to enlarge inside the panicked house, but we notice that clogging smoke encompasses the interior more than flames.

None of us are noticeably harmed as we stand in the vacant lot across from the smoke-filled house looking on in awe as cloud-like smoke once again attempts to burn our place of residence to the bare ground. We curiously look around for our old man to ask him somethin' about the destruction, but he is nowhere to be found.

As news of a fire quickly spreads throughout the neighborhood, then to the town, the Buckley fire department arrives at the currently tragic and sorrowful scene in a timely manner, managing to save the house well enough that we can still occupy it.

My old man is gone when everyone arrives on the scene.

Where is he?

Does he not care about his own family?

What a silly and already knowing question for me to ask myself.

The police and fire department thoroughly investigate the partly burnt house after the flames subside, attempting to solve the cause of the "unexpected" fire, and they cannot discover it. We have nowhere else to reside except for the charcoaled house, so we go back in and begin cleaning it the best we can.

WE have lived in this partly burnt house all summer long, and we reek of dirty smoke every day, and takin' a bath doesn't take away the sticky smell.

In the weeks following the fire, our kind, sacrificing neighbors feel sorry for us, so they generously share food, clothing, and blankets.

One of our compassionate neighbors that gave us some fresh vegetables and sweet fruit from their colorful garden, informed my brother Mart about a government truck that comes by the neighborhood every so often.

"The government truck gives food away to the needy," he told Mart. "It's called '**Working People of America**.'"

Mart decides to investigate the neighbor's claims, and sure enough, after going to meet the government truck, Mart is coming home with much needed food.

Mart exclaims to us, "The government truck gave me a bag of enriched white flour, heavy lard, and pale, pink bologna, the kind with the red strip of plastic surrounding it."

WE have now run out of government food, and our neighbors can no longer be givin' away what they barely possess, so it is time, we decide, to go searchin' for the necessary food that we need for our very survival.

It is the end of a blistering summer, and today Mart and I had intentionally snuck fresh, succulent fruit off the nearby fruit trees that grow on nearby fruit farms. We have one cherry tree in our yard, but we ate most the cherries off it before Summer ended.

My old man, after some time, finally came home. He was absent for most of the Summer. The reason he is home is to collect insurance money on the house.

When my old man finally came back to the house, the expectin' police were waitin' for him, so they could question him. A neighbor informed the police of his comin' back, and the police took him into custody.

The police had no evidence that my old man started the almost deadly fire, so they were required to release him. He was only in jail a short day or so. When he came back home that night, he never did mention to anyone if insurance money was received on the house. We assumed he didn't receive insurance, because our circumstances did not improve.

Grandmother graciously wired Mom some needed money, so we can all travel back to Red Lodge. Mom is about to give birth to her fifth child, and we need a place to stay as the burnt house cannot keep us warm in the chillier winter months.

School will be startin' soon, and Mart will be needin' to start second grade. He is eight now, Irene is six, and Bill is five.

CHAPTER 5

The Trip To Red lodge

TRAVELIN' with me on this new, shiny, black train with green and yellow stripes is my courageous mom, my beautiful sister, my two brave brothers, and my helpful aunt Ruth. Ruth stayed with us this Summer, so she was here when the fire occurred, and she is twelve now. My old man plans on meetin' us in Red Lodge. He is bringing the black Ford back to Montana, because we can't all fit in it.

Sadly, one important family member we had to unwillingly leave behind in Buckley is our German Sheppard, Rascal.

We are not allowed to take Rascal with us because the mean stewardess on this fancy train says, "In order to take your dog on the train, you are required to place a mussel on him."

We do not have enough money to purchase a constricting mussel, and we don't own one because Rascal is the kindest canine you would ever know; therefore, we wouldn't think of placing such a confining object on him, and Grandmother sent us just enough money to travel to Red Lodge on this here train.

I don't know how my wonderful grandma can afford to keep sending us money. She faithfully bails the deceiving old man out when he gets into terrible trouble. I know Grandma must be so kind in this matter because she loves Mom and us kids. I'm sure it isn't because she takes a likin' to my old man, because he's nothin' but trouble.

I love Rascal, because he is an exceptional pet. He bravely rescued my beautiful sister Irene once from eminent danger in an attempted kidnappin'. I'll tell you how the fascinatin' rescue story unfolds. It's a good one.

At the time of the attempted kidnappin', which was near our smokey home in Buckley, Irene was six, and I was three. Mind you, I don't recall the brave Rascal rescue story in its entirety myself, I just often hear Irene telling her friends about it. Mom often mentions it too when talking to her friends in the neighborhood.

IRENE and I are happily exploring along the dusty, rusted-out railroad tracks which we found about a half of a mile behind our house right after moving here.

Keep in mind, won't you, that we don't live in the best of circumstances. We live on the poorer side of town which is usually where we reside when living in a town, not where all those rich folk live with the expensive houses and cars. Our house be lucky that it is still standin' considerin' the fire and all; and our car; well, I'll explain about the old black Ford later on. I'm attemptin' to get through my dog rescue story, but I keep gettin' distracted.

Irene and I were walkin' along the tracks with Rascal when suddenly we see some staggerin', booze reeking, crazy ol' man comin' directly our way. He don't look like someone we want to be talkin' to or should be talkin' to for that matter, so we mind our own business by going on our own way. The ol' drunk doesn't mind his own business though which is how this rescue story comes into existence.

We are poor, but his circumstance appears to be worse off than our own. How someone could be worse off than my family, I don't know, but I'm looking at this guy and seeing that it is possible. I guess anything is possible—at least that's what my imagination tells me most the time.

This strange man seems like he could quickly become a nuisance to our pleasant day, and as he walks a little closer to us, it's obvious beyond a measure of a doubt that he has been heavily drinking—smelling as if he spent the whole of the night in a stinky skunk hole.

Slurrin' his words together, he suddenly speaks to us sayin', "You know, it is illegal to drink alcohol. They call it the Prohibition. Many countries such as Russia, Finland, and Canada also have banned alcohol. The Prohibition started in the United States in 1920 as an 18th Amendment to the Constitution, sayin' that alcohol should be illegal."

Why this crazy, ol' fool is explainin' to us the facts of the Prohibition; I'm not sure, but Irene and I get the uneasy feeling he might intentionally attack one of us which knowledge comes apparent as he attempts to place his sticky beer arms around Irene. This scary guy is not only drinkin' illegally, but he is also tryin' to cause deliberate harm to two innocent, beautiful, young girls.

As soon as the ol' drunk attempts to snatch Irene, she immediately begins a screamin'. I start yellin' too, and all the screamin' gives an immediate signal to Rascal that Irene is in danger. There is not a livin' soul around the train tracks to save us from our dangerous situation, so our brave dog begins chewin' on that drunkin' bum's leg.

Rascal's long canines are now permanently lodged into the nasty ol' bum's leg when suddenly, he lets out a horrendous yelp. It must be mighty painful for him having ol' Rascal's razor-sharp teeth sink deep into his rough skin, because as soon as they do, he quickly releases Irene and switches his attention to gettin' Rascal off of his now bloody leg and ripped trousers.

Bright red, thick liquid begins to instantly pour out of the open, two-inch wound being created in the ol' bum's leg. You can sense how much pain he is in when he falls quickly to the hot, dusty ground in agony bellowing words that I am not permitted to speak.

Irene and I don't stay and wait to see what actions the drunkin' bum is going to take next, so while Rascal is chewin', we go runnin'. We race back home as quick as our short, wirily legs can scurry.

Irene and I are young and can't run so swiftly as if we were older, and sometimes Irene must carry me while Rascal buys us time.

As we arrive close to the house, we see Rascal running closely behind us. That ol' bum must have run back down the tracks from where he came. I presume he had to be in an extreme amount of pain.

Rascal is our hero savin' us in what could have been a most dreadful day.

Relief sweeps over our beating hearts as soon as we step upon the rickety, crooked steps. Rascal arrives shortly after us, and we give him a lot of lovin' and praise for what he'd just gone and done for us.

After Irene and I walk through the front door it falls off the hinges a little more, definitely not a stable door which is able to keep any strangers out during the night if anyone was thinking about robbing the place, even if a lock was put on it.

As soon as we walk through the house to the kitchen and sit down on the kitchen stools, Irene's shaky, but determined voice relays the whole frightful kidnapping story to Mom.

Irene is done explaining the story, so Mom calls the police, and they come to our house quickly. They ask Irene and I some questions; mostly Irene, since she is older than me, and the polite policemen write down the description we give them of the ol' bum.

The police immediately go out searchin' the area lookin' for the attempted kidnapper, but they never do find that creep. I just hope he don't go try stealin' some other young, innocent girl.

My heart breaks as we leave the train station and see Rascal sitting on the train station deck, wonderin' what's going on. If it wasn't for his bravery and self-sacrifice, maybe, my lovely sister and I wouldn't even be here today.

Us girls cried all the way out of Buckley about leavin' Rascal. The brave boys probably wanted to cry, but they must act all strong and brave ya know. Rascal sadly watches us leavin' him. He is probably wonderin' when we are goin' to come back.

"We aren't coming back," I silently tell Rascal. "We aren't coming back."

CHAPTER 6

My Grandparents

THIS fast-moving train is leaving Buckley—traveling to Red Lodge. Red Lodge is where my sweet grandmother and grandfather Fogleman live. I've never met my grandmother and grandfather which is who we are going to live with temporarily.

Here is a bit of history about my grandparents.

My grandparents battled a devastatin' divorce in 1924, a short while before Irene was born into this world. Divorce was not looked upon as a good and proper decision in those years and was extremely difficult for women to immediately obtain in those descriminatin' days.

Grandmother attempted many times to stay married to Grandfather and gave him multiple opportunities to change his ways, but he wasn't always too nice and was often lazy around the house.

Grandfather worked hard when he felt like working, so sometimes they had quite a bit of living money and sometimes none.

Grandfather was never excited about my sweet grandmother having all five girls and no boys to carry on his name. Oh, she was pregnant with boys once—twin boys. She didn't know she was carrying twin boys though till they were born.

Grandpa wanted a boy more than any girl, so he was weary of Grandmother producin' all girls and no boys. It seems that from the stories I've heard, Grandfather didn't even want his girls, telling Grandmother that he would rather she just give them away.

First, my mom was born. Then, Frances Ella Fogleman blessed their family on January 7, 1904. Next, Grandmother gave birth to twins on October 26, 1905: Louise Fogleman and Lois Beatrice Fogleman. After that, Grandmother gave birth to tiny twin boys, but they were not blessed to live in this world with their other siblings. They immediately died after their fatal birth.

Grandmother and Grandfather must have been awful sad to have lost those sweet baby boys. They could have carried the Fogleman name twice into the world instead of just once, but it ultimately was not meant to be. God must have had a unique plan for them. Maybe, they were the family's guardian angles.

I think Grandfather would have liked to have a boy because then he could have help with his carpentry business. Grandfather is an experienced and well-known carpenter. His highly sought-after expertise and quality grade workmanship is well known and appreciated around Red Lodge and the immediate surrounding areas. People are always requesting Grandfather to build somethin'.

In 1904 my grandparents migrated to Red Lodge, Montana, and Grandfather built Grandmother a beautiful well-to-do house with a quality amount of acreage. He built the house in the popular and well-respected part of town.

First, Grandfather built a large. The barn was where Grandmother, Grandfather, and their two girls lived until he could make enough money to build a respectable home.

Grandfather made money to build the house by charging people to haul their stuff around. He would hitch up his sturdy horses to a large red wagon, and people would pay him generously to move stuff for them. A lot of his success from the uprising business came from the busy and wealthy mines, but he also received golden opportunities and business from affluent private parties.

After saving money for a home, he built Grandmother a nice, more than modest home with square, white pillars supporting the front and left side of the house creating a charming porch.

Their house was much nicer than most of the homes in the immediate area, or at least just as fancy, and as most couples are, they were extremely happy when they first began their exciting journey together. Eventually though, but not in all situations, reality and mood swings set in and gets to a marriage.

In 1919, Grandfather unexpectedly left Grandmother and went to live with his parents in Iowa for a little more than three years. Grandfather did not provide financial help or encouragement to Grandmother in these years which is why she built her own business boarding miners. She needed money somehow as she found out she was pregnant with another child. That child was my Aunt Ruth. Grandmother was in her low forties at the time she was told the news she was pregnant with Aunt Ruth.

Grandmother boarded seven men at a time, and it wasn't an easy life havin' those boarders live with her and her daughters.

Coal miners, and men in general, weren't always the most respectful in those days to women. Women were often treated as second class citizens. Grandmother cooked, made lunch buckets, and cleaned laundry for those dirty boarders. Washing clothes on a worn-out, wooden wash board was a grievous and tenacious task that the girls undertook for the boarders as their attire would get extremely soiled from underground mining.

Mom was an excellent guide for her younger siblings. She happily helped Grandmother by gingerly taking care of them while Grandmother worked the house. Mom's sisters would also help around the bustling house.

Mom wasn't physically capable of participatin' in physical labor because of her crutches, but her upbeat attitude and guidance were essential in the combined efforts of the overall organization and functionality concerning the boarders demands and needs.

The large house was warmed on cool nights and on chilly winter days by an iron wood burning stove. Mom's sister, Frances, joyfully played the cherry wood, glossy piano, entertainin' the family and boarders on the sometimes-dreary winter weekdays and weekends. Mom said that she played the piano beautifully.

In 1923, Grandfather decided to grace the family back with his presence and came back to live with Grandmother and my aunts. My aunts did not desire him to come back, but Grandmother allowed him too and gave him another opportunity to change.

Realizing that Grandfather was not going to change because of his continual laziness and harshness towards the family, she decided it was best to seek for a divorce. She already knew she could make a good living on her own because she had done it for three years. The experiences with the boarders prepared her for the opportunity to leave Grandfather for good this time.

Grandfather did not make the unwanted divorce easy on Grandmother. The entire town and surrounding areas were busy bodying their nose into my grandparent's affairs, and Grandmother received unfavored ridicule for her thoughtful decision.

Grandfather and Grandmother were required to attend the court and eventually the Judge ruled in favor of my grandmother. Grandfather was very unhappy about the court's decision. I heard that Grandfather always was asking my grandmother to come back to him, but she always said, "No."

In 1924, my grandmother received a maid and cook job working at Mrs. Brophry's. Grandmother was given her own living quarters directly beside the house, and her immediate responsibilities to the Brophry residence was the responsibilities of cleaning, cooking, and taking care of the children.

Grandfather was born on November 9, 1874. Grandmother was born on April 22, 1881. They were married on March 28, 1900. Before they came to live in beautiful Montana, they resided in the state of Iowa. Mount Ayers, Ringold County, Iowa was where they were born and raised.

My grandfather's parents, David Fogleman and Lavinia Ella Ayers—her maiden name—had a prominent farm in Iowa.

My Grandmother's parents, William Absolum McClurg and Caroline Grady—her maiden name—lived most of their lives in Iowa. Iowa is where my grandparents met.

Towards the turn of the twentieth century, they moved to Montana to obtain free land, and after they claimed their free land in beautiful Montana, they settled in here and live here until today. Mom says that they will never leave the town of Red Lodge.

All I know about my grandparents is what I hear from my mom and siblings, and of course Ruth. I hope to get to know them personally while living in Red Lodge. They don't live together, but they do live in the same town.

WE have almost arrived in Red Lodge. I must say, I am excited to finally meet my grandparents. The Old Man told us before we left Buckley that from the money he made in Buckley, he's going to start a new business.

Is he talking about the money he made working in Buckley, or the money he made from the fire? I am not too sure. I really don't desire to inquire about where the money came from. It is probably better if I don't know. I do know, however, if he is starting a new business, we won't see him much.

Every time my old man begins a new business venture, or a new one of his escapades, he leaves for a while. It won't even matter that Mom is about to give birth. At least grandma is going to be there to help Mom.

One of these days, I imagine Mom will leave my old man and not take him back. He doesn't deserve her.

Mom, especially for having to use crutches most of her life, is certainly a strong woman; although, I'm not exactly sure how I feel about her. She works exceptionally hard to take care of us sometimes unruly children, and it is obvious she loves us. I would say more than anything I admire and respect about her is her courage, strength, and determination.

For some odd and unknown reason, I don't necessarily feel exceptionally close to her. Irene seems to get along and connect with Mom well. They seem really close to each other.

I do know if mom wasn't here for us, we probably wouldn't even have a chance at a decent life. I sure am grateful that she puts up with us.

"There's Grandmothers house," says Mom.

CHAPTER 7

Katherine Is Born

SUMMER is almost over, and Fall is inviting itself into the vibrant town of Red Lodge.

It is September 7, 1931, and Oh! I just can't stand the suspense of it! Mom has been in the small 40X40 foot bedroom all night with Dr. Adams, Irene, Ruth, and Grandmother.

What is going on, I wonder to myself?

When I plead to help, they just said, "You're just too young Mary."

Well, I might be young, but I think I can help out a whole lot.

One day, I won't be so little and they will all say, "Oh, I guess Mary is capable of doin' a few things."

Yahh, they'll see, I'll show em'.

They all say, "Irene is at a good age to help Mom."

Well, I believe I am too.

What will I do when that tiny human is born? I don't know the rules on how to be a helpful big sister. I'm still learning how to be a little sister, and no one thinks I do it properly. I overhear Irene telling her friends now and then that I can be a big bug sometimes.

Lord, please help me be a good big sister. My biggest worry is that I won't know how to take care of a little baby, and I am worried I might possibly break it. I aint never had a baby doll before, and a real baby is sort a like a baby doll, cept it can move without you movin' it.

I would have to be real careful not to press too hard on those small baby fingers and toes. They would be awful temptin' to press down on though.

I always wished to have a baby doll, but we never have enough money for one. Irene got a hand me down once, and it wasn't much to look at, but at least it was something. Irene never does let me play with it. She said that a witch would come down and spite me if I ever was caught playin' with her fake baby doll. I'm not real sure what spite means, but it can't be all that good if Irene is threaten' me about it.

Now that I'm goin' to be a big sister, I am probably goin' to have to teach the little one how to use the bathroom.

Those small babies go do their business in the clean diaper and get it all dirty. And what about the diapers? I aint never changed a diaper on a real baby before, and I really don't look forward to doing so. It's only been a couple years since I was in those dirty things myself.

Maybe, since everyone thinks Irene is so much more responsible than me, she can be in charge of changing the baby's stinky diaper. That is somethin' I won't complain about! She can do all the diaper changin' she desires.

I tell you what, those diapers are not fun to be around. The babies outgoin's are always sticken' to those cloth diapers and ya have to really scrub hard to get the stains out of 'em. The smell aint somethin' that I want to deal with neither. I would probably go and poke the baby with one of those sharp, little pins that go on the immediate side of the soft white cloth—on accident of course. I would never do any harm to no cute, tiny baby on purpose. I think those babies are all so cute. Even the ones I hear the grown-up men call homely and kind of ugly.

I need to apologize for the way I am talkin'. Grandmother noticed right off that I don't speak properly.

Grandmother went and told me, "Mary, you got the desired looks that a man is lookin' for, but if you do not learn to talk like a proper, pretty young lady, no decent good-looking man is going to choose to marry you. He'll just think of you as white trash."

I know I need to get to talkin' more proper, but I don't live in those rich neighborhoods. I live in poor neighborhoods, and how I speak is the way people talk. I have two parents that speak distinctly different. I hear one speakin' broken English and the other speaking good English. I suppose I got to choose which parent I'm going to speak like.

I am going to work on speakin' like Mom.

I kinda like that Grandmother said I was a looker though. We never have to many mirrors in the houses we live in, but whenever we go to town in Red Lodge, I look in those big mirrors in the department store. I must say I aint bad lookin' for a three in a half year old. There I go again, gettin', or [getting] distracted, when I should be tellin' ya about Mom and the baby.

We arrived in Red Lodge just about a week ago. The Old Man left us with Grandmother so he could go look for some prospects.

He said, "I need to find a suitable house and a god paying job."

Well, we haven't seen him since. And here Mom is—going into labor.

That's what everyone is sayin'. Labour.

I know whenever I hear someone talkin' about labor, they usually are talkin' about a job or someone workin'.

Someone could say what mom is doin' in that room is most definitely work. I wish she didn't have to go through that specific work, but I am sure glad it is her and not me.

That's a shameful thing to say, isn't it? But her little screams sound like she's being tortured—like someone's pinchin' her all over the place—those tiny little pinches that leave big red marks all over your tender body.

How long does it take to get a baby out anyways?

Grandma said, "Sometimes, it takes ladies Three Whole Days!"

I think I'll pass on the labor thing. Mom has already been in that room for a whole long day and excruciating night. I wish that baby would come soon, so she don't have to be in anymore pain. I hope I didn't put her through that much pain when I was born. It would make me extremely sad if I did.

Now everyone's a screamin' in the room. Somethin' exciting is happening in there.

"The baby is almost here," I hear someone say.

"Get some warm and clean, blankets," I hear another one say.

So many people are talkin'. I can't hear who's sayin' what. Then, I hear it, a sweet, faint cry.

That precious baby must be out of Mom's bulgin' tummy. I wonder how they got that baby out anyways. I mean, it must come directly out of some hole, but mom doesn't have any holes in her body. I wonder if they must cut a hole into her body to get it out. I am curious, but not likely curious enough to ask the question, because I'm not sure I want to know the answer, yet. Maybe, when I am older, all this baby stuff will make more sense.

Suddenly, I hear someone say what I have been waitin' to hear. "It's a girl!"

I hear Grandmother say, "Wow! A baby girl."

This is excitin'. I try to go in to see what the sweet baby girl looks like, but as soon as I push a little crack in the door, someone quickly slams it shut.

Oh, darn. I guess I'm goin' to have to wait a little longer.

Grandmother finally peaks her head out the door and says to me, "Mary, would you like to see her?"

Even though I'm real nervous, of course I would like to see her.

"Yes," I say to Grandmother.

You are probably wondering where we all are as this special baby girl arrives into this wonderful world. We are behind the Brophry's house, where my grandmother lives.

THE STORYBOOK ADVENTURES OF MARY MILLER

I heard Mart say that the Brophry's must be the richest well-to-do people in the entire town of Red Lodge.

He said, "The Brophry's have a huge coal mine here, and their fancy house is one of the finest houses you ever saw."

The hot Summer is coming to its end, and every plant in the Brophry's magical yard is splendid, shining with emerald-colored leaves attached to flowers coming up in all kinds of hidden and obvious places. Walking into their backyard is like being in a landscape painting of the most beautiful flower gardens. Deciduous, fir, and evergreen trees surround the large three-story, part brick house, and they are the prettiest, most well-manicured trees I ever laid my eyes on.

This entire town is real pretty to look at. I've only been in Red Lodge a week, but I've been doing a bit of investigatin', and I discovered where Grandfather lives. He lives down by the pea factory. That's about a half of an hour walk from where we are stayin' now.

I like to walk to his house; he gives me food to eat that I usually never get the pleasure of eatin'. I'm going to like getting' to know Grandfather. I know that he and Grandmother had past troubles, but he and I get along real well.

Well, back to my cute, new baby sister.

I slowly slide myself through the two-foot crack in the narrow, open door and see everyone is happily surrounding Mom as she peacefully lays in a newly made comfortable bed fluffed with white sheets and soft pillows around her head and back. She is lookin' (looking) like she crashed into a wagon full of water containers that broke from the dreadful crash. Beads of sweat slowly drip down her tired face which explains why her attire and hair is soaked with wetness.

Everyone in the room seems to be trying to make her as comfortable as possible. Mom instantly smiles widely at me after she notices me shyly walking into the full, small room, and as I step next to her bed, I see this sweet baby girl.

The new baby appears so small all wrapped up in a thin, light pink, crocheted blanket. The pink blanket is squeezed so tight around the baby, and I wonder how she is even breathing properly. Her little chest is going up and down, so I know she's alive.

Standing cautiously next to Mom, I place my own petite fingers on the baby's soft, miniature, warm head.

"She sure is a cutie," I say. "Mom, what you going to call her."

"I think we'll give her the name of Katherine Joyce. What do you think Mary?"

It probably doesn't make a difference what my opinion is, because I am absolutely sure Mom's probably going to call the baby Katherine no matter what I may suggest.

I personally wouldn't call one of my babies Katherine, not because it isn't a nice name—mind you—I just would choose a different one.

"She looks like a Katherine Joyce, and that name will probably suit her just fine."

Mom smiles, and her smile makes my heart happy.

The doctor says, "It's time for everyone to leave the room now, because Monta needs her rest."

This house isn't too big, and you can hear just about everything everyone says, even if they think ya can't hear 'em, but now all is quite as I am the last one to leave the cozy room full of forever memories.

I am thinking about life in a new way today, and after everyone leaves the room to go outside and get some fresh air, I purposefully stay behind and place my ear nosily to the inch cracked door.

I hear the doctor say to Mom, "Monta, you can't have any more children."

Mom doesn't seem upset about this information. I don't think she was thinking about having anymore anyhow. Five kids are a lot to handle for a woman that uses awkward crutches. Not only that; she is usually raisin' us kids on her own. She's probably glad she can't have any more of us.

CHAPTER 8

Living In Red Lodge
(Fall 1931)

IT'S just after Thanksgiving, and Winter breezes are in the now cool air as the first, white snowfall lightly blankets the once dry ground in Red Lodge. There sure is a lot of snow that accumulates here in Red Lodge. Snow is not something I'm used to growing up in as I lived in Washington and all. We sure received an accumulation of rain in Washington but no snow. At certain times of the year, there's so much thick, damp, white snow that you must slowly tunnel through it just to get to the other side of the street. Many residents carry their metal shovels wherever they go—just in case they get stuck.

I sure do enjoy playing in the white, fluffy-like clouds. At the first snowfall, I went and made me a white, three-balled snowman—placing two black, shiny coals on the first ball to make eyes, one to make a nose, and seven to make a mouth.

Making heavenly snow angels is one of my new favorite activities. When makin' a good and lasting angel, ya must make sure where ya step when you are makin' (making) it. First, you carefully step your foot down where your leg of the angel is going to be. Next, you slowly and carefully plop yourself down into the snow where you plan on layin' down with your back in the snow. After that, ya move your arms and legs wildly up and down from side to side. Then, very carefully, when ya are done, ya slowly get up, makin' sure your feet and hands are inside the angel. Finally, you must quickly jump out of your fantastic creation looking back to see a beautiful sight. Snow angels are the prettiest angels.

Talking so much about pretty angels is making me remember Grandmother taking us to church. You do notice don't you that my language is getting better. The first month and a half I was in Red Lodge, I was living with Grandma, and she was always correcting me, but she doesn't correct me as much anymore, because I'm beginning to recognize my mistakes on my own and am getting good at quickly correcting them.

We are not living with Grandma any longer, because my old man came back to Mom a few weeks after the baby was born and informed us saying, "I found a fine-looking house to rent about a mile away from where Grandma lives."

Well, it's not much of a house, but at least it's by Grandmother and Grandfather.

GRANDMOTHER has been taking us to the Methodist church since we've been living here. I do enjoy going to church and learning about God and things. I've never known anything about religion before we began going with Grandmother.

Grandmother told Mom, "Monta, you know that your children are going to all be needing to be baptized soon."

I honestly believe Mom wants us to be properly baptized. I sure wouldn't mind being dunked into a pool of living, righteous water, and I fully enjoy listening to the preacher talk about God every Sunday morning.

Grandmother is a handsome gal. She is straight and tall and has beautiful naturally curly, dark locks with deep, short waves. Her quiet laugh brings an instant wide smile to my face, and I love listening to her tell us funny stories and am always laughing about what she's saying.

Grandfather is round and sturdy, standing at almost six feet, and is coupled with a bald, often shiny head. His left eye is slightly lazy, so when you look at him, one eye looks in the other direction.

Mom and Grandpa are extremely close.

Mom is a real pretty gal, not so much handsome like Grandmother, but pretty enough just the same, especially, when she was in her teenage years. I remember seeing a couple of her younger pictures and thinking—she is so pretty. She probably could have gotten a better husband than she got, but she probably was afraid no man would want her because of her clumsy crutches.

Mart has been in public school for a couple of short months now, and as I ease drop with my ear against Mart's bedroom door, I hear him telling Mom about the frustrations of going to school in all this heavy snow.

He says, "I must walk two miles following the broken-down railroad tracks. It's not easy when your waist up full of cumbersome snow. Sometimes, friends will pick me up on a sleigh and bring me where there's snow and then with the snow being useful and to our advantage, we slide quickly behind the wooden sleigh. When there's no snow, it takes us about twenty minutes to get to school, unless someone picks us up in their car."

Mart is currently in the second grade. He is nine now. Irene is seven, and Bill is five. Irene is not old enough for first grade, so she stays home with Bill, me, and Katherine.

My old man's new business venture was to open a meat market in October. I don't know how long this will last, but I'm sure something's bound to go wrong.

Everyone seems to be excited about Christmas. I must say, I'm excited too. I don't remember ever having a Christmas in our house. Of course, I am only three and a half.

The reason we don't usually have a Christmas, even before I was born, is because our old man always spends the money on something besides presents.

Grandpa, that's what I call him now, told me that we could have a real Christmas at his house this year, and he is going to give me a special gift. My excitement and anticipation overwhelm my curiosity, and I wonder how I can possibly wait so long. I hope it's a pretty dolly. I don't expect anything from my old man, and Mom will probably sew us something if she can find some material.

During the Winter days, I try to help Mom with baby Kay. We have been calling Katherine, Kay. Mom has been helping Grandma at the Brophry's, so I help with Kay when she is busy.

The Brophry's are awful kind and generous folk. Oftentimes, while we were living with Grandma, the Brophry's would give us quality red meat. Good meat, not bologna.

Mrs. Brophry also allowed us to choose various clothes we needed from her downstairs selection. She is the president of a club of ladies and is in charge of the clothing drive in town. People bring unneeded clothes to her house, and she gives the clothes to the less fortunate.

We are unquestionably considered less fortunate, so she invited us to come over and take what we needed.

Maybe, since we've been attending church on a regular basis, God is helping us.

The educated preacher says, "If you go to church, you'll be blessed."

I think the preacher has the right idea, and Mrs. Brophry will be blessed even more since she goes to church and continually helps people in the community.

I gather I better begin doing some community service in order to receive a few of those special blessings the good preacher is talking about. Service is when you purposefully do good deeds. That's what Grandma tells me.

CHAPTER 9

My First Real Christmas (Fall 1931)

CHRISTMAS Day is finally here. I've waited all Winter for this glorious day. We are going to Grandpa's for dinner, and he told me that after dinner we could open the wonderful gift's he bought us."

We are living with Grandpa now, because last week we had to get our old man out of jail. He mysteriously disappeared for a week, and we didn't know what happened to him. Well, he was in the city jail, because the government caught him in one of his failing schemes again. He is back in Red Lodge now.

Yes, you're probably wonderin' what the old man went to jail for. I sure will tell ya.

My old man ended up losing a whopping $3,000.00 at the meat market. The government took it all away from him. Come to find out, he was knowingly selling the meat black market. When the government found out, they come and shut the meat market down right away.

The old man lost all that money because he was fined. You see, the government don't want people selling too much meat. You can only buy so much meat and you take off a stamp and give it to the government. So, since the old man was limited in his meat sales, he decided to sell it under the table and was getting a higher price for it. This is the black market.

Mom and Bill went to the small jail house to bail him out.

When they came home Bill said to the rest of us siblings, "I'll never forget going with Mom to the jailhouse and seeing our old man behind bars."

I tell ya, I think after Bill gone and told us that, it made us all not want to get into any kind of trouble. Our old man's always getting into trouble. That's why we are always moving from one place to the next. People in the town that we are residing in catch on to what he's up to, and he gets run out a town after each failed scheme.

I can't believe all the times my family has moved already. None of us kids have even been born in the same town, and there is only nine years between all five of us. I hope we don't get run out of town this time. I like spending time with Grandma and Grandpa. It's also nice eating better food.

Grandma had a little garden when we came to live with her, and we stored a lot of good veggies for the chilly Winter months. Grandpa's always giving us sweet goodies too.

Well, after Mom used all our resources to get our old man out of the jail house, he left again. I don't know where he went to, but I hope he stays away. We lost our place we were renting, so Grandpa is letting us stay with him.

Well, dinner was most delicious, and I'm ready for presents.

"Can we open our gifts Grandpa?" I ask.

"Yes, we can," says Grandpa as he gives me a nice warm squeeze.

Grandpa's house is real nice. He's a carpenter, so it would have to be nice. It's nicer than all the houses I've ever stayed in.

I wish I could have a normal life. I get nervous about going to school someday. I'm so embarrassed about my old man. Many people are now already aware of him and his destructive plots, and when people know about deceptive people, they warn their children to stay away from the likes of the people's children. I don't want anyone to find out we are related to The Old Man, but some town folk already are aware of my direct relations to him. I suppose as soon as I would get any friends anyways, we would probably have to move, because he would get caught participating in some crazy, wild scheme and get kicked out of town.

Wow, I did get a beautiful baby doll. I'm good with babies now, since I've been helping with Kay. I'll treat this baby real nice.

CHAPTER 10

My Summer In Red Lodge (Summer 1932)

SPRINGTIME in Red Lodge is bursting out with fruit blossoms all over town. It's the end of April, and the year is 1932. Soon, I'll be four years old, and Bill will be six.

Well, we didn't get run out of town concerning the meat market; thank goodness. Mart will be off from school in a month, and I'm excited for a hot Summer, because Grandma said I could help her with her garden, and I am beyond excited.

Kay is growing by leaps and bounds. She's already activity crawling around trying to lift herself up. She's drooling a lot too. Mom says that she drools because she's cutting teeth. I really don't understand why Mom says such weird things. I mean, it doesn't look like Kay's ever cutting her teeth, but it is apparent that her tiny teeth are quickly growing. She's continually trying to chew on my fingers. She acts like they taste like sweet, delicious candy.

I must tell you about Mart's friend. Mart has a peculiar friend whose name is Ted Brasemgame. The first couple months living in Red Lodge, Mart and Ted started to hang out together and became close friends.

The Old Man didn't want Mart and Ted being friends because he said, "Ted's oldest brother is a criminal."

I hear if you are a criminal, and if you were put in Deer Lodge, that is a bad thing. That's where Ted's brother is—in Deer Lodge, Montana.

"That is quite a distance from here though," I heard Mart say after The Old Man told him to stop hanging out with Ted.

Well, if someone lives in Deer Lodge, I guess you're supposed to stay away from the rest of the family too. This is what The Old Man and Mart were arguing about one day in October of 1931. The Old Man didn't know it, because Mart told him that he would stop hanging out with Ted, but Mart kept hanging out with Ted.

Just the other day, I saw them down by the narrow creek in town. They were talking about how they were going to go fishing together the next day and where they're going to meet. I heard them, because I'm curious, and followed them.

I also heard Mom and Grandma talking today about my old man. Mom told Grandma that he called her up yesterday and told her that he got a good job. He's apparently living on a hog farm near the two-mile bridge area. A farmer who owns the land is letting him rent a house on the land, and in turn, the farmer is letting him take care of his hogs and get all the profit from them.

Supposedly it's a modest hog farm. The Old Man borrowed some money from a guy for the rent. We don't know who, but it can't be good, especially, since most often all of his ventures go belly. He wants my brothers to help him with the hogs for the Summer.

Summer is drawing to an end, and it has been one of the best Summer's I've ever experienced. The weather in Red Lodge is seasonably warm. I helped Grandma grow a beautiful garden. The highlight of my summer weekdays was helping her make things grow.

I helped with the magnificent, colorful flowers in Mrs. Brophry's yard too. She has the most beautiful flowers. Some day when I get a nice little house of my own, I'm going to plant me a beautiful flower garden. I'll plant many amazing, flowering trees too. I feel like it's part of me to see things grow.

I had lots of fun playing to.

There is a special, almost magical swing at the Brophry's, and after I was done helping things grow in Mrs. Brophry's flower garden, I would swing for a time. The beautiful swing is nestled, purposefully it seems, in the midst of the mystifying flowers and is attached to the biggest tree in the gigantic garden. It's like a fairytale being in their magical garden, and when I am happily swinging, my imaginative mind is taken away to magical places that have yet to be discovered and explored.

I also made a few friends in town, and Kay's almost walking now.

I am sad today though. It's the end of Summer and we are leaving Red Lodge. The Old Man is taking us back to Butte. Well, this is the first time I will be going to Butte.

Why is he taking us to Butte, do you ask?

He lost another job here, and no one will hire him because news of his reputation has gotten around the entire town. I'll tell you about the hog job that he lost. He thought he was really something having them hogs running around that hog farm.

Well, a few days ago, my old man, Mart, and Bill were all out at the farm feeding the dirty, smelly, old hogs and cleaning up after them. You know what he feeds them hogs? Horse meat. He bought cheap, old horses that were about ready to give up the ghost, and he would cut the horses up and feed the meat to the hogs.

The farmer gave The Old Man money every month to buy food for the hogs. There was a set price every month, but my old man thought he would be able to pocket a bit of money if he bought cheap food which is why he used the horse meat, they were practically free.

While my old man was cutting up some horse meat, Mart and

Bill were out cleaning after the pigs. They were throwing rocks against the farm buildings, and the hogs got a good fright when Bill threw his rock. It was a big rock and made a thunderous noise which caused the hogs to instantly stampede. They were so affright that they broke down their simple pens and got loose.

Mart and Bill couldn't find all the hogs, and one of the hogs got such a fright that he went and broke his leg. The farmer found out about it when he went to check on the hogs that day and fired my old man because of it.

The farmer lost a bit of money, because he could never find all his hogs, and when the farmer found out that my old man was feeding the hogs old horse meat; that was the end of his schemas adventure.

We give hugs to Grandma and Grandpa and say our goodbyes. I suppose we'll probably see them soon. The next time they must bail our old man out of trouble or take us in because he is in jail.

CHAPTER 11

Good Old Whitehall Brings Us Back To Red Lodge (1932-33)

THE old man brought us back to Butte right before the school year started. Mart will be in the third grade. Irene will be in the first grade, and Bill, me, and Kay will be at home with Mom. I'm only four and a half.

Kay is beginning to speak many words, and we can more clearly understand what it is she's saying to us.

Currently, we live on 8 Rose Street. This house is in Walkerville. Walkerville is way uptown. As far as you can travel on the road to the mountain. I did not see Butte on our way into town, because I was asleep. Butte sure is an interesting place though. Things are not so green as they were in Red Lodge, or in Renton. Here there is mostly dirt.

Mom says, "It is a mining town Mary."

The black, metal Gallows Frames seem to be on every corner in this place. It's not all that huge as far as the land goes, but it contains many more people than Red Lodge or Renton. Over 100,000 people live here in this little place. You can see the 100-foot metal Gallows

Frames by just standing outside our house. Some of them seem like a mile long going up into the sky. There are more than 5 open mines here in Butte.

Well, it's now Christmas day, and we have been downright freezing the last few months.

I am jealous that Mart and Irene are going to school every day, not because I want to go to school necessarily, but at least the schools are heated. This house is frigid.

As for a Christmas Tree or any Christmas at all, we have none. It is so miserable here. We have made lots of friends though. The Old Man keeps on talking to Mom about moving to Whitehall. We just arrived here, and he wants to move again. If he wants to move, I wish we could go back to Red Lodge and live with Grandpa. His house was always warm, and we had a nice Christmas there.

WE survived the Butte Winter. Spring is now starting to reveal and proudly show her colors. Well, as much color as you will see in Butte.

It is 1933, and as our old man is again waking us all up again in the middle of the night, the only rational thought that comes to my immediate mind is that he's burning down the house again.

So sad isn't it, that my first rational thought was that the house was on fire, and I think he is burning the house down?

The softly lit night air is seasonably comfortable as we are all rushing frantically out of the burning house, and our whole family is now outside watching the flames light up the dark, night sky. The red, orange ascending flames are rising higher and higher, like red and gold ribbons flowing in the wind.

This fire reminds me of Fall in Red Lodge when all the burnt leaves on the sleeping trees are turning their brilliant autumn colors. I especially liked when the leaves fell. We would rake them up and play in them for hours, burying ourselves over and over again.

Red Lodge, though, is a whole different and other place as I stand outside watching our house burn to the leveled ground.

The icy snow is almost gone, so it's not so cold outside tonight.

The flames of the fire are keeping me somewhat warm as I hear Irene asking our old man, "Where we going to live?"

He says to her, "I got me a plan."

The timely fire department is here trying to save the burning structure that used to be a house, but the sneaky flames consume the broken-down home as quickly as a frog brings in his prey with its snatching tongue.

As the once blazing red and orange flames begin to die down a bit, our curious neighbor comes by and says, "Stay with us for a few days until you know what you're going to do next."

Mom replies, "That that would be nice of you."

We stayed at our neighbors until our old man was able to meet with the insurance agents. That figures, he must have set fire to the building so he could get money out of it. It is so embarrassing being his child. This is the third house that has been set on fire by him.

To his credit, the first fire blazed house was an innocent accident, but it sure has given him some creative ideas about setting random houses on fire in various towns and getting insurance money from them. At least, he tells us to get out of the house first instead of burning us to the ground too. I am thinking that if our lives were part of the insurance money, he would most definitely leave us in there too.

Next month, it's my birthday, and I'm going to be five, Bill is going to be seven, Mart is ten and Irene is eight, and Kay is one and a half.

I have no idea where we are headed next, but I know it's going to be some crazy place with and even wilder adventure I don't want to have any part of.

CHAPTER 12

Cactus Junction (Summer 1933)

THE Old Man found a house on Carter Street, 3034 Carter to be exact. This is where we lived for a couple of months after the fire.

We are now headed to Whitehall. Whitehall, Montana.

The Old Man says to us, "There's a place there that I bought. I am going to fix it up and sell it."

I ask, "Where we going to live after that?"

"Don't worry, Mary, I got a plan."

Well, his plan must have to do with buying this new car. This is a nice car, almost a brand-new Ford Model T. He must have used the insurance money from the burnt house to buy it. He says he's making payments on it. We've never owned any vehicle so strikingly beautiful and sleek.

I ask my old man, "Where are we headed to?"

"It's called, Cactus Junction."

This worries me, because I have seen cactus' and have been poked by a few. I don't look forward to living in a place with sharp poky cactus'.

He says, "The house was practically free."

I ask, "How much did it cost?"

"A couple hundred dollars. This house is just an investment. In a few months we are going to move to a different place and have a little farm. Don't ya all worry, I'm goin' to take care of everything."

His words do not comfort my worried heart or make me feel any safer.

The drive to Whitehall from Butte isn't that far—about thirty-five miles or so.

It's the first week of a warm July, and the year is 1933. Mart and Irene will be going to school in Whitehall—if we are still there that is. We never know how long these "unexpected" trips will last.

I have been told that the Whitehall School is the closest school to where Cactus Junction is.

I think, since we have a while to get there, I'll sleep a little.

Well, we did made it to Cactus Junction. I was pretty sure we would considering the fact that we have a new car. I can't believe what I'm seeing. This can't be the place. No wonder it was practically free, it's made of pink-orange mud and stucco, but I do notice real quickly that it does not have so many cactus'.

Is my old man insane?

Maybe, Mom should have him institutionalized at the insane hospital located in Warm Springs, Montana. Why can't he just get a normal job and work and save his money like a normal person?

I wish I was still asleep, and this was all just a horrible, scary nightmare and I would soon wake up. I would take a horrible, scary nightmare that kept me scared my entire life over living just a day in this place. I don't even want to think about sleeping in that mud mess. I would rather sleep outside or in the car. Yes, the car would be comfy. It is new after all.

Mom is telling us all to get unpacked. The neighbors in Butte were kind to give us some clothes and food for our new journey. I will miss them all; they were so kind to us. They even gave us warm, fancy blankets and puffy, white pillows. We don't have any beds to put them on though. We will probably all be sleeping on this hard stucco floor.

Cactus Junction has become one of my least favorite places. There is nothing but dry, olive colored sagebrush spreading across the wide-open fields of grass and wheat, and not one person within miles. We have a few neighbors, but it looks like an open range; like in the western movies when cowboys are taking their journey across the wild, dry western plains.

Well, I have not yet gone to a movie, but I have heard about them, and they look like something interesting. A moving picture. Seems amazing and unconceivable to me. In Butte they had pictures of movies that were playing outside of the movie houses. In Butte, Bill would take me around town and show me all the fancy theaters. Outside the theatre's would be colorful posters of actors that play in the movies. Those fancy actresses and handsome actors sure looked glamorous.

Well, I don't quite know what glamorous means, but I would hear people saying it as they stared at the colored pictures.

I think, I want to be a glamorous actress one day.

DO you want to know what the old man's plan was in this Cactus Junction—burn everything to the bare ground. Mart is starting to call him the firebug.

Mart says, "If the insurance ever catches up with him, he's going to be in a load of trouble."

Mart's exact words, "They'd fix him."

We have only been here a couple weeks, and yes, our old man again burnt down another house. I don't know how he burnt this one down since most of it was pale, dried-up stucco mud.

He not only burnt the house down—he started the car on fire

and sent it over the cliff nearby. There is a corner just down the road from our now burnt down house, and a high cliff of about 100 feet descends below the sharp, unexpected corner. I'm sure many a people have traveled to their all to soon death down that unawares cliff. The corner is so sharp that if you weren't already aware of it, and you were speeding too fast, you'd miss turning it entirely.

Well, our old man only made two payments on that newer car. It was the only nice thing we owned. I was wondering why he came home last week in our old, beat-up Ford. He knew he'd need a vehicle after he set the new one on fire.

WE are heading back to Red Lodge. Thank goodness. I really did not want to go back to Butte. It is much warmer at Grandpa's house in Red Lodge.

THE Old Man dropped us off at Grandpa's and says to us, "I will be back soon. I'm going to be working in Butte. I will be living on Carter Street."

Carter Street was the last place we were living at in Butte, and while we were living at the Cactus Junction, he would go over to Butte a lot and stay for days at a time there. We hardly ever saw him, so he must have kept that house in Butte knowing he would need to live in it again.

I guess Mart and Irene will be going to school in Red Lodge instead of Whitehall.

CHAPTER 13

1934

SINCE we left Cactus junction, we have been moving around a whole lot—Butte, Bozeman, and Red Lodge.

Mom and my old man have been off and on together, so Mom has been moving us around with her—mostly moving in the Summer. Irene had to go to school, and so did Bill. Bill will be finishing up the first grade and Irene the third. Mart has been working a bit here and there to help support Mom, so he had to miss the fifth grade this year.

I remember Mom loading us all up and going over to Bozeman to visit Aunt Lois.

We always get an enormous meal when we go to Aunt Lois's. It is always so exciting when we get to visit her and her family. She sets her dining room table with everything all decorated looking nice.

You can't imagine the table she sets, but she always knows that it is always a treat for us and that we really enjoy and appreciate it. You can seat about 20 people at her table, and oh, the food.

In her garden, I always pick out the little, orange, sweet carrots and fresh, pale green peas. I end up gorging myself on their goodness—they taste so delicious.

Aunt Lois's kids have everything. They have their own fancy leather cowboy boots and beautiful first-class horses. They even own their own, almost new cars and have their own bedrooms. I can't imagine having my own bedroom. I would like to even just have my own bed and share a bedroom. But we always must share. I wonder what it might be like being so rich.

Our old man never was with us when we visited Aunt Lois's, because he was never allowed on the place. Mom is on her own right now anyways. Mom always enjoys going to visit her sister Lois. We always have a pretty good time here, and I love watching the horses running around. What a site; the kids in their leather saddles, and all the yummy goodies they have to eat.

One thing about Mom—she has the guts to go places. She has the model Ford now. My old man left it to her while he was away. A lot of people, especially women, are scared to drive, but not mom. I admire her courage.

On one of our trips going to Butte, when we were coming back from Red Lodge in the middle of Winter, we were driving on Harding Way, or Nine Mile as it's sometimes called, and on the highest part of the road, the Ford began sliding, and the back wheels on the edge of the road were just barely hanging there off the slippery, dangerous, wintery road.

How we never went off that mountain, I'll never know, there must've been somebody above looking over Mom that night.

I have been hearing in church about guardian angels and how they sometimes protect us from danger. I don't understand all the information I hear about them though. Well, someone driving by on their way to Butte stopped when they saw we were hanging off the cliff and said they would send word once they arrived in Butte. I would consider this a guardian angel, wouldn't you?

Later, a life-saving wrecker came and pulled the hanging car back onto the slippery road. The car was just balancing the back wheels over the side of the mountain. None of this bothered Mom though, she just got back in the car and drove back to Butte.

One thing, I must say about Mom—she isn't afraid of anything. At least, far as I can tell nothing seems to bother her. She really enjoys herself—that is for sure, especially, when she is away from her old man. When she is away from him, her spirit comes alive. I learned about spirits in church and how they influence the things our bodies and minds do, and her spirit sure is a strong, lively one.

CHAPTER 14

Getting Baptized And Robbing Banks (1935)

MART, Irene, and Bill have been going to school in Red Lodge this past year. Mart is done with the fifth grade, and Irene is done with the fourth. Mart is twelve, and Irene is ten. Bill just turned nine, and in May, he just finished the second grade. Kay is three, and she is still home with me.

Today, is a glorious day, and I just know those guardian angels are rejoicing over me and my beautiful sisters. I am getting baptized today. It is June 15, 1935, almost a month after my birthday, and I am not the only one getting sprinkled with water today.

Grandma said to Mom after I turned seven, Monta, "Before Jo comes back, those girls should all be baptized."

Grandma has been taking us all to church while we have been here, and I must say, I really like going. That God-fearing preacher sure gets involved in his saintly sermons. Sermons, in case you don't know, are when a spiritual man of the good Lord speaks about the Lord's words that are found in the Bible.

The Bible is a large, usually black book. I don't quite know how to read yet, so I can't read the Bible, but I think it would take a long time to read. I see Grandma reading the Bible and even Ruth.

Grandma says, "The Bible will save you if you read it enough times."

I am not quite sure what she means by that statement, but I believe her, because she says it with such conviction. When she says it, I feel truth coming from her educated words. I just wonder though, how many times we have to read it to be saved?

I want to be baptized, because the preacher says if you don't get baptized, you will go to a fiery, burning hell. He was preaching a couple weeks ago about Hell and how we will burn up in Hell if we do bad, awful things.

I've experienced many fires in my life, and almost burned in some of them, so Hell doesn't seem like a place that fits my personality. It doesn't seem to be a place that is too much fun to be in. I was begging and pleading Mom to baptize me after I found out all about Hell.

So, my sisters and I are all going down to the river to get baptized. We are all beautifully dressed in all white, sheer dresses.

When I asked Grandma why we had to wear white she said, "White means purity Mary, and after you are baptized, you will be pure and clean."

Grandma made all our magnificent dresses.

She said, "This is a special occasion, and you all must look nice and proper for God."

Mom looked so pretty. Her dark, brown, thick hair is flowing just past her ears, and she curled up the ends. She has on this pretty, cream-colored dress with ruffles in the front and a pretty, white sweater that is so gracefully wrapped around her wide shoulders.

Irene's hair was just recently cut, and it is curled just right around her ears. She also has dark, thick hair like Mom. She has beautiful puff sleeves that just cover the top of her bare arms, and there is a white ribbon tied around her waist. She has wonderfully tiered ruffles at the bottom of her dress, and her dress flows just below her knees. She sure looks magnificent.

Kay's dress is simple with wavy sleeves. Her dress starts covering her high at the neck and flows straight all the way to her knees, although, her hair is in sort of a disarray.

My dress is similar to Irene's, except I have a ribbon tie in the front and instead of puff sleeves, I have layered, wavy sleeves. My hair is not as dark as Mom's, Irene's, and Kays. It is light brown. They all have brown eyes too. My eyes are as blue as the ocean on a sunny day.

I still have memories of the magical, blue ocean in Washington. Sometimes, I think all that was a dream—being in Renton.

Us girls, except for Mom have big white bows tied in our thick hair. All little girls love to wear fancy bows in their hair. My hair is the same length as Irene's. I like my hair longer though.

We are walking down to the narrow river, and the air is a little cold still being the first part of Summer and all. Ruth is also with us. She has already been baptized, but she wants to join us on this occasion.

The Godly preacher is already in the water waiting for us. We all walk slowly, carefully, and a little nervously through the cool water. We have to take our shoes off, of course. I can feel the sand squishing between my small toes as I walk.

Irene is going to go first. The Preacher is saying something—I am not quite sure what. Then, he goes and sprinkles some water on Irene, and says, "You are now baptized."

The good preacher repeats the same actions to Kay and me.

Grandma has a wide, satisfied smile on her pretty, gracefully, aging face. I can tell she feels more secure about where we are going to go when we die. I too feel a little bit cooler now that I'm baptized, and it isn't just because the now muddy water's cold. I just know now that I have a ticket up to Heaven now, unless, of course, I murder someone, because murder is the only decision you can make to have a void baptism.

I am a bit confused about my baptism though. The preacher says in the Bible Jesus was baptized. I am confused about that too. He was supposed to be perfect, but he still had to be baptized. Why?

His cousin John, who they called John the Baptist, baptized Jesus. John baptized Jesus in the River Jordan, and when he did, he put him all the way under the water, and after he came out of the water, a magnificent, white dove appeared.

So, I kind of feel like I did what Jesus did, but different because I was just sprinkled with water. If we are supposed to do the things Jesus did, I think the preacher should have dunked us all the way under so not a stitch of us was above the water. This would have reassured me that the baptism was effective and real. And I'm thinking we might have even seen a glorious, white dove appear directly above our heads if we did it the way Jesus did.

When I asked Mom about it, she said things are done different now days. This doesn't make sense to me neither, because in the Bible it says that Jesus never changes His ways. At least, that was in one of the preacher's sermons.

All this is a bit confusing to me; except, I know now that I can go to Heaven, and that is what matters.

WE are going back to Butte now. My old man came back and wants us to go with him. He told Mom that he has a house on Sanders Street.

"3201 Sanders," he said. "It is a nice place, and I got me a good job working in the mines."

Mom tells Grandma, "We have been in Red Lodge too long burdening you."

Grandma says to Mom, "You are not a burden Mary."

But Mom is going to go.

IT has been a few months since we have lived in Butte. I have a story to tell. It was just Thanksgiving and the kids in the neighborhood sure were thankful for what they received.

It was a crazy, exciting day today. Everyone was talking—passing the word swiftly down the busy street that someone had robbed a bank. As the story was told, the bank in Whitehall was robbed. That is close to where we were when we lived in the Cactus Junction. Just 8 miles outside of Whitehall.

The story is that the dangerous robbers were sticking up the place with real live guns, threatening the people who worked in the bank and the people that were there getting out their money, telling them to go into the vault. Well, the people listened to the hideous robbers. Then, those mean robbers locked those people in the vault. After locking them in the vault, they took all the money.

The word on the street yesterday was that these bank robbers had a generous sack full of coins, and they came over to Butte trying to hide themselves, and the stolen coins. Well, the police ended up finding out where their secret hiding place was and took out after them.

While on the desperate run from the police officers, the robbers dropped one of their bags of coins, and when the first kid found it there were plenty more kids who came after trying to find coins. Word traveled fast about where those coins were dropped, and well, everyone ran in the street to collect the coins—including me. Everyone was savagely pushing each other greedily picking up the stolen money and quickly placing the coins in their pockets.

There were some kids already in the narrow, now dusty, dirt street when I arrived. The coins were laying all over in the trampled down dirt. There were about a hundred or so kids reaching down trying to find the coins that fell out of the robber's bags. I reached down and found a few of those coins for myself, and after I did, I ran as fast as my scrawny seven-year-old legs could carry me.

I don't know what happened to those robbers, I didn't hear much about them after that day, but I know that the bank didn't get all their money back because all the kids from the neighborhood got handfuls of them coins.

I don't know much about what a sin is and what it isn't, but I do know that I didn't rob the bank, and some other kid would have gotten the coins if I hadn't picked them up.

I am not sure why I am even thinking about taking those coins as a sin—Maybe, because I recently got baptized. Since, I have been in Butte, I haven't been to church once. I am fairly sure that I am still okay with the Lord, and this is not one of those sins the preacher talks about.

CHAPTER 15

Back To Good Old Whitehall (1936)

THE smell of sweet fruit tree blossoms fill the warm Summer air as I notice a hairy spider scurrying across the new piece of dusty ground that inhabits the house we will be calling home.

It's 1936, and my old man has brought us back to Whitehall, or on the "outskirts," he says.

We didn't live in Butte long before we came out here. I wonder if I will ever have a place to call home for more than a couple years.

July is always an eventful month in beautiful Red Lodge and even in Butte, but I am afraid that this July, being in Whitehall, is going to be very uneventful considering we are eight miles away from the nearest town gatherings. I am now eight, Kay is four, Bill is ten, Irene is eleven, and Mart is thirteen.

Mom says, "Mary, you will be starting the second grade in Whitehall. Mart will be in the seventh grade. Irene with be in the sixth grade and Bill in the fourth grade."

As we thoroughly investigate this sagebrush filled land that is new to us, we notice about ten acres surrounding the house that apparently is ours.

"It's a farm and ranch," says Irene.

"Yes," I say. "And it feels like we are in the middle of no man's land."

Irene laughs at me and runs to catch up to Mom to see if she needs any help packing things into the house. Irene is always trying to be helpful. This is a good quality that she naturally possesses.

The warm, sweet air steadily blows through my sticky, brown hair as I breathe in the fresh and overabounding scent of sagebrush and fresh water. Wondering where the scent of fresh water is coming from, I begin to walk over past a small hill directly below the one-story house.

Below the grassy hill, I see a narrow, slow, flowing creek running through the bottom of the rich farmland.

The Old Man must have had this move planned for some time— probably while we were living in Butte, because there are already animals on the land. Chickens are gobbling up some of the fresh creek water as well as a few reddish-brown cows. In the not so far distance, walking along the creek, are a couple brown and white goats and about four white, fluffy, baa-ing sheep.

My old man surprises me with his appearance as he sneaks up behind me saying, "Those clucking, egg layin' chickens are going to be a big money maker for us, Mary."

He looks out at the blue, smokey mountains in the far distance as he continues to walk farther down the calm, flowing creek. I see him lazily walking toward an old run-down chicken house in the back of the dusty yard. I imagine the chicken house should be painted, but paint is expensive and no doubt, we won't be here long enough to make the farm decent.

I follow my old man, and as I get closer to the chicken house, I see that I was correct in it needing fresh paint. The dry, cracking paint is quickly chipping off, and the bare wood is turning grey from the previous winds, rains, and snowfalls. All colors of chickens: red, white, and green and black are busily and noisily clucking away at us as we maneuver around their place of residence.

The ancient house, which is on the very top of the insignificant hill from the creek, is surrounded by mostly dirt, not a lot of full trees or green grass around it, but there is an abundance of bendy brown and green willows that run along the playful creek. I recognize that the hot wind here is strong as it has picked up speed already since our arrival.

As I walk toward the house, scratchy sagebrush rubs against my bare, skinny legs. Sagebrush is two-foot by two-foot bushes of ugly greenish grey that look like sticks and dry leaves—definitely not my favorite plant.

When I arrive at the torn down house, I notice it looks sort of like a lost in the forest log house. I'm not sure you can call it homey, because as I immediately walk inside of it, it's bare of any evidence of previous life. Walking through the house, I quickly notice there are three small bedrooms. Mart is already trying to fix the broken front door, which is currently falling off at the hinges, if you could call them hinges.

Mom is excitedly rushing us around telling us, "Empty the luggage and the stuff we brought in the car and bring it into the house."

We don't have many personal possessions to bring into this old house, so I am not sure why mom is so anxious about it all anyways. We never did get anything new while living in Butte. Even the precious dolly that grandpa gave me for Christmas is gone because of the fire my old man started in Cactus Junction. She went up in red, hot flames just like the fancy car.

Mostly, the only clothes we have are the ones we are wearing; although, Grandma did send us a few old things from the Brophry's clothing drive a few months ago. Grandma loves us so much, and Mrs. Brophry is so kind—knowing we lack enough clothes to wear, but even those worn clothes are almost useless. We have all been growing like giant beanstalks the last few months. It seems when Spring comes, and every living plant begins to blossom and grow, so do us kids.

I kneel cautiously down, carefully placing my narrow hand in the partly brick fireplace, and as my thin, long fingers rub old black and grey ash between them, I notice the kitchen. The kitchen is about 12 X 36 feet, and I get the idea quickly that there is no bathroom. It looks like we'll be using the stinky outhouse.

Because my view already tires of the log cabin house, I walk outside and see a cute little barn in the back pasture where all the farm animals apparently reside. It is a little way past the chicken house.

Even though, I'm not at all happy to be here, it will be fun playing with all the lovely animals. I love animals. I've learned though, not to get too attached to animals—ever since we had to leave our dog in Buckley and since my old man sold my wonderful baby calf just before that. I'm thinking, in the near future, we'll probably be butchering most of the animals on this farm.

I hear my old man say to Mom as I make my way back to the broken porch of the log cabin, "Monta, we are going to be rentin' this place."

The fourth of July is almost upon us, and Mom says to The Old Man, "Summer will soon be ending, and the Winter's in Whitehall are even worse than the Winter's in Red Lodge and Butte. Snow drifts sometimes will reach the top eves of the houses, and the ferocious winds in these fields will blow the drifts to 40-50 feet high."

That's one thing I'm not looking forward to. In Red Lodge and Butte, the snow was okay since we were living close to town. Out here, in no man's land, we are far from just about everything and the town assistance won't be coming to plow the snow away for us. I don't even have warm socks to wear. I hope I get some before I start school, and I hope they match. Most the socks I get from the thrift stores don't match, and I am afraid kids will make fun of me for it.

I'll be starting the second grade in just a couple months, and I don't own a decent warm coat or nice dress yet. I know I'm going to be so embarrassed going to school, but one day, I'll be a famous dress designer and have all the pretty dresses and coats I need.

One day.

At this vital point in my history, I would happily settle for anything that didn't look like torn-up, overused rags.

I grab a few things from the car attempting to make my contribution to bringing things into the cabin, and as I look at the bedrooms, I notice there are a grand total of three dusty beds. The beds look like someone had gone to the local dump—quickly snatching them up before they were forever buried in the landfill never to be used again.

Looks like cleaning is going to be our jobs all week. There is always so much cleaning work to do when we move into a new-old house that I think I am an expert janitor now. Cleaning will keep us busy all week.

I guess the girls will be sharing a bed and room, and the boys will be sharing one. Mom and our old man have their own room.

As I try to be upbeat and change my negative attitude into my positive imagination, I look in the house for Katherine to see if she wants to go exploring with me; when suddenly, I hear her scream.

"AAAAA," yells Katherine, who is outside.

I swiftly run out of the cabin to see what the matter is.

"What is it, Katherine?" I ask.

Katherine is almost five now.

"Bugs! Bugs!" She hollers.

Oh my, were there bunches of bugs, creeping crickets, and hopping green and yellow grasshoppers. They are everywhere—hundreds of them—surrounding all sides of the chicken house.

Katherine doesn't much like bugs. When we were living in Butte, in that ugly green house, the brown, blood sucking bed bugs were absolutely awful. We'd angrily wake up in the early morning full of bloody sores on our tender legs and arms. Since having to confront bloody bed bugs, Katherine can't take any kinds of bugs, and as soon as I reach the chicken house, she just as quickly runs towards the cabin hoping to find her quick pavilion of safety. She is so cute, her and her little skinny legs running as quick as they can travel.

Everyone calls Katherine, Kay, but I still like to call her Katherine sometimes. She is special to me, because she is my baby sister and the first sibling I was ever able to take care of. I feel all grown up when I am around Katherine.

I follow Katherine back to the house, attempting to get her to come back out and come play with me at the beautiful creek, but no matter what I say to her to try to get her to come out, she won't budge away from Mom's legs.

"No!" she states firmly, "I won't go."

As I go back outside in the now scorching, windy summer air thinking I will explore and imagine all alone, I notice Mart and Bill walking over to the neighbor's house. There's another farm about a half a mile up from where our farm is. It is a much fancier and much more manicured farm than this one. The two-story house is real fancy surrounded by lovely, full fruit trees and green, emerald shrubs. In their back yard, a huge plentiful garden is apparent, and the obvious and perceptive eye can already see most of the growth of the sweet fruits and delicious looking vegetables.

Mart and Bill are real social and get to know our neighbors right off. They don't waste time. I love their confidence and courage; they are great examples to me on how to be more social.

My old man says as I walk away to follow Mart and Bill, "Monta, we need to begin plantin' crops."

I'm only eight, and I know that it's already too late in the season for planting crops that will grow and flourish. The neighbors will soon be harvesting their bountiful, luscious crops in just another month. We don't even have any machinery and tools to till the dry, hard ground that exists here with, and we don't even know how the irrigation works.

Mart is almost fourteen years old, and he hasn't farmed a day in his life. Our old man—I'm sure will not be here most the time, and Winter is going to set in soon, so I know Mom won't start planting no crops.

I leave the cabin and all my old man's talking nonsense, and as I get closer to the neighbor's house, my curious eyes land on some boys playing in the beautiful yard. I soon figure out that's probably why Mart and Bill walked over there.

Mart and Bill are real good at making friends whenever we move places. Them and those other boys are all talking now. My curious eyes don't see any girls hanging about—except for the mother of the boys who also comes out to greet Mart and Bill.

CHAPTER 16

The Kiss (September 1936)

SCHOOL begins today, and I'm more nervous than a man and woman's first kiss.

It's September, and the year is 1936. The big, yellow school bus is supposed to be coming out here to pick us all up. At least my siblings are going to be on the bus with me; then, I won't be as nervous.

I have a used, blue dress on that my old man bought me from a thrift store in town last month. He brought it home thinking he went and did something special and nice for me, but it's a whole size to big, and I must pin part of the back in so it don't fall off of me. Mom would have sewn it for me, but she lost her sewing machine in the last fire.

You think if he knew he was going to start the stucco house on fire, he would have purposefully grabbed Mom's much needed sewing machine. Maybe, he thought he was going to get insurance on that too.

I've never had a pretty, new dress, except for the one my wonderful grandma made me specially for my healing baptism. Irene has had a few, and I always inherit her hand-me-downs, or I get used thrift store dresses.

Going to school today—I do have some socks from the thrift store, but they both have holes in them. Looking on the positive side, as I try to do most often, the socks are the same color. They are not a perfect match, but almost. My brown, Mary Jane shoes are all worn down. There's an inch hole in the left top foot and a centimeter hole in the back of the right one. I wish the respective holes were reversed, so the front of my toes protruding out wouldn't be so noticeable.

My light, brown, shoulder length hair is up in four-inch piggy tails, and I have no coat—as of yet. It's not too cold yet, but I know it's going to be soon. Hopefully, I have a cosey warm coat by then.

My sister Katherine musts stay home with Mom. She doesn't mind though, because since we saw the various pesky bugs outside, she hasn't wanted to go out since. She has been in the cabin most the hot Summer. Nothing anyone says can convince her that the hot, windy outdoors full of pesky bugs is better than the stale, moldy cabin.

The Summer in this old cabin was quite interesting. A couple days after we arrived here—it was the fourth of July, and I was unhappily woken up from a wonderful dream.

"What is all that noise?" I wondered out loud.

I'll tell you what happened.

The hungry brown and white spotted goat, in the middle of the night, got out of her stinky pen and somehow managed to get herself into our broken-down kitchen. Mom was attempting to get the apparently starving goat out of the kitchen; when, before we knew it, the famished goat got a quick hold of the holey, sun faded, green curtains. She was hurriedly ripping those curtains down one by one chewing them up just as fast as she could get them down, knowing full well that her breakfast would be confiscated as soon as she was found out by one of her human owners.

I've never seen any living thing gobble something up so fast in all my life. I don't suppose you could call those pieces of material curtains anyways. They had so many holes, stains, and rips in them, it's not like they were helping us with our privacy which is the entire purpose of curtains.

That goat was in such a fright because all of us were yelling at it that it ran out of the house, into the back yard, and towards the mountains over across the creek. It came back a few hours later though. The whole scenario reminded me of my old man's story of when he lost his ol' mule, except the goat was not injured, and we didn't burn a fire underneath it to get it going.

I looked around after the goat incident, and someone was missing.

I asked Mom, "Where is The Old Man?

"He went into town to try and find some buyers for chicken eggs. He will be back soon, and we need to start taking care of this farm."

I guess that was the start of us taking care of the farm.

Our old man did come back. Every few days he would come and gather chicken eggs and bring them into town. Mart would go with him. I heard Mart telling Mom at the beginning of August that he didn't want to go selling eggs with our old man no more.

Mom asked, "Why not, Mart?"

"Because, he is cheating people, and it's embarrassing when they find out what he is up to."

Mom asked, "How is he cheating the people."

"He's been putting good large eggs in the first half of the egg carton, and in the bottom half, he puts nothing. By the time the people figure out what he has gone and done to cheat them, we've already gone out of their yard, and he never goes to the same customer twice."

I think our old man got caught selling those eggs though, because not too many days after that, he came home and said, "I got me a buyer for those chickens, a meat market in town said they would buy the whole lot of them."

You think, I would be surprised by now concerning and knowing about all the sneaky schemes and non-full proof plots I have heard my old man contrive over the years, but I am still unpleasantly surprised when I hear of his most recent scam.

Farm living created many opportunities to explore and imagine all Summer. I guess sagebrush comes in real handy when you want to make imaginary castles and fight off angry water serpents, that are actually snakes, in the oceans of Antarctica—which is actually the creek down below the house. I was even included when Mart and Bill and the boys next door built a tree house down by the creek with all those malleable, yellow and green willow trees.

We really didn't do much farming. Our old man was gone to town most the time, and he always took the old black Ford, so we had no way to go to town unless we walked. It would take most the day to walk eight miles, so we just stayed on the farm. The closest thing to farming we did was collect eggs, until our old man sold all the chickens. He did not even keep one chicken so we would have eggs to cook with.

Mom milked the cow so we could drink milk, and we had to butcher the goat and one of the sheep for food. Food was scarce, which meant instead of feeding the animals, we had to eat them.

Well, back to my very first day of school. I do try to stay on the topic when I'm telling you my stories, but my thoughts distract me, and I must stop and inform you about what's going on in them.

Mart says, "That's a woman thing."

I ask, "What do you mean by that?"

"Mary, I'll explain when you're older."

Of course he will.

After getting off the bus, I look towards a grey and red brick building. The building is not so large, but since it is the only one, I assume this is the school. It seems as if grades one through twelve are all in it, which is good if I need to talk to my sister or brothers, I will be able to easily find them. It's a cute little place.

Ringggg! Ringggg!

That's the bell. Time for school to start.

When we get in the school building everyone heads for their classrooms. I don't have any idea where I'm supposed to go, so I ask someone who looks like a teacher.

"Where is my classroom?" I ask the kind looking lady.

She says to me, "What is your name young lady?"

"Mary."

"And how old are you?"

"Why, I'm eight and half years old."

She points to the place I'm supposed to be going, and I go the way she is pointing.

As soon as I arrive to the place she was pointing, I notice a class full of excited boys and girls. Such a variety of kids, I think to myself.

The teacher sternly commands me, "Go find a seat!"

Then she starts talking—telling us all the rules of the classroom.

"Everyone introduce themselves—beginning from the left front," she instructs.

When it's my turn to do the introducing, I stand up courageously and say, "My name is Mary Janette Miller."

I sit down after introducing myself, and everyone else that is left introduces themselves.

I think I'm going to like this teacher. She's not such a looker, but she has a nice disposition. I've heard Mom and Grandma use that word when they are talking about someone who is not such a looker. I'm not sure what it means, but I think it means something nice.

The bell rings for our first recess, and I'm excited about this new experience. Learning is good, but I really want to make me some good friends. All the excited girls are heading straight for the four blue swings and the rambunctious boys are going for the one slide.

The shiny, silver slide looks more entertaining than the swings, and even though there is an extremely long line to the slide, I choose to go to the slide. I just happen to get in the back of the slide line, because I was the last one out of the classroom.

I was the last one in the classroom before class began, so I had to sit in back of the classroom; therefore, the last one out of the door for recess. The last row of chairs in the classroom is farthest from the classroom door.

Well, back to the slide. I'm waiting in line forever it seems and am getting frustrated, thinking I made the completely wrong choice in my recess entertainment. I am extremely worried that the bell's going to ring before I even get a chance to slide. Especially, when all those rowdy boys keep trying to climb up the slippery part of the slide after they had already had their turn going down.

I'm not saying I wouldn't do the same thing, because it does look like fun, but I want a turn before the bell rings.

Finally, the recess assistant comes over to the slide and tells the stingy boys to stop double sliding, and after the recess assistant prohibits the boys from not playing fair, the line begins to move much quicker, and it's my turn to slide.

Finally! I think to myself.

I slowly and carefully step up the slide steps and am soon at the top. I suspiciously look down before sitting my tiny bottom on the top of the solid, slippery slide.

I take the plunge.

"Wheee!" I scream as I feel the wind rush through my four-inch piggy tails making them slightly fall from their supposed place of security.

As soon as my now fiery bottom stops on the edge of the slippery slide, a boy about three feet in length, Walter Jap, is facing me. I know his name because I remember him introducing himself in class, and he sits directly across from me, so it was easy to remember; plus, I want to purposefully remember everyone's name as to make friends easier. It seems that Walter is intentionally waiting for me at the bottom of the now mysterious slide.

What happened next was not expected and took me surely by surprise.

Before I even had the opportunity to get off the bottom of the slick slide and contest of Walter Japs not offered offering, he was standing more directly over me.

I look up and see him just as quickly leaning over me planting directly on my small childlike, suddenly pink flushed, soft cheek, a great big, slightly wet kiss.

As he leans back to his first position, I just look at him in bewilderment and awe-stricken surprise. Mom told me I should smack a boy if one ever tried to kiss me, but I was just too stunned to say a word, except for, "What you done that for?"

He smiles at me and says, "I think your awful cute, and I want to be your boyfriend."

I did not think this was something I would have to worry about on the first day of school, but without thinking too long or too much about it, I say, "Okay, I'll be your girlfriend."

I am sure Mom would not approve, but she isn't here is she?

CHAPTER 17

Almost Dead (February 1937)

"I'M soooo cold," is an anguish cry that is presently heard in our frigid cabin.

Before I get to the present, you're probably wondering what happened with Walter and me. Well, of course we never spoke one word to each other after the first day of school, but he still told the entire class that I was his beautiful and amazing girlfriend, bragging to everyone that I am such a good kisser. He told everyone that I was the prettiest girl he has ever seen. Well, those are the rumors I heard anyways.

The older I get—the more people tell me that I am beautiful. Even though I don't have the prettiest clothes, it seems like my looks are pretty good.

The Old Man has been gone for a couple months now. Ever since he sold all the sheep, most of the goats, and all the cows, except the milking cow, we haven't seen nor heard a stitch from him.

We had to butcher the milking cow, because we were starving. We aren't large people anyway, so when I say starving, I mean our bones are beginning to protrude out of our thin skin.

February has come all too suddenly upon us and with it freezing forty-five degrees below zero temperatures. Three weeks before Christmas, our old man came by to give us some potatoes, carrots, flour, and salt.

He told us, "This food should last you all Winter."

Before this, we didn't see him for three weeks.

Mom wasn't too happy with The Old Man the first time he left, and she said to him, "What do you expect us to do when all the snow comes down?"

But he had no instant or reasonable answer for Mom.

The Old Man wasn't too happy when he was about to leave either, because the goat started eating the cloth on the seats in the model T he was driving. Yes, he takes the car every time he leaves and leaves us stranded.

The cold, bitter wind bites through our thin, goose-bumpy skin and clattering bones as it creeps its way into the thin walled, partly holey cabin. It's so cold, and the snow is so high that the school bus hasn't stopped here for almost three weeks.

The snow is as high as the eaves—just like Mom said it would be. We have almost no burning wood left. Mart and Bill have been tirelessly tearing and chopping the wood off the old sheds and the barn, so we have wood to burn in the fire—attempting to keep us warm as the wind and the fire fight against each other in a ferocious battle. If we didn't have the barn and shed wood, our lives would have probably ceased to survive by today, and we would be as frozen as the icicles that hoover down past the eaves of the igloo cabin.

We have not been able to send word to Grandma and Grandpa. The post man hasn't been able to come out because of the below zero temperatures, so there have been no letters coming in, and we can't send any letters out. Mom and Grandpa usually write to each other a few times a month. They became real close after she got married, and they really love each other.

Uncle Walter Fogleman hasn't been out here for a while either. He lives in Butte and comes to check on us, because he is always worried about our situation. Uncle Walter is Grandpa's brother. He sometimes brings us food to eat.

Even the creaky water pump in the kitchen has frozen, so we are melting snow to get water. We haven't been able to clean ourselves for weeks. We have a tin tub in which we would normally fill up with water from the kitchen pump, and three of us would share the water one after another, because the tub was too hard to fill up all the time. Since the pump has frozen, we are all dirty. We couldn't possibly take a bath anyways, because the water would be difficult to warm up, and collecting snow would take us out into the freezing cold.

I guess if I die that will be the end of me being Walter Jap's beautiful girl. I suppose being dead might not make me ugly—not at first anyways. I mean, after I decompose back into the earth, I might be ugly, but it might take a few days.

Bill interrupts my thoughts and says, "It's got to be at least forty below zero out there, and that's not including the wind shield."

It's been difficult to keep warm. We have almost used up the shed and barn wood, and once you move away from the stove, the rest of the house is freezing. The bitter wind blows through the ½ inch cracks of the house. There are plenty of cracks too. I think if no one comes to save us, we will probably starve or freeze to death— whichever one comes first.

Mart comes in from the outside and announces to Mom, "I am going to hitchhike to Butte and try to find Uncle Walter. The neighbor said he would bring me part of the way."

The neighbors have been as kind as they could be, but they have families to feed and to keep warm too. Mom has tears streaming down her eyes, because she doesn't want Mart to go out in that cold weather, but she knows if we don't do something and quick, we are all going to be frozen, hard icicles. There is so much snowy frost on the frozen windows, and if we are not right next to the stove, we can see our breath in the cabin.

Mart is so brave. Yet again, he is my example of courage and what a man should really behave like. Even though it's icy cold, he is going to risk his young, tender life and good looks in a fearless attempt to reach Butte to find our uncle to come get us.

Mart doesn't have much for clothes, so we all give him as many clothes as we can find.

As he goes out the door, I say a little prayer to the Lord, "Please Lord, keep care of my brother and watch over him."

It's been two long, lonesome, worry filled days since Mart walked out the cabin door, and the weather has not let up. All I can do is dream about being in a nice warm house with a warm, blaring fire, keeping warm in a bed all my own with a hot water bottle stuffed snug into the fluffy, clean, crimson linen covers.

When you live like I do, all you got is your dreams.

I won't live like this though, and I'll make sure I marry a good man—a man who will take care of his children.

Just now, when I've gone all dreaming, Mart and Uncle Walter are walking through the door.

"Oh, I'm so glad to see you both," I say as I give them both a big bear hug.

Everyone is so excited. Uncle Walter brought his car, and we are all going with him. He's bringing us to Red Lodge to stay with Grandpa.

Before we leave, I say a little prayer of thanks to the Lord for protecting Mart, "Thank you, Lord, for protecting my brother. I know you love him too."

I don't know the Lord too well yet, but I'm trying my best to get to know Him. The coins still hoover over my mind sometimes, and

I'm still not sure if I have sinned. One day, I'll have to get enough courage to ask the preacher—maybe, when Grandma takes us to church again in Red Lodge.

I think I already know the answer. The courage to talk to the preacher about it is what I am lacking. What will God do to me when I confess?

As we drive away from the almost grave that was our home, I feel so glad—glad to leave this place—hopefully forever.

CHAPTER 18

Back In Red Lodge (1937)

I overhear Uncle Walter and Mom talking on the way to Red Lodge as everyone is soundly sleeping in the warm Model T, but I am pretending to be asleep.

"I've been seeing Joe around town."

I can sense the hurt in Mom's cracked voice as she tells Uncle Walter, "I am leaving him for good this time."

This isn't the first time I've heard Mom say those all to famous words—well deserved too. I just hope she means it this time. Uncle Walter was telling her how Mart got a hold of him.

He says to her and technically to me too since I can hear him, "The neighbor drove Mart about a third of the way on the pass when he had to go back, he was worried about the gas running out in the car. He waited long enough for Mart to hitch a ride. The man he hitched the ride from was going to Butte, so he gave Mart a ride the rest of the way. It took Mart a whole day to find me, and when he did find me, we wired a message to your mother in Red Lodge. She sent some money for gas, and as soon as we received it, Mart and I left Butte and came to get you."

I'm excited to go to Red Lodge, because I know we'll get some good food and have a warm house. As I think about how nice it will be to be in Red Lodge again, my eyelids begin to droop and give up.

"GRANDPA!" I happily say.

"Hello Mary, I'm so glad you all are here."

He is telling Mom that since we were here last, he did some re-modeling. Grandpa figured we'd be back, so he converted the garage into two rooms for us, so we could have some privacy.

Everyone is saying their hello's, and Uncle Walter is saying his goodbye's.

He says, "I need to head back to Butte, and I better get a start."

Grandpa says, "I am going into town to get us some food to eat, do you want to come Mary?"

I say excitedly, "Of course, I do!"

"What are you making for dinner, Grandpa?" I ask.

"I'm going to cook a warm soup."

As he talks about the soup, I begin licking my lips hungrily.

Grandpa must go to all the grocery stores to find the best price of meat. He always feeds us real good, but he makes sure that he's getting the best price for his dollar. Mom says that he's a bit of a cheap skate, but he has never been cheap with me.

Mom told us kids that Grandpa's a bit of a hypochondriac too.

A hypochondriac is someone who thinks they are always sick or that they are going to be sick. They are always thinking that there is a problem with them and their health. Mom says this because Grandpa has cupboards and cupboards full of pills. But she told us that he is as healthy as a horse. I am not sure what healthy as a horse is. I have seen plenty of horses that are not too healthy, but Mom always says strange things like this. I know she went to school and is smart, but I don't know about all these other references she talks about sometimes.

When we get back to the house, Mom is getting ready to leave to see Grandma.

"Can I come, Mom?" I ask.

"Sure, Mary."

When we arrive at the Brophry's house, we head to the back of the house; we are not supposed to enter in the front of the house. Even though the Brophry's are kind people, we are not allowed in the front door.

Grandma gives us all a big hug, and she has made some good smelling cookies. Grandma must keep a full cupboard of cookies, cakes, and breads in the Brophry's house at all times. She doesn't even get to have Sunday's off, because she must have dinner waiting when the Brophry's get home from church. She gets to go to church, but after church, she is required to prepare dinner.

Grandma is attempting to console Mom. She tells her that the Brophry's just received a bunch of clothes for the drive, and we can pick some out. I am so excited about this news. We are going to have to finish our education this year in Red Lodge, and we do not have anything to wear but what we have on.

Grandma says, "Go ahead downstairs and pick out some clothes. Mrs. Brophry already said it was okay."

Irene must use the bathroom, and Grandma points to the outhouse. Even though the Brophry's have indoor plumbing, Grandma is the help, and she must go outside to use the bathroom. The little house that is hers in the back doesn't have indoor plumbing. I'm so sick of outhouses. Grandpa has indoor plumbing, so that's nice.

WE are done eating Grandpa's soup. It is nice and warm considering it's so cold outside. Not as cold as it was in Whitehall, but it's still cold. I'd say about negative ten degrees.

Mom is telling us, "You all must start school on Monday. I must come with you so you can be enrolled."

Mart says, "The schools here are separate and much larger than the ones in Whitehall."

I say, "I'm so excited to go to school now. I have new, hand-me-down clothes and not one hole in my shoes or socks. I hope, I meet a new friend."

IT'S been six months since we came to Red Lodge.

I did enjoy going to school in Red Lodge. My teacher was Mrs. Barbara Sanderson, and my principle was Mrs. Mayme Anderson. They were all nice, and I made a nice, new friend. The only problem was, I got all D's and C's on my report card. It seems like they were teaching different things than what Whitehall was teaching, and I did not go to school for one month while we were stranded. So, yes, that will be my excuse.

This Summer, Mart was able to go to a boy's camp with the other boys in town. He needed quite a few dollars to go to this camp, and we didn't have the money. He charmed the rich ladies down at church so much the first two months that we were here that they decided to raise some money for him to go.

Mart was gone about a month in the summer at that camp. It was a church camp for boys, and they got to do a lot of fun activities. Mart gets to do lots of fun things.

Some of the things Mart does, Mom doesn't even know about. Mart got hooked back up with his friend Ted too, and she didn't know about that.

Well, while there was still snow on the ground, Mart would go hunting with Ted and Ted's dad. They didn't have a license though. They didn't need one I guess—at least that's what Mart told me when I overheard him and Ted talking by the creek. I'm not sure if he is telling me the truth, but I will assume he is because he is my brother.

Anyways, I heard Mart and Ted talking about how they were going to go hunting by the old timberline above Red Lodge. They were talking about how they shot an elk up there and how they brought it down with one shot through the head.

Sounds like they were pretty proud of themselves. They were also talking about how they got a hold of a couple wild horses running around in the hills. They roped the horses down and got a saddle on them, and they were going to ride them all summer.

They said they would just keep the horses until summer was over and then let them loose again. I saw those horses, and they sure were pretty. Mart and Ted kept them tied up near the hills all summer and fed them grains from Ted's dad's small farm. He has a farm of cows.

Mart and Ted also did something they weren't supposed to do this Summer, and they did it right before camp. No one found out, but me, because I like to follow Mart and Ted. They seem to always be doing some interesting activity, and I like knowing about interesting activities going on.

So, again I followed them to the creek. The creek is where they meet, because it's away from town, and it's about a mile away from Grandpa's. Remember, Mart is not supposed to be hanging around Ted because of Ted's criminal brother. I don't think people should judge people by what their families do, though. Just because you're from the same family doesn't mean you are going to do all the same kind of activities, whether they be legal or illegal.

Mart and Ted decided to hitchhike up the old dirt road all the way to Cook City. Cook City is far away, like 7 hours away by car. You must travel past Bozeman and into part of Wyoming, then you come back into Montana. But if you go way of the mountains, it cuts off a third of the time. I'm not sure which way they are taking though.

Ted told his parents, and Mart told Mom that they were going to take a blanket, a frying pan, and a few potatoes and camp down by Rock Creek for a couple days with friends from school. They said all the other parents said it was okay, so Ted's parents said it was okay, and so did Mom.

Mart and Ted called the River Rock a creek, but it is actually a river. This is the river I follow them to every time I want information on what those two are up to. I don't ever tell Mom, because I want Mart to have fun, and I wish I was big enough to do some of those things.

So, they headed to Cook City. They were gone a few days, and when Mart got back, I ask him, "What did you do in Cook City?"

"How did you know I went to Cook City?"

"Because I heard you down by Rock Creek before you left."

"You little eavesdropper, I'm going to have to watch who's following me next time."

"Oh, please Mart, just tell me, I won't tell nobody." I plead. "I just want to hear something exciting."

"Okay," he says as he ruffles the hair on my head.

So, he told me all about it saying, "Me and Ted got a ride by someone driving a Model T Ford. About four of those cars go by every hour. We stayed and camped overnight in Cook City and hitchhiked home. Cook city is about sixty-six or so miles from Red Lodge."

I guess he took the short way to Cook City.

We sat there for about an hour as he went on to tell me all about his wonderful, exciting adventures.

AS a family, we took a trip this Summer to Custards Battlefield. Custards Battlefield is on the East side of the Big Horn River and our great-grandparents live on the West side of the Big Horn River. Our great-grandparents have a big place with lots of fruitful, beautiful land and amazing horses.

We took their beautiful horses and rode to Custards Battlefield. We stayed the night in between time. We would stay the night by the Big Horn River and fish. Uncle Walter came with us too. The most common fish in the river is a catfish. We fried those fish up over the open flamed fire, and they tasted so good.

We saw many grey gravestones along the way—all those gravestones sticking out of the ground, not like anything they have in the towns. There were graves underneath those stones. We couldn't walk around there too much because the place was crowded and full of dangerous, poisonous rattlesnakes.

Uncle John and Uncle Jack, Grandma's brothers, would meet us at our great-grandparents and come camping with us. They live around the Lodge Grass area. I have a story about Lodge Grass, but that comes in the picture when I am ten.

CHAPTER 19

Goodbye, Red Lodge
(August of 1937)

THE Old Man is back. Oh, it makes me want to cry, because I know it means we are leaving Red Lodge. He's trying to convince Mom to take him back—pleading with her—telling her he's a changed man.

Grandma and Grandpa tell her she can continue to stay with them in Red Lodge and to not go back to him.

Mom says, "I know that we are all a burden on you, so we must go."

That's why she is always taking him back, because she feels like she's burdening her parents. The Old Man wants to go back to Butte. He says he has a steady job working in the mines and that he's done with schemes. If I had my way, I would stay with my grandparents forever.

It kind of upsets me that Mom's going back to him, because we almost died the last time he left us.

My grandpa tells us, "Now come and stay anytime. You can always come back when you need to."

"Goodbye again Red Lodge," I say as I sadly wave goodbye.

TRAVELING in the car with me is Mom, The Old Man, my sisters, and my brothers.

We have a long way to travel in this beat up tin car. This is the same car that my old man brought after he burnt the mud house down. It's old and ready to fall apart. I'll be surprised if we even make it to Butte, Montana. I'll tell you a little bit more about Butte when we get there, but right now, I must tell you about this car.

This rusty model T is so rusty it looks as if bed bugs got a hold of it and instead of sucking the blood out of it, they gone and sucked all the good metal out, leaving all the sores and blisters behind. It is a stick shift and the tires, with wooden spokes, are not something I would brag about as the wood is looking like it's going to rot off soon.

We must stop every ten miles or whenever we see a ditch full of water. Mart, who is fourteen years old; well, in about a month he'll be turning fifteen, must pour water in the radiator of our car because it keeps getting too darn hot.

The only thing we have on this trip to eat is pink bologna sandwiches, which is normal when we are with our old man. When we are with him, we almost never have any money to buy anything really good to eat. I have been so used to good food the last six months that I don't even want to look at a pink bologna sandwich. I'm surprised us kids haven't turned into a bologna sandwich through the years, because we have eaten so many of them.

Grandpa was going to give us some food for the trip, but our old man said he had food for us.

You know what I wish? I wish I was on one of them fancy trains that the rich travel on. Well, sometimes the poorer folk travel on them trains, but they got to sit in the sections that don't have nice seats and where all the baggage is. I've seen where the rich people sit on trains, and it is pretty nice. They have nice soft chairs and tables that are shiny and clean. They get to eat nice, warm, steaming cinnamon buns for breakfast and drink fresh squeezed orange juice.

Mmm, Mmm, Mmm—sounds good, don't it? In my imagination, I can taste all that delicious food and hear the wheels of the train scalping against the railroad tracks, metal against metal.

Oh, snap out of it, Mary.

There I go dreaming again. At least I do have my dreams. It is quite hard to dream, when the reality is the exhaust in this car is making it difficult for me to breathe, and the only thing I can hear is the crimson metal on this car rubbing together as if it will soon fall apart.

I wonder if we are going to make it to Butte. It is 230 miles to get to Butte from Red Lodge.

It's been close to a year since I lived in Butte, and I can't remember exactly what Butte looks like. I just stayed near the house and apartments, and we weren't there for too long, so I didn't do too much exploring.

Our old man says, "We'll be living in a different part of town than before. On Faucett Street. 907 Faucett Street."

I'll be starting the third grade in Butte.

CHAPTER 20

A City On A Hill
(August 1937)

WE are almost to Butte, and it's getting dark and scary on this highway.

We just passed Whitehall and the so-called farm we lived on, and thank goodness, we are not stopping. Goose bumps instantly pop up all over my skinny, pale arms as I think about how we lived there and were almost sent to our heavenly home.

This highway is a two-lane narrow road and steep on one side. It is the only mountain pass to get from Whitehall to Butte. The steep side is about 100 yards down to the next landing, and the road is full of squishy, dark mud. The rain hits the windshield like sheets which makes seeing clearly out the windows almost impossible. We are traveling very slow, so we don't spill over off the edge. What a horrible death that would be to fall off one of these cliffs.

At least, if I die, I know I ain't going to Hell. While I was in Red Lodge, I explained to Grandma about the coins, and she swiftly brought me to the preacher that baptized me in the holy water. I sorrowfully explained to him what happened, and after I did, he told me to say a few hail Mary's and do some good deeds. My good deed was to help Mart go on his church trip, so I helped the old ladies at church raise the money. Now I know I'm not going to Hell.

We are all squeezed tightly in the old Ford. We had to leave a lot of personal stuff behind, because we couldn't fit it all in the car. The car probably would collapse if there was too much weight in it.

Wow, I'm starting to see lights up ahead.

Ohh, how amazing! What a sight!

My Uncle said Butte was a city on a hill that looked like a bright candle lit up at night, but until you actually see it yourself coming off the high mountain pass late at night when it is dark as pitch, you can't believe your star gazed eyes.

Butte is a glorious sight coming into it when the night is at its darkest. I am thinking, it's like the brightest star that shines high in the sky. I shall never forget this moment—as long as I live—August 27, 1937.

WE are driving through town, and I can't believe all the people cumbering about in the dusty, paved streets. Last time I was here, we did not go this far up, and I can't quite remember the people the time before.

The Old Man says, "About one hundred thousand people live here."

That number is amazing, because you wouldn't think that there would be enough room here to fit all those people in such a small space. All these people in this itty bit of space, and everyone looks so busy—like little gathering ants going in and out of their dusty ant hill as fast as they can, and it's pretty late at night too. It's about midnight.

We are traveling on Main Street, about ready to turn onto Park Street.

Everything is so bright and interesting. We just went by a Theater.

"What's the name of that Theater?" I ask whoever wants to answer me.

My old man says, "That's the Realto Theater. They show all kinds of movies and plays there. There are about ten theaters' here in Butte, and people are always going to watch movies at all hours of the night. The businesses never halt."

"The lights are so beautiful," exclaims Katherine in wonder and awe as her bugging, child-wondering eyes look out the stained, dusty window.

The sprinkling rain subsided right before we saw the lights on the pass.

"See all those men with the lunch buckets, they are all going to work in the mine tonight. That's what keeps this town so busy, the mines. Mining is big business here in Butte. That's where I've been working the last eight months," my old man says pointing to one of the mines.

We turn sharply into the drive of our new home. I notice something about this neighborhood. There's a different kind of people.

I ask, "Mom, who are these people?"

"They are the Chinese, Mary."

"What are the Chinese?"

"The Chinese are people from China, a land far from here and over the ocean, and they have come to Butte to live."

"Where is China?"

"China is on the other side of the Pacific Ocean—5,000 miles away."

These people look so different—I'm thinking to myself. It seems like our house is right smack in the middle of all these strange, unfamiliar, slanted eyed Chinese people.

My old man says, "This part of town is called Finn Town."

I ask, "Why is it called Finn Town?"

"Because the people that come over from Finland settle in this part of town. There are many parts of town that belong to different races of people. During the day, all creeds are mostly okay going into the different parts of town, but at night, especially late at night, you want to stay in your own section, because people don't like you much on their territory."

He went on to say, "We live on the East Side of the city, and we are close to Finn town."

This new house on Faucett Street is an awful green color.

"Everyone that lives in this area has a different accent," says The Old Man.

It is so crazy; I have passed just a short distance and have seen so many different types of people passing by. It seems like everyone is of a different nationality. Like a melting pot as I have heard many people say when a bunch of something is compiled together into one.

My old man says, "I got this place, so we could rent the apartments to people."

"He thinks he's going to get rich by renters," whispers Mart in my ear. "He got the apartments for practically no money at all and had to pay a dollar down and then twenty dollars a month. That does seem like a fairly decent price, but I don't see who's going to pay more than five dollars a month to stay in these run-down, moldy apartments."

I must agree with Mart.

WE have been living on Faucett Street for a week, and it's starting to get chilly at night. This house does not have any insulation. Our old man said he has been collecting cardboard boxes all over town the last few months and bringing them home before Winter starts.

Why does he need cardboard boxes you're probably wondering?

I'll tell you. He has been hanging them on the walls in this ugly, green house thinking they will act like insulation. He thinks by putting them boxes on the walls it's going to keep us nice and cozy warm during Winter.

I'm living in a constant nightmare.

One good thing is, I have already made a friend. Mom seems to know a few people. Mom is always real friendly with people. I hope I can be as friendly as her one day.

Our neighbor is a real nice man. When we first moved in, he says to me, "When you get settled—come on over—and I have a job for you."

"I'm not old enough to work," I tell him.

"You come directly over, and I will tell you what I need. For what I need, you're old enough."

So, here I am a week later, and I am going over to my neighbor's house. As I arrive, I see he is on a wide, white porch, so I ask him, "What job do you have for me."

"What is your name little one?"

"My name is Mary."

"Mary, I'll give you some money if you go take this fancy bucket and run up to the bar on the corner and have the bartender fill it up with deep brown, rich, foamy beer."

I thought—this isn't too hard, although, this bucket isn't as fancy as he imagines it to be.

"I have to go ask my mom if it's okay."

"Go ask her."

I run quickly home, and as I burst excitedly into the house, I ask mom, "Mom, the neighbor told me if I take a fancy bucket, which really isn't so fancy, of his up the street to the bar and get it filled with beer, he'll pay me. Is that alright?"

She says, "Go ahead."

I guess beer and whiskey are legal now.

Mart told me after we arrived in Butte, "The Prohibition has been over for a few years now, Mary. On April 7, 1933, beer was again legalized in Butte, and on December 21, 1933, whiskey was legalized."

I don't much remember what life was like when beer and whiskey were illegal, but when the country outlawed drinking alcohol there was a lot of bootlegging going on. We learned about bootlegging in school and how much crime there was because of it. Bootlegging is when you sell something illegally.

So, I guess to solve crime problems, there was no other real choice than to make alcohol legal again. Although, I don't really see how that solved crime. It seems there is just as much crime from people getting drunk legally as there is drinking illegally. But what does a young girl like myself know about that.

After discussing the beer carrying job with Mom, I quickly run back to the neighbor's and say, "My mom said it is okay that I work for you."

He smiles wide as he gives me the rusty bucket, and right off, I take that bucket and run up the street until I see the fancy, new bar he was telling me about.

I walk into the fully occupied bar and walk shyly over to the counter where I see the greasy haired, sweaty bartender. I am so little though that I can barely see over the wet, sticky counter.

I am not sure if the bartender can even see me, so a guy sitting next to where I'm standing says, "Hey Joe," that's the bartenders name, "There's a little one here payin' you a visit."

The sweat dripping bartender looks over the sticky bar, down at me, and says, "What you want little one."

I look up at the old bartender with a kind smile and say, "I need this bucket filled with beer."

I tell him who it is for as I attempt to barely lift the bucket up past my head and onto the slimy bar.

The bartender takes the bucket and says, "I can do that for ya."

I give him the money from my neighbor, and after he is done filling up the bucket, he gives me the bucket full of beer.

Watching him fill up the wooden, metal hinged bucket makes me think of a flowing, downward waterfall. As the frothy beer goes into the brown bucket, it creates foam like the foam at the bottom of waterfalls. Mind you, I have never actually seen a waterfall in real life, but I have seen fancy pictures, and from what I have witnessed, I imagine that is what it would look like."

As I walk down the street back to my neighbor's house, I must hold the bucket with both hands, because it's so heavy. I hope I can make it back to my neighbor's without spilling any of the sloshing beer.

Boy, each step I take this bucket gets heavier and heavier, but it sure will be nice to get some money. Hey, I am thinking to myself, I forgot to ask how much he was going to pay me. I hope all this trouble is worth the cash.

As I walk, I enjoy watching the foamy beer slosh around like waves on the sea. The bucket was a lard bucket. Lard is animal fat. That is what we use for cooking. Some lard tastes good, but that kind is expensive. We get the cheap lard, because that is all we can afford, and depending on what animal it comes from and how old the animal was, depends on the taste being good or nasty. There doesn't seem to be an in-between taste when it comes to dealing with lard.

When I finally reach my neighbor's house, I notice that just a little bit of the beer has splashed out.

"Here's your bucket of beer," I announce to the neighbor as I hand over the bucket to him.

He gives me a big smile and asks, "Did you carry this bucket all by yourself Mary."

"I sure did," I reply as I purposely stand up straight and proper and with confidence.

He says to me, "That is a whole lot of work for such a little girl."

I thought to myself, little. I am so sick and tired of people telling me how little I am. In this case however, as I calm my racing, angry mind and heart down, playing the 'little' card might do me some good. Maybe, he'll pay me more money if he thinks I did a lot of work, or it could backfire on me—maybe, he won't ask me to do it again.

"How much do you think your work is worth?" my neighbor asks me.

I must think a minute. No one has ever asked me how much my work is worth. Probably, because I've never had a job before.

I thought I would take a chance at it, so I say, "Five cents."

That's what I say with confidence in my voice, "Five cents, if you please."

The neighbor looks me up and down curiously, and I think to myself, I don't even know this man's name. I thought that I would ask him his name after he gives me the money. He takes a shiny coin from his pocket and places it in my hand.

He asks me, "Will this do?"

I look down at the shiny, wonderful coin and see that it is a whole dime.

I say to him, "It sure will do. Thank you very much sir."

He ruffles up my hair with his hand and asks, "Will you do that whenever I call on ya?"

"Of course, I will."

I am about to run home, when I suddenly remember that I was going to ask him his name.

I turn swiftly around and ask, "What is your name, neighbor?"

"My name is Ted," the neighbor replies with a chuckle in his voice.

I take off for home, and every few days now, I wait around the corner of Ted's house hoping he sees me and asks me to fetch him a sloshy bucket of foamy beer.

CHAPTER 21

Pasties, And Third Grade
(September 1937)

THE Old Man isn't too happy as of recently, because he has had nobody renting the apartments from him.

I heard Mart say to Bill, "Our old man is in a bad situation, because he can't pay the rent on this house or the apartments."

It's September and the first day of school. We are going to the Grant School which has grades one through eight.

Mart is starting the seventh grade, Irene the seventh grade, Bill the fifth grade, and I am entering the third grade.

My old man went to the thrift store in town and bought us some used clothes for school. I don't think he pays much attention to what size we are. He's always buying me something to big. Irene's clothes fit her the best, and the boys' clothes are a little too small. Kay gets the worst of it. She inherits clothes from me, the same ones I inherit from Irene. Poor, Kay.

The Grant School is close to where we live, so we can just walk. Mom tells us to come home for lunch since we live so close. We didn't have any breakfast this morning. Usually, we don't eat breakfast anyways. The only time we get a hearty breakfast is when we live with Grandpa.

Mart, Irene, Bill, and I are walking to school. I am still amazed at all the people here. It's hard to get sleep sometimes, because people are up at all hours of the night.

A couple days ago, Uncle Walter came by our house to see how we were all getting along. We had cleaned the house up to look quite livable. Almost like a real home. Almost!

Uncle Walter wanted to take us to see the boarding houses that the miners go to, to eat. He was going to get us some yummy lunch, which sounded tasty considering when we are with our old man, we do not eat a lot of good food. This is probably the reason we are all so skinny.

Uncle Walter has a wife and children, but I have never seen them.

Mom says, "He doesn't really talk about them. I don't ever see much of them neither."

Uncle Walter lives on Park Street. Part Street is a main street uptown and a very busy one. Uncle Walter loves to take fancy pictures—every time I've been with him—he always has his needed camera supplies. So, he took a picture of my family before we left to go get pasties at the boarding house.

He picked us up and drove us to this large boarding house. Quite a bit larger than the one Grandma used for boarders. I saw the house she used when we lived in Red Lodge. She told me all about what she used to do one day when we were having lunch outside of the Brophry's house.

This boarding house that Uncle Walter is taking us to is called, Mary Buckley's Boarding House. It is on 526 North Wyoming Street.

Mary, the woman who runs the house, has six kids that she raised herself. She feeds about fifty men and rooms around twenty. Well, that is what Uncle Walter is telling us. He says that most boarders must pay about 8-10 dollars a week.

The first object of fancy that catches my immediate attention in Mary Buckley's Boarding House is a long table that seems to stretch for miles in my imaginative thoughts. This lengthy table seems to be almost as large as the fancy house. There is so much good-looking food. All these miners are sitting at the table eating.

Uncle Walter says, "Pick out anything that you want to eat. It costs a quarter a person, and I am paying."

Many of the men are eating something that looks like an apple turnover, but instead of apples contained in the soft dough, there is thick meat and cubed potatoes inside.

I ask Uncle Walter, "What is that food?"

"O, Mary, have you never had a pasty."

"I have no idea what a pasty is," I respond.

"A pasty is so good! There's chopped up meat, potatoes, and onion in the middle and it has sort of like a pie crust on the outside that's wrapped around the meat and potatoes. If you pour a little beef gravy on that yummy pasty, it makes a wonderful, satisfying meal."

I whisper in Uncle Walter's ear as I point wantingly at the pasty, "I would like to try one of those."

In fact, we all get a pasty.

O, my—is this pastie good. I've never tasted anything like it. I think I better enjoy it, because I probably won't be getting one again for a while.

"Where did they come up with the pasty," I ask Uncle Walter?

"The English are the ones that made pasties popular. I have only heard of pasties being sold in Butte. I've never seen them sold anywhere else. Mary, do you see the miner's buying pasties and putting them in their lunch buckets?"

"Sure, I do."

"They take them down in the mines with them, and those fill-ing, delicious pasties will last them the whole day."

They are quite large; I think to myself.

∞

WELL, back to going to school. I have a few squirrely monarch but-terflies in my upset stomach. The Grant School is just about eight blocks from our house, and I am wearing—my getting to be darker brown hair—in a ponytail bun.

Irene had her hair up in rollers all night, so now her hair is nice and curly.

"She's older, so she gets the rollers," Mom said.

I guess we need more rollers considering we have four girls living in the house. I'm sure they have some at the thrift store. I am an older child and a younger child, which means I get no advantage. I either get the old worn-out stuff or nothing at all.

Kay is still not in school. She will be six tomorrow, but she is still too young for school. She has a couple more years until she can go to first grade. Kay is becoming quite the pesky pest, so I am sort of glad she is not attending school with me yet.

The Grant School faces the street from where we live. It is made of pale brick and has two rectangular sides with a depression of about four-feet deep and twenty-feet wide in the middle of the sides. It is a three-story building with a brick twelve step stairway going to the main door. There is brick lined down below the first story and green grass covers the grounds. On the side there are three rectangles shaped like the front of the building and an arc doorway to enter the school. It's a much fancier school than the one I attended in Red Lodge.

As soon as we all walk through the double doors, we go our sepa-rate ways. I know where I'm going this time, because we came here a couple days ago with Mom to see where all our classrooms would be.

When I arrive to class, and after I sit down and so does everyone else, we are asked to introduce ourselves like you always do when it's the first day of school. There are a couple kids here that I recognize from my neighborhood. There is also a Chinese girl that lives in the rentals where we live.

We must wear dresses to school. The girls are not allowed to wear pants like the boys. I don't know what Kay is going to do when she must wear a dress every day. Kay loves wearing jeans. Most every day she will put on a pair of skinny blue jeans.

Kay is a bit of a Tom Boy. Maybe, that is why she is becoming such a pest. Don't get me wrong, mind you, I love Kay, and I am glad she is my sister, but she teases like a boy and gets me in trouble many a time.

Today, I have on a pinkish, purplish dress. Mom had to pin it this morning, but in a few months, I'll probably grow into it, and it will fit just fine. I have a white pair of cloth shoes, and I am grateful that there are no holes in them. I also have a pair of socks that are a whitish cream color.

When I introduce myself to the class, and tell them where I live—on the East Side—one of the girls says, "That's the Cabbage Patch area."

Another girl says, "She lives by the Chinese and Mexicans."

Then a boy blurts out, "Those Chinese eat all the cats in town."

After this extremely rude boy's comment, the little China girl that is in class with us, kind of shrinks down deep in her wooden, yellow chair.

I say boldly and with courage to all the kids in class, "They do not eat cats!"

The only problem is, I really didn't know if they eat cats. I guess it probably wouldn't surprise me if they did. I'll have to ask Irene if it's true.

Mart, Irene, Bill, and I all went home for lunch. Mom is giving us a quarter to go get some bologna and three cupcakes at the corner

store. Along our street, there is a small grocery store and three saloons. Butte has a lot of saloons, too many to count really.

I must give Mom a dime back in change, because the food I
bought was just fifteen cents. It's sounds like everyone had a good
morning, except me. I just hope I can find at least one friend.

CHAPTER 22

Oh, No, Irene!

THIS week has been unusually long, so almost immediately after school, Irene and I go in the back of the yard to play.

In the backyard, where we want to play, is a long, deep, dusty ditch running through the yard. We haven't played back here yet, but we are curious. There is no water in the sandy ditch, but there are a lot of rocks in the back yard, so being bored, Irene and I begin throwing all the heavy rocks in the dried-up ditch. Throwing rocks is fun and sometimes our only entertainment and we think, since there isn't any water in the ditch, we might as well fill it with rocks.

We are attempting to see how strong we are by picking up and throwing the biggest rock—when Irene picks up one of the biggest rocks in the yard—hurling it into the ditch. Soon after Irene hurls the heavy rock, and before we know what is happening, Irene is on the ground in uncontrollable tears.

The huge rock didn't make it to the ditch, and as soon as the rock hit the ground, we hear an ear-splitting, booming explosion where the hefty rock landed.

Grey, black smoke immediately fills the once clear air and combines with dusty earth particles creating a mushroom cloud in the once clear, blue sky. Irene is exactly next to the great explosion; I am a little way away from it, so I can't feel the effects like Irene does.

Irene weakly requests of me, "Mary, go get Mom."

I run as fast as I can up to the house. Once I reach the entryway, I run swiftly down the stairs and into the house.

"Mom, Irene is hurt real bad, come quick!" I scream.

Mom quickly rushes out of the house, and on the way out she commands Mart, "Go run to Dr. Monahan's office, and tell him to come quick."

Mart quickly runs out the door immediately after we do.

Mom finally reaches the ditch and is attempting to carefully help Irene up. When I get a closer look at Irene, I notice that three of her fingers are barely connected to her hand, and her knee is bleeding like a swift, running river flowing down a mountain valley that has melting snow in the Spring.

The Doctor and Mart finally arrive at the terrible scene. Mom is ablet to lift Irene onto her lap as she is attempting to keep Irene from going into immediate shock while we waited for Dr. Monahan.

After Dr. Monahan and Mart arrive, they carefully lift a broken Irene up, gently carrying her into the house.

They instantly take her into our bedroom. The Doctor says to everyone, "Leave the room, except Monta."

Dr. Monahan, Mom, and Irene are in the bedroom a long time. Irene is crying but not too much. She's pretty tough. She is also so pretty. Most people might think she is not tough, but she is, and she is one of the most kindest people I know. Sure, she won't share the curlers with me, but other than that she sure is the giving kind.

"Please, God," I plead, "Help Irene, and don't let her lose her precious, beautiful hand. She is a good sister and deserves good things."

After a long hour, the Doctor is coming out of the bedroom and so is Mom.

I urgently ask, "Is Irene all right, Mom?"

"She needs some rest, Mary. Dr. Monahan gave her something for the pain, and she's asleep right now."

Mom and the Doctor are talking seriously at the open door, but I can't clearly hear what they are saying.

After Doctor Monahan leaves, Mom tells Mart and I, "You should never go down in that ditch, because the ditch is full of mine caps."

"What are mine caps?" I ask.

Mart says, "They are used to prevent access to old, abandoned mines." (Wikipedia)

I don't quite understand, but don't ask the question again, because Mom is telling us what is going on with Irene.

"Irene blew off part of her three fingers on her left hand and part of her kneecap," explains Mom.

Tears begin to stream down my face as I think about poor Irene and how sad I feel for her. I will help her get better though, and I'll help her pick stuff up if she has trouble. That's probably what a good little sister would do, and I want to be a good little sister.

Mom goes on to say, "Dr. Monahan said that Irene will probably always have trouble with her knees and fingers."

CHAPTER 23

Christmas At Grant School (December 1937)

IT'S the end of November, right after Thanksgiving, and at school today we are going to decorate the amazingly beautiful, evergreen tree that will be our school Christmas tree. We don't have a tree at our house, so this will be the highlight of my Christmas. Mom tries to make things special around the holidays as well as she can, but we don't have a whole lot of money right now.

Halloween was last month, and it was fun. We didn't have fancy bags to go trick or treating, so me and my siblings took the faded green pillowcases off our pillows and used them for trick or treating bags. In my opinion, the large pillowcases are better, because you can fit a lot more yummy, sweet candy in them. We went around to the same areas about two or three times. Halloween is the only time we get some sweet things, so we take advantage of it as best we can.

For Thanksgiving, we didn't have any turkey or ham. We usually don't unless we are at Grandpas. Mom made us some potato soup. If Mom doesn't have a quarter to pay for bologna and cupcakes at the corner store for our lunch, she usually makes a potato soup, or another kind of soup, or we have plain old red beans or white rice.

Well, back to decorating the beautiful Grant School Christmas tree. Yesterday, everyone in grades one through four made paper Christmas decorations for Christmas. We are going to use some of the decorations for the walls of the school and some for this magnificent tree. I am supposed to help. We made so many Christmas decorations, and the town is getting ready for Christmas too.

The town of Butte takes Christmas seriously. The people in charge of the city, whoever they are, are already putting up the magical decorations around town and making everything festive, and they begin the celebrations right after Thanksgiving. The school Christmas tree is beginning to look magical. We are also putting shiny lights and tinsel on the tree. The principle just put the star on.

Speaking of my principle, she is a great gal. She is always so nice to me. She knows my life is hard financially, and she doesn't talk to me like I am white trash.

Winter air is starting to creep into the town and into our house. It's not in the negatives yet, but everyone is saying that it will be after Christmas.

My principle's name is Mrs. Kelly, and she calls me into her office every morning when the Winter sets in and makes me take a teaspoon of cod liver oil. I hate that stuff. It's supposed to help with colds and sicknesses though.

The principle is nice, but the kids aren't so nice. They tease me about my clothes and make fun of me. Well, most the girls do. I don't have too much trouble with the boys. They don't seem to mind my clothes. I even get whistled at a few times a week. Mom says it's because I don't look my age. She says I seem to be maturing faster than a lot of girls. She also told me that the boys whistle because I'm such a pretty girl.

My old man tells me that too. He has always told me how pretty I am.

Mom told me a fabulous story about how pretty I was after I was born.

She said, "Mary, after you were born in Renton, there were two quite older ladies that lived close by in the rich neighborhood. Well, you see, when your father and I were taking a walk one day, maybe, a month or so after I gave birth to you, these old, handsome ladies saw us taking a walk with you and said, 'That baby is so cute, we would like to adopt her.'

Those wealthy ladies were willing to pay good money for you, and your father was willing to give you away for the small fortune, but I would have never given you away for any amount of money. Sadly, I had to keep you close by me that first year so your father wouldn't get any ideas. I mean, you know how he is?"

"Yes, I know how he is," I replied.

Anyways back to the mean girls at my school. Mom says the girls are just jealous and that's why they tease me. I guess that's what I'm going to believe.

We usually don't get Christmas presents, but we did get a special surprise after Halloween. We received a wonderful little puppy. Mart brought the puppy home. He got it from someone on his paper route.

He said, "I got this dog from the gal I work for. The gal had extra puppies, so she gave me one of them."

It is such a special white puppy with brown spots, and she looks like a beagle. I don't think she is a full beagle, but just to describe her properly, I would say she is most like a beagle.

The sweet, well-mannered puppy is a girl, and us kids and Mom all decided that the name Penny would fit her perfectly. I'm so glad Mart brought us Penny. Pretty Penny likes to sleep at the bottom of the bed with us girls. She keeps our cold feet warm, and she warns us when the blood sucking bed bugs are coming to attack. Sometimes, she's too late, and she and us get bitten. Most the time though, she does a proper job of warning us.

When those darn bed bugs come out, it must be dark. They like the dark. Penny wakes us up when she notices them, and we switch on the light. After we switch on the light, what you see is an awful sight. Those nasty bugs go scurrying up the old, cracked walls and into whatever crevice's they came out of.

When we first arrived in this house, Mom and Irene wanted to change the wallpaper and paint the walls. Well, you can't even believe what was under the wallpaper they were attempting to take off.

Yes, you guessed it. Dead bed bugs all over in-between the dirty wall and the wallpaper. Mom and Irene instantly put that wallpaper back up faster than a chetah can catch a fox or a rabbit, and we never did speak of it again.

O, I hate those bed bugs. They always keep you scratching.

CHAPTER 24

Bill Gets Tied Up
(Spring 1938)

I met a real nice friend at school this year. In fact, I'm sure we might just be best friends. Her name is Becky.

All year, the girls in school were teasing me un-mercilessly about living next to the Cabbage Patch.

So, I asked Mart, "Why is everyone always teasing us about living next to the Cabbage Patch?"

"Maybe, it's because we can grow a lot of cabbages."

Then, he laughed.

The peculiar thing is, I never see any cabbages growing in our neighborhood. I guess I'll never know what that means, because obviously, Mart is not going to tell me a darn thing.

When I asked Mom, she just said, "What nonsense."

Winter this year showed no mercy either—I would say it was almost heartless as the last two weeks the temperature has been twenty below zero, and the few weeks before that about negative thirty.

The Old Man says, "Mary, you know the temperature can get down to fifty below zero sometimes."

Temperatures are not as bad this week as everything is starting to thaw out now, so much so that Mom is hanging her laundry out to dry. The sun is shining bright, and it's a real beautiful, sunny afternoon. It's funny how fast the weather can change here. The bright, lemon sun must be warming the earth to about 40 degrees this beautiful day.

Mom doesn't have a laundry machine like the Chinese laundry down by the school. She must wash all our laundry by hand. The soiled, stubborn laundry can take painstaking hours to finish oftentimes. Mom's done it all her life, so she can do it much faster than me. Whenever I do laundry, it takes me so long that the clothes on the line are dry before I get my first piece washed.

Bill got into trouble today, so Mom tied him tight to the wire clothesline in the back of our yard while she was washing the laundry—she does that sometimes when he gets unruly and out of hand, and boy is he screaming up a storm like hurricane today.

When Bill is causing trouble, and when Mom is busy, and the weather is warm enough, and we are all outside to watch him, she ties him to the clothesline.

Some up to do people might think this is somewhat of a cruel act of punishment, but Mom is on crutches, and if Bill runs off when he is upset, there is just no way Mom is going to catch him.

"Be quite!" Mom tells Bill.

Bill will be twelve next week—on the fifth of May. It's 1938. My birthday is a couple weeks later than his. We are almost exactly two years apart in age, so I'm going to be ten.

I can't believe, I am going to be ten years old, but we won't get anything for our birthday's. We never have enough money coming in. Of course, if our old man didn't spend so much money on booze, we might be doing a little bit better with our finances. Mom will surely try to get something at the Salvation Army for a copper penny, but there's not much you can get at the Salvation Army, even for a penny.

The Salvation Army is a thrift store. In case I haven't told you what a thrift store is, I'll tell you now. A thrift store is a place where people donate items they have in their house or yard that they don't care to have anymore, and depending on who is donating, depends on how good the stuff is.

It would be nice, and I think more practical, if those rich people that are purposefully donating things would just put in the newspaper: Free Stuff, Come and Get It.

The thrift stores charge people money who are buying the donated items, but if we were able to just go to someone's house that was giving away their things, then we would get them for free. Doesn't that sound like a better plan—than to have those poor folks like us pay for it?

Like at the Brophry's, all of them clothes were free. I think if well to do folks want to help the needy and the poor, giving like the Brophry's would be the best way to give. The government should have a house that people can give their things away to and just invite the public to come get it.

Mom's almost done with the laundry.

"Wrrrr, Wrrrr."

"What's all that racket?" Mom asks.

"I hear it too," I say, "It's coming close to us."

We find out soon enough what the noise is, because all too suddenly, a couple of police cars are pulling up to our house.

"I wonder which neighbor is in trouble this time?" I say to Mom.

The policeman is getting out of his car and walking towards our house.

I whisper slyly to Mom, "It looks like we are the neighbor that is in trouble."

"What's going on here?" says the police to Mom.

"There's no trouble here, officer."

"We received a call from a neighbor that some poor, little boy was being abused at this address."

THE STORYBOOK ADVENTURES OF MARY MILLER ~ 129 ~

Bill was as quiet as he could be while still tied to the clothesline.

"There's nobody being abused here," replies Mom.

"Why is this young boy tied to the wire clothesline?" asks the policeman.

"Because, he isn't being too good," says Mom sternly and with confidence. "And I'm on crutches, and I can't worry about him running off when I got chores to do."

I guess the policeman is satisfied enough, because he's getting back into his police car and is driving away.

Mom says to me, "Now who gone and called the cops on me?"

Mom didn't seem so happy that someone called her in, and Bill was quiet for the whole rest of the day. I have a feeling he's not going to throw such a fuss next time he's tied to the clothesline. I wouldn't be surprised neither if that's the last time Mom ties him to the clothesline.

CHAPTER 25

Kidnapped (Summer 1938)

I have a short, interesting story to tell you about my summer. Well, there are many stories I must tell about this summer in 1938, but I'll start with this one.

I suppose I must take the total blame on this one. Well, maybe my friend Becky can take a little bit of the blame. My old man wasn't too happy about what happened in this particular story, and neither was Mom. It goes a little like this.

School ended the beginning of June, and our old man announced that we are all going to Cardwell, Montana for most of Summer. Cardwell is about ten miles away from the town of Whitehall and is towards Bozeman. You must travel through Bozeman to get to Red Lodge.

Mart's not going to Cardwell. He got himself a good job out of town with our aunt, but I'll tell you about that sometime later after I'm done telling this story.

The Old Man said someone hired him to take care of their place in Cardwell while they were visiting friends and family out of their town for the Summer. I guess we're going on another adventure. I've never been to Cardwell, Montana, so this adventure will be new and interesting. Lots of imagining can happen on a bright, new adventure.

I don't mind going to Cardwell, but I was looking forward to playing with Becky all Summer. Becky is the girl I made friends with at school. I am just so worried that if I'm gone all Summer; maybe, Becky will find her a new best friend. Since I was worried, I asked Becky if she wanted to go to Cardwell with me for a couple weeks.

A bunch of kids are over at our house when I ask Mom, "Mom, can Becky come to Cardwell with us?"

Mom says, "Sure."

Kids are always spending the night at our house. Most the time, Mom never knows how many kids there are here at night. Mart and Bill always got their friends coming over. Irene too. They make friends real easy. The grown-up neighbors oftentimes come over and play cards with Mom and my old man too. Well, whenever he is around. He actually stuck around more this year than he normally does.

Becky told me the day after I asked her to come to Cardwell with us that she could go. I thought—well, this is sure going to be a fun adventure, so we loaded up our car full of people, clothes, and a few things from the house and headed to Cardwell.

It is a nice drive along the Harding Pass in Summer. As we are passing by Whitehall, my memory of Walter Jap crosses my mind.

"I wonder what Walter is up to this Summer," I think to myself.

The one thing about Whitehall is that it's much warmer here in the summertime than in Butte, because the town isn't on a big hill surrounded by a big mountain. Butte looks like a giant bowl at the end of a mountain, and the elevation is significantly lower in Whitehall and things seem to grow real good here, so it sure is a pretty town. The trees are all blooming flowers, and the warm air smells so sweet.

We finally arrive at the house we are supposed to watch over, and it is nice. The whole area surrounding the house is pretty and comfortable. Plants and trees are almost done blooming, and the grass is a sweet, emerald green—looking as soft as a blanket to lie down on and be happy as you take pictures of the white clouds with your imagination.

The people had already gone by the time we arrived at their house. They left a key in the barn. As we drive up to the house, I see one large horse, it looks like about ten cows, and a few sheep.

One exciting thing is that we got to bring Penny. I'm glad we don't have to leave our new dog Penny behind like we had to with Rascal. I think she is really going to enjoy being out on this farm these next few weeks. We are now passing by a little creek full of flowing, clear water down below the quaint house.

The Old Man decides to drive right through the creek, saying, "It's faster than taking the road."

Of course, we are now stuck, but I guess this Summer wouldn't be an adventure if there were no unpleasant surprises. Getting through the unplanned surprises are usually the experiences we end up telling stories about and laughing about later in life.

The clear creek is just a little too muddy on the bottom, so we are stuck firmly in the sticky, brown mud.

"Get out of the car!" bellows our old man.

We all quickly exit the car, and some of us begin digging mud away from the tires, while others push the car forward from behind.

Mart and Bill are the ones pushing, and Becky, Irene, and I get enough mud away from the car wheels, as our old man slams on the gas which sends mucky mud into the clear creek dirtying it all up and onto us kids.

Splat!

Mud covers all our clothes and some of our hair, but we are finally unstuck. It's about a whole half hour since we started digging.

Becky and I decide not to get back in the dirty car and run up to the house. My siblings have the same idea as excitement fills our childlike, adventurous minds. As we arrive closer to the house, I notice there is a hidden root cellar by the back of the house and a small barn for the few animals that are in the field.

Emerald evergreens and white birch trees surround the yard and field while bendy, green and gold willows line the narrow creek.

"Look!" I say to Becky, pointing to the flower garden right up next to the house. "I'll take the job of watering the flowers. I love flowers so much that I would like to own my own shop one day."

"That would be lovely," responds Becky.

Walking in the house, I notice that there is indoor plumbing.

"I am so glad we don't have to use an outhouse," says Becky.

"You took the words straight out of my mouth," I say.

This blue, new, constructed house is one-story with a little basement and is very clean and orderly. Comfortable looking couches, chairs, and beds are all in the rooms, and there is a modest size white porch outside the front door with a swing attached.

Becky and I have a fun week exploring and playing in the root cellar. The root cellar is so dark that we would play the boogey man game and scare ourselves to screaming out loud. My old man was always telling us to keep the racket down, but I was thinking—what does it matter what racket we make, we don't have neighbors living close enough to be bothering them.

Then, it happened. Today, Becky and I are in the clear, shallow creek having so much fun playing with the squiggly water snakes and hyper skip bugs when we see them; the police.

"Boy, how did they find us all the way out here?" I say to Becky. "And who did something wrong?"

"Mary, come here!" screams my old man ferociously.

"He does not sound very happy," I say to Becky as I swiftly run up the trail and wonder out loud, "What did I do now without knowing what I did?"

Becky follows closely, but cautiously behind me, as if she understands the sudden commotion and uproar.

I quickly recognize by the deep tone in my old man's voice that I am in some kind of serious trouble.

When I get up to the house, I see Becky's parents and the police.

"Becky's parents have been looking for her all week," says my old man.

Becky's parents are hugging Becky like they thought she died and came back to life. I guess Becky told her parents that she was going to stay the night with me, but she didn't tell them where and for how long.

I give Becky a dirty look, like I am saying, "What were you thinking?"

I guess she was worried I'd find a new friend this Summer too.

CHAPTER 26

The Rest Of The Summer Of The 1938 Story

A few weeks after the unfortunate Becky incident, my family took a quick trip to Bozeman, Montana to visit my mom's sister Lois. This is where we are now.

Lois is one of my mom's twin sisters. She is married to Raymond Henry Menard. They were married, in Bozeman, on November 7, 1924. Aunt Lois and Uncle Ray have five children and live on a huge ranch just outside of Bozeman.

Aunt Lois is a hospital nurse, and so is her twin sister, Louise. Aunt Louise married Don Roby Cadwallader on December 31, 1926. Aunt Louise and Uncle Don live in Red Lodge—close to where Grandma lives. They have three children: Beverly, Donna, and Royal—two girls and one boy. We visit them when we see Grandma and Grandpa in Red Lodge.

The ranch is a joyous time, like always. The spacious ranch has many acres. I don't know how many, but the land seems to go on forever. There are mostly white, fluffy sheep on this farm, but they have many chickens too, because they sell their chickens eggs to a grocery store in Bozeman and to people around the area. Selling chicken eggs is a good money maker when done appropriately.

I like helping with the noisy, pecking chickens. The blue and reddish-brown chickens live in an enormous, red chicken house the size of a small horse barn and they have little two-by-two feet nests set up with stiff, golden straw inside each comfortable nest. The chickens sit in the nest and lay eggs.

I wonder how those eggs come out of the chicken? It's from the bottom somewhere—I know that. I am still utterly confused about the entire birthing process. I'll sit and wait for the brown and white, sometimes green eggs to come out, but I can't catch them in time to see where they're coming from.

As Mom and I are helping gather the eggs this morning, I ask her, "Mom, how do eggs come out of a chicken? They must come out of their bottom because that is where the chickens are sitting and where we pick up and gather the eggs from."

Mom says, "Mary, I will tell you when you are older."

Why does everyone say that they will tell me when I am older. They keep saying this year after year, and every year I get older, no one answers my questions.

After carefully gathering all the eggs, Mom and I see Uncle Don appear with a sharp axe. Then, he captures a-clucking-like-crazy chicken and quickly whacks the frightened chicken's head off after carefully placing the chicken's head between two pounded, silver nails on a short, wooden stump. We are having chicken stew for dinner, and we need a chicken to stew. Chicken meat is so slimy. I don't really like chicken, especially, after seeing how they die, so I'll stay away from eating another one.

After our families prepare for dinner, helping gather scrumptious vegetables and oh, so sweet fruit—and of course—a chicken, my cousins and me play in the open field covered graciously with emerald grass blades. Penny has fun running around after us as we play tag before dinner.

My Aunt is always very kind to us, but I get the feeling that Uncle Ray would have been happy if we had never showed up. Mom never gets to see her sisters very often, so it was a treat for her to visit her sister this week.

I heard Uncle Ray say to Aunt Lois, "Those relatives of yours are all just white trash."

I think he says that because of our old man, and maybe, because our clothes aren't always too nice.

Aunt Lois doesn't care what he says though—she always makes us feel real welcome. Aunt Lois cooked us a wonderful meal tonight and every night we have been here. Uncle Ray would always give The Old Man dirty looks when we were sitting at the eating table.

It was like he was saying with his eyes, "Get out of my house you dirty crook."

I can't blame him for thinking that way, but Mom isn't that way and neither are us kids. For having such an awful old man, us kids are all kind and nice. We take after our mom in that respect.

My rich, spoiled cousins have so many things. They have no indoor plumbing or electricity, but they have a lot of clothes, shoes, and toys. I know they must have a nice Christmas and Birthday's every year. I like the food, the land, and Aunt Lois when we come here, but I don't much like my nasty cousins. They get along real well with Irene, but they aren't too nice to me.

Those girls haven't said hardly two words to me the whole time I've been staying here. Kay and I just go and raid the garden that is behind the house when we are ignored, because there are so many good things to eat in the acre garden. We must stock up our usually empty bellies with good food—you know—considering when we leave, we will have nothing good to eat.

All Summer we've been going back and forth from the house in

Cardwell to other fascinating places. It has been a fun and memorable hot Summer.

TODAY, Mom received a letter from Mart. Summer is almost over, and we'll have to go pick him up soon. Mart is in Bozeman. I told you I would get to this part of the story soon.

Mart stayed with Great Aunt Abby and Great Uncle George Sinnok, who lives in Bozeman.

Mart told Mom in the letter, "They are treating me real well, and they are even going to buy me some clothes for school."

At least one of the five of us is going to have nice clothes when school starts. Mart will be turning fifteen soon and starting the eighth grade. Irene will be in the eighth grade too. Bill will be in the sixth grade, and I'll be starting the fourth grade.

School starts in a few weeks, and I'm excited to see Becky again. I kind of miss even being around those Chinese.

MY Summer stories and adventures are drawing to an end as this is our last weekend in Cardwell.

We picked Mart up in Bozeman yesterday. We thought if we stayed for two weeks at Aunt Lois's and Uncle Ray's we would pick up Mart afterwards and bring him home with us. Our old man isn't with us, so Uncle Ray wasn't too bothered by us staying with him again.

It's cold tonight. Even though it's Summer, we still get some cold days. Last week, it was eighty degrees in the day and fifty at night. As you can tell, Montana weather changes on a dime. The rain is pounding on the roof of the house like buffalo tumbling down a buffalo jump in Lodge Grass, and the temperature is about thirty degrees.

The weather in Montana is never what you expect it to be. Sometimes, we'll get a heavy snow in July that is so heavy the tree branches break off from the stressful weight of the cumbersome, white snow.

The Old Man went to Whitehall for some groceries to take home before we head back to Butte. Well, that's what he says, but every time he says that we don't see any groceries, and all we smell is stinky, stale alcohol on his already skunk smelling bad breath.

Crash!!

"What's all that noise?" I hear Mom asking.

Everyone quickly runs to where the initial, noisy crash was sounding. Looking at the evidence, we see that Mart was playing baseball with rocks inside the house—using the roundish, grey rocks for a round baseball. If you're playing baseball with rocks and an old wooden spoon in the house, something is bound to get broke. I wonder what boys think about sometimes.

"What are you doing?" yells Mom.

"It was raining, so I was playing baseball in the house," says Mart.

"Well, now you're going to have to go to town and get a new window. With all this rain, the house is going to get all wet," she explains to Mart.

It is about two miles to the supply store in Cardwell.

Mom tells Mart, "You better hurry back before your old man gets home and sees what's happened."

I must remind you that this is not our house. We are just supposed to be taking care of it, which doesn't make much sense to me considering the owners of the house were to be back about a month ago. The strange thing is, every time we come back to this house on the weekends, after we were visiting extended family, more animals are gone missing. There are only a few animals left now, a red cow and a couple of white sheep are all I see.

Mart reluctantly agrees to go to the small supply store in Cardwell, so he can buy a new window with his own money. He takes off running and is running super-fast. He's going to get so wet. I feel bad that he must go out into that chilly, rainy weather, so I say a little prayer for Mart. I think the Lord will listen more closely to me now that I've been baptized for a good year now and repented for taking those bank coins.

"Please Lord, protect my brave and courageous brother from getting sick from the cool rain and blistering, rigid wind. Amen." I plead.

It's about three hours later, and here comes Mart with a brand-new shiny window. He looks so cold. Irene and I have already been heating up water after we saw him coming up the drive. We figure he'll be needing a warm, cozy bath.

After I said a prayer to the good Lord, He gave me the idea of a warming bath. I'm learning I need to pray, but I also need to listen to how I can help my prayer come true. I have learned; even if we don't get formal church learning every week, if we want to have a relationship with God, He will be there to listen and talk to us if we desire it.

Mart quickly puts the new window in, because he is cold and wants to get into the comfortable hot bath. He learned how to do a lot of fixing stuff like that when we were living with Grandpa. Grandpa is a carpenter and told Mart and Bill that they need to learn how to fix things around the house when those things get broke.

He said to them, "Your old man can't do any kind of carpentry work, so you are going to have to help your mom when she needs you."

Well, I think the window Mart put in is better than the one that was in there in the first place.

IT'S been a couple days since the broken window incident, and our old man didn't notice a thing. Mart paid for the window himself, since he made money working this summer.

It is eighty degrees out again, and everything has dried up from the rain. Our old man is telling us to get into the car, because we are going back to Butte.

"School is starting in a couple of days, and we need to head back," he says.

We are all waiting in the car, but our old man is taking forever to get in here.

"What is he doing?" asks Mom in irritation.

She seems frustrated.

"Here he comes!" exclaims Kay happily.

Kay is getting so darn cute. She is almost seven now but won't be starting school yet. She will have to wait another year.

The Old Man finally arrives in the already compacted car and starts the old engine, and as we are heading down the dirt lane and then past the now empty, dry creek, which is empty because the water was all used up irrigating this land and the land around us, we notice a smokey, grey like cloud coming from the house.

"Hey, where is all that smoke coming from?" asks Mart.

I look back and see that the little red and white barn and the blue, once lovely house are now on fire. Red and orange, golden flames ascend into the blue sky from the roof of the house.

I say to my old man in exacerbation, "The house is on fire!"

All he says is, "Well, Mary, I was actually just renting the house, and those people don't really live there, and I am taking care of everything."

I just can't believe what I am hearing and what I am seeing. Mom is just shaking her head in disbelief, and I'm so utterly embarrassed, even if no one knows me here. I just want to get away from this place and never come here again; not because I didn't have fun this summer, but because of how it ultimately ended.

∞

WE are back in Butte. The silent drive home was exhausting as the highest of tensions in the air was as thick as wet mud after a summer snowstorm, and after we arrived home; the old man left immediately to go drinking,

Mart says to Mom after our old man leaves the house, "I'm leaving for a while. I know of a job in Bozeman that a man I met offered me, and I need to get away from my old man."

He says, "I am also getting tired of him beating on me."

Mart is going to be sixteen, and he is telling Mom, "There are so many things to see in the world. The guy's name that I am going to work for is Old Man Grooter. He is a Dutchman. I met him while I was working with Aunt and Uncle."

Mom didn't argue with Mart, because I think she understands all too well how nice it would be if our old man no longer existed and how she herself would like to get out on her own one day so she could also be free.

I am going to miss Mart. He is all packed and ready to go. Before leaving Cardwell, he had already made this going away decision and packed for this occasion.

I won't cry. I must be tough. Mart is leaving today, because our old man is gone, and Mart doesn't want him to know where he is going. He won't be able to go to school, so he is going to miss his eighth-grade year.

He tells Mom, "I can make up the school year later."

We are all sadly watching him go. We quietly follow him to the busy train station, and he boards the noisy train as we are all wildly waving goodbye.

CHAPTER 27

The Halloween
Prank (1938)

SINCE Mart has been gone, Bill has been taking on Mart's paper route. Mart is now sixteen, Irene is fourteen, Bill is twelve, and Kay is seven. Irene is in eighth grade, Bill is in sixth grade, and I am in the fourth grade.

Today is Halloween, and even though Halloween is fun because of the candy, there is always a little magical trickery that goes along with the scary holiday. In my opinion, the trickery is the best part.

Tonight, I have an extraordinary and splendid plan. My friend, Becky, and I are going to soap up some unexpecting windows at the Grant School. Or maybe, they are expecting someone to soap them up—who knows what windows think and remember.

We have the prepared design already, and I am sure, no one will find out. I mean, last year, and every year before that, that I can remember, there are memorable pranks done on Halloween. Of course, I don't know if people get into trouble pranking, but I haven't heard of them doing so. I will just figure that they don't get into trouble for it.

I would say it is a tradition to do some sort of Halloween prank-ing in Butte. You can't call it an official Halloween without tradi-tional pranks. The older I get, the more I want to do these fun ac-tivities I have always heard the older kids doing. I think, I am finally an older kid, which hopefully means, many of my questions I have been asking all these years will be answered real soon.

Some kids will purposefully empty stinky, ol' garbage cans and stack them in the streets. They even pull the lights down from the arc light that is attached to the telephone poles. It is pretty safe to do this, because most people walk instead of drive. People also tip over outhouses, and boy, when people go to the outhouse to do their business and it is tipped over, you'll hear some yelling to high heaven in the neighborhood that is for sure. Haha, it is so funny.

The prank that makes people the maddest though would be when kids soap up the windows from the outside. They get a clean-ing bucket of cool water and a bar of soap and soap up the cool night windows real good. The cool weather seals the slippery soap to the windows, and it is just about impossible to get it off.

Painting up windows is my bright idea. I mean, I have never done any pranking before now, and I think it is about high time I do.

Well, I am going to meet Betty.

Bill and his sneaky friends already have their gunny sacks to collect candy in. They get so much candy that after they had filled up their sacks once, they go empty them in our washtub and go back out again. They might get three sacks tonight, because I have a feel-ing this night is going to be the best Halloween yet, and everyone is going to get something good.

I see Becky.

"Hi Becky," I say.

"Hi Mary," she tells me as we begin walking.

"Are you really going to do it?" Becky asks me.

"Yes, Becky, I am!"

We walk up to all the houses in the neighborhood and feel lucky at all the goodies we are acquiring. I am trying to use big words now. Have you noticed? The older I get, the more exposed I get to different words on the school spelling tests and as I read books from the library. I like the big, fancy, educated words I use; they make me feel like I am important somehow.

Becky and I are not going to empty out our sacks in an attempt to get more candy. We are satisfied with just one sack tonight.

"It's time Becky. Are you ready?" I ask her.

"Mary, I am sorry, I just don't think I am going to do it."

"Why not," I ask disappointed and a little angry.

"What if we get caught?"

"O, we won't get caught, you sissy. No one is at the school this late."

"Sorry, Mary, I'm just not going to help you. I will watch you from a distance though."

"No matter. I'm not a sissy and won't back out of my word, even if my word is to myself. It is important, I think, to keep the promises you make to yourself."

As I walk to the school windows, I'm thinking—I can't believe Becky bailed on me.

I decide to forget about Becky and grab my bag of candy. I am going to take it with me, because I don't want anyone to steal it.

I walk over to the 4x4 foot windows by my classroom when someone says, "Don't do it, Mary!"

I turn quickly around while I am saying, "So, you decided to come with me Becky," but after I turn around, no one is there.

I see scared ol' Becky, but she is far behind in the bushes trying not to be seen.

I hear the voice again but a little louder say, "DON'T DO IT MARY!"

I am looking around again, but no one is there.

I think to myself, "Are there ghost's out tonight? Am I being haunted for pranking?"

I say angrily as I am a bit annoyed, "Who is talking to me?"

But no one answers.

I have heard of things like this. When I went to church last time, the preacher was preaching about our conscience.

He said, "We all have a conscience. It sometimes sounds like a voice talking to us."

I did not understand a word he was saying then, but now I am thinking about his invisible talking voice sermon, and I think this might be what he was meaning.

I say to my conscience, "Go and leave me alone. I am going to write on this window with all this slimy soap, and you are not going to stop me!"

So, determined, I gladly grab my slippery bar of soap from my right coat pocket and nervously dip it in the cool water. I bring the slick bar of soap out of the water and begin marking up the school window. Suds begin to cover the windows, and so much joy fills my soul that I forget that I was nervous before, and of course, it is my classroom window.

Haha, I want to see the reaction of all the kids tomorrow morning, and as I think about their reaction—finding happiness in my thoughts—I smile to myself.

I am just about done, so I back up to see my fancy pranking artwork, and to my surprise, I back up into a stiff, tall tree. I am thinking, I did not know there was a tree there. I mean, I have been going to this school for a while now, and I don't remember a tree.

Well, the more I feel and place my hands around me, investigating the tree, the more I realize this is no tree. I quickly turn around, and who is standing there? Well, one of my most favorite people in the whole world, Mrs. Kelly. The look on her face is not so good though, and she seems a little, or maybe, a lot upset with what she just witnessed. I have never seen her be devil like mad, but I think I do now, and I wonder how long she has been standing there watching me with sharp, eagle eyes.

I see Becky running in the distance and think, "What a support she is."

I guess I should have listened to that little voice that was in my head saying, "Mary, don't do it!"

Man, I need to attend church more often, so I don't make so many mistakes.

"What are you doing Mary?" asks Mrs. Kelly.

My costume must not be disguising me good enough. See, disguising, that is a good, smart word to use, isn't it?

"I am just pranking, Mrs. Kelly. You know, everyone does it."

"Well, Mary, I am going to let this soap sit overnight, and in the early morning, I want you to come early to school and wash it all off."

And as if that is not punishment enough, she continues saying, "You can also wash all the windows on this side of the school every night after school for the next week."

Well, that is something Mrs. Kelly would do. That is just the way she is. Even though she loves me, she wants me to learn an important lesson that will stick into my sometimes-stubborn brain and thoughts throughout all of time. O, the sad disappointment in Mrs. Kelly's beautiful, kind eyes. I will never forget it.

IT'S the next day, and I am washing all the soap off the windows.

Becky comes up next to me as I am washing and says, "Sorry for running off Mary, but I did not want to get into trouble."

"O, it is okay Becky," I say. Even though in my head I am saying, "Bawk, Bawk, Chicken!"

The kids are all watching me as I wash the windows and making fun of me for getting caught. Some people are saying it was a great idea though. Those comments almost make it worth it, except for one thing, Mrs. Kelly, and her disappointment.

The rest of the day was miserable. Every time I would see Mrs.

Kelly, she would give me a sad look. I tried to purposely avoid her the whole day, but it seemed as if she was everywhere I went. You know how that works, don't you? The very thing you try to avoid is always popping up in your life, so you remember the lesson you need to be learning.

I know tomorrow the looks will stop, and Mrs. Kelly will love me just as much as she did before this tragic incident. See, another spelling word, tragic. I am getting good at incorporating important spelling words into my vocabulary.

I am finally done washing windows, and I decide that I will leave pranks to other people in future Halloween escapades. I just think God wants me to be good. Lately, I have not been as good as I should be, and maybe, He's trying to teach me lessons. I better listen and then behave, or one day, I might find myself in some real kind of trouble.

CHAPTER 28

Mart Is Back
(February 1939)

MART came back yesterday, and I am so happy, but he seems real disappointed in his working for Mr. Grooder.

This is what he told Mom when he came home, "I worked for that guy for five months, and he was supposed to pay me a dollar a day and give me good meals, but every time I would go and ask for my check or for a couple dollars to buy shoes or things like that, he would say, 'No, I am putting the money in the bank for you son, my boy, and at the end of your time here, I will give you all the money that you got coming to you.'

Instead of buying new shoes for me, he took my old shoes out in the ford shed and hammered some old tire casing on the bottoms of them. I walked around in those shoes for the rest of the time I was there, and the only compensation he gave me at the end of my time there, was a ten-pound ham."

I heard Mart talking to one of his friends later that day behind the house saying, "I didn't want to stay there, because I wasn't getting paid, plus my mom told me she wanted me to come back home. My old man was beating her and Bill, and she needed some protection. I didn't want to come back to Butte because of my old man, but I am older and stronger now, and I need to protect my mother and brother. I saw the black and blue marks all over her body and couldn't not come back."

I am glad he is here. I don't see it when Mom gets beat. And my old man never touches us girls. I don't have much to do with him. I don't see him much and don't care too, but I guess he is beating Mom, and I am so glad Mart came back to protect us.

IT'S March 1939, and Mart began working in the copper mines today. He is going to school, but on his days off, he works in the mines. Since he missed a couple years working, he will be graduating the same time as Irene from eighth grade. The school is letting him finish.

The Old Man said to Mart last month, "Boy, I am going to get you a job in the mines."

And, well, he did.

Mart said that he was standing outside the mine with all the other 800 men that stand around the gates of the mine trying to russel a job, and the hiring foreman came out and says, "You back here again? How old are you son?"

"I am sixteen, Sir."

"You are a bit skinny, and it doesn't look like you could lift a shovel, but your old man said you were needing a job, so I am going to give you a job and see if you can make it."

The mine he is working at is called the Bellmont Mine—one of the best paying mines in town. Mart seems to be okay with this. He gets a good paycheck from it.

Mart told his friend, "Since working in the mines and being a little older, I've been getting strong, and my old man hasn't been beating my mom, me, or Bill so much. He is strictly a drunkard. He goes to work and makes $28.00 a week and wastes it before he arrives home. Sometimes, he doesn't come home for weeks at a time, and when he goes to the bars, he buys all his buddies drinks. I am going to give my mom seven dollars a week out of my wages, then I'll keep the twenty-one and use it to buy my own things. I'll try to save some of it too."

Mart said, "My mom can buy a truckload of groceries with seven dollars a week. She can use some of it to pay the light bill, the water bill, and gas bill too."

Wow, I did not realize that Mart and our old man made that much money. I am thinking we could be living better if he didn't squander so much of it on his own selfishness. Poor Mom. And how wonderful is Mart being so unselfish.

Mart also was saying to his friend, "The best place I ever worked was for my Aunt Abby in the Gallatin Gateway. Yes, those were some of the happiest years of my life. I learned so much from that woman. She taught me more than anybody in this world could have taught anybody. It was a pleasure working for her. I shingled barns, mucked out chicken coops and barns, learned how to milk the cow, and took care of a garden. She was so wonderful. She was good to everyone around her."

I wish I would have known her that way. I never knew her the way Mart seems too. I wonder why our given life experiences are so different, even when we live in the same house and are around the same people. It's a curious wonder.

Mart seems to be able to do many important and valuable actions. He lives like he is in an adventure movie that is constantly being continued. He gets to get out and experience life, while I am just stuck here doing the same things every day.

I don't mean to seem ungrateful for all the things I do have, but I want to experience an exciting, adventurous life. I want to sometimes live like I am in a memorable movie participating in magical, wonderful adventures.

CHAPTER 29

Root Beer Explosion, Bones and Graduation

(Moved to Store—Gaylord Street, May 1939)

IT is May 1939, and many exciting events, opportunities, and new stories about my life have happened since Mart came back.

Our crazy old man decided he was going to open a grocery store in November 1938, so he bought a grocery store, or rather, is renting it trying to make a good go of it. There are three apartments upstairs from the grocery store, and we live in one of them. A large Irish family lives in one of the apartments, and one is vacant. Look, another big word, vacant. My vocabulary is increasing daily, and I am happy about this.

I love using my new vocabulary around Mom—she has a happy look on her face when I do, and I feel like she just might be proud of me. I don't often feel like Mom is proud of me. I know she is proud of Irene and my brothers, and even Kay, but I always get the feeling that I am her disappointment. Of course, I don't know if that is true, but it's just how I feel most the time.

Our old man had high hopes for a profitable grocery store, but he never did get it going. It is still just a big, ugly, empty room downstairs.

The neighborhood is pretty much the same as where we lived before—having every nationality around. Most of the parents living in Butte, who are of different nationalities, can't speak English, but the kids know how to. Learning a new language seems easy for young kids to learn, and it helps that English is the only language taught in school.

An interesting fact about this grocery store, is that a lot of the kids in the neighborhood come here to hang out. After dark, many kids in the neighborhood come here and spend the night. It has come to be the regular meeting place for the whole gang that live on this part of the east side.

When I say gang, I really mean gang. In this neighborhood there is two to three gangs, and you don't step over each other's designated territory. Most the time, everyone gets along real well though.

This house and neighborhood ain't so bad. The house is a little closer to the school, and it's about five blocks away from our old living quarters on Faucett street. We have a quaint little yard too. It is comfortable.

Our old man didn't get the grocery store going, but he did attempt to make root beer.

Attempt is valuable word in this particular adventure.

In January—it's now 1939—our old man decided to make some extra money. He learned how to make root beer. Don't ask me who taught him, because I do not know. Believe me, I wish I knew. I would have a few words of wisdom to say to them.

He thought he would sell the root beer and make a small fortune, so he mixed the required ingredients together, and put the concoction into bottles. Making and mixing the root beer is the hardest I've ever seen him work. He was really thinking he would pull in some cash on this absurd venture.

Mom said to him, "Those bottles look old—like you got them second hand."

He said to her, "Don't worry, Monta, the root beer needs to mature, and then everything will be fine."

He told us that he was going to put the bottles in the grocery store to mature, but he ran out of room and said, "Some are going to have to go in the apartment. We need them in the closets and under the beds. In a few months they will be mature and then we will sell them."

I guess they need to mature in a dark area and that's why he put them in the gloomy, dark closets and under the mysterious, shadowy beds.

I knew something would be brewing in the few months those bottles of root beer were maturing, but it wasn't going to be good old foaming, tasty root beer."

IT'S now the middle of May, and us kids are soundly sleeping in our cold, barely sheeted covered beds, when suddenly, we hear a gunfire or explosion.

Well, we are not sure if we hear gunfire or an explosion.

Bang, Bang, Bang!!

Mart says, "What are they blasting at the mines in the middle of the night?"

Bill screams, "We are under attack, the mob has finally reached The Old Man."

We hear an explosion that sounds like mine blasting's and gunfire all right. The sound we hear could very well have been the sound of gunfire, but the explosion isn't coming from the copper mines or the mob.

As we all quickly rush to turn on the lights, what a sight our sore, tired eyes behold. Root beer has violently blasted all their pending tops off, and I don't know why they decided to do it all at once, but isn't life, like that, the problems blast off all at once most the time.

I think to myself—this life of mine really must be just a dream. It must be a dream, because this can't be real life. I sometimes think, I must be living in a dream when it comes to my real life, or rather a horrible nightmare—whatever you would call it, but I always wake up knowing it is my reality when I happen to see sticky, foamy, root beer exploded bottles covering every inch of our already worn-out home.

After the bottles explode, we hear the slamming of a door.

Our front door.

Our old man is leaving his mess for us to take care of.

Mom says, "Get up everyone. Grab some towels and soap—we have some cleaning to do."

As I think about how calm she is, telling us to get up and begin cleaning, I think, but don't say out loud, "Mom, don't you want to scream and fill the air with frustrated noise? Don't you want to cry out, Why me? Why me?"

But that is not what she does. She has a demeanor of the strongest of steels. It's what I admire about her. She has every right to scream and holler and even get mad at God—like some people do. But she calmly just fixes what needs to be fixed. I want to be like her in this way.

You can't even imagine how sticky everything is. It's going to take a good two weeks to get the sticky out of our house. We immediately listen to Mom and get to work.

IT is the beginning of May, and we are experiencing yet another adventure.

Our old man took us down to the nine-mile today to look for skeleton bones. There are no houses at the nine-mile. It is about ten miles from where we live, so we must take the car.

He is telling us, "I can get good money for bones."

All I can do is shake my head when words like "I can get good money for ...." come out of his mouth.

There is a big, blue lake located in the vicinity of the nine-mile, and it is fun playing in the cool water but not too much fun looking for bones. The last time we were here, we found lots of bones.

Who gives you money for bones anyways, I wonder to myself?

There are many wild animals in these high mountains, and I am assuming that the bones come from the wild animals. The mountains start at the nine-mile. The nine-mile is a road, and in order to go to Red Lodge you must take this road, and on your journey to Red Lodge, you must pass through Whitehall.

This road has many sharp twists and turns and can be dangerous when traveling in the wrong weather as I have mentioned many times in our travels to and from Butte. Many people have accidently fallen off because of the narrowness—coming to face their untimely deaths. At some points there is more than a two hundred foot drop down the side, and the side is just inches away from the road.

We have not traveled on this death trap lately, because Mom has not been to Red Lodge for a while. Mom writes Grandma and Grandpa letters regularly, and they write her too. She says she plans on taking a trip there soon. I can't wait. I love my grandma and grandpa.

I am finding some good bones, and so are my siblings. Our old man is happy with our finds, but the sky is beginning to darken and finding bones in the dark is difficult, so The Old Man says, "It's time to go. Get in the car, kids."

Then he says, "You should have worked harder. We need more bones to get the money I need."

Yes, it is all about him, because he spends the money on things we don't need and things he wants—mostly beer.

As we drive back home, I think about how in a few weeks Mart and Irene are going to graduate from eighth grade. It is a good thing.

Irene says she is going to go to High School, but Mart says, "I am going to just work at the mines."

I wonder what I will do after I graduate eighth grade?

I wonder if I will graduate eighth grade?

I have a few years yet to think about it. I should further my education, but I just hate school, except for Mrs. Kelly.

CHAPTER 30

Miss Papas, And The Papas Boys (Summer 1939)

I must say that this summer started off on a good foot, but then a devastating tragedy happened. I met a new friend in our neighborhood before Summer began, and I guess he is Mexican. That is what Mom says. He also goes to school with me. We had made many plans on what kind of Summer we were going to have.

Then it happened.

Mom says out of the clear blue sky, "Mary, you are going to go to Lodge Grass for the Summer."

"What, why are you sending me there?" I ask in a fright.

"Mary, you are spending too much time with that Mexican boy, and I am going to put a stop to it."

"Where am I going to stay, and why is it a bad thing that I am spending time with a Mexican boy."

"With Mrs. Papas and her sons, and one day you will understand."

I remember Mrs. Papas from when we were in Lodge Grass before, which seems like an eternity ago.

Mom says, "She is willing to take you in for the months of June and July."

"I won't go, and one day I will not understand!" I scream.

"You have no choice."

I was thinking—now I know for sure Mom does not love me or even like me. She always thinks I am going to cause trouble.

"Mary," she often says, "You are going to get into trouble one of these days, and I am just protecting you from it."

Now, just because I don't get good grades, and just because the teacher is always sending bad behavior notes home because of my actions in class, and just because I get involved in some things around the neighborhood that cause the police to come around with their sirens wailing, does not mean that I am bad.

I come to understand quickly that this is one argument I am not going to win with my mom.

So, it is now the beginning of June, and I am now stepping on narrow steps of the long 100-foot train that is traveling directly from Butte and going to Lodge Grass. I just know this is going to be the worst memory of my life.

AFTER arriving in Lodge Grass, I had to be around the boys at Miss Papas' house, and they were absolutely horrible. All Summer, I had to put up with their teasing's. I was so unhappy. I pretty much stayed to myself or rather hid from those awful boys for two whole months. Mom was worried about that Mexican boy, but she should have been more worried about the influence of those Papas boys.

I can't even talk about my experiences in Lodge Grass at this present time, because I want my time there to just disappear. I felt so abandoned by my mom these last two months, and I wonder; does she even love me?

I am on the way home to Butte from Lodge Grass, and the conductor on the train helps me get back home. He is so kind, and I am scared to death, because when I arrive at the train station in Butte, no one is there to meet me. I suppose I must walk all the way up the hill by myself.

When I walk in the door, Mom just says, "You finally got home?"

I do not utter a single word. I just walk into my familiar room, shut the door, stoop down against the door, and silently cry.

I never did see my Mexican friend again. His family must have moved away. I am sure that made Mom happy.

CHAPTER 31

Butte's Playground
(Summer-August 1939)

IT is August, and thank goodness, I am not in Lodge Grass. I want
to permanently erase that horrid time away from my now troubled
mind and life forever.

But my positive attitude is good again, and I am going to make
August a good part of my Summer, mostly, so I can forget that I was
ever shipped off to Lodge Grass. That memory is going to stay hidden away in my head for forever and a day. I won't allow it to ever
surface again.

Today, my siblings and I, are driving Mom crazy, so she tells us,
"Go play outside, and don't come in until dark."

All the other mothers must have said the same thing, because
the neighborhood kids are playing on the streets and at the mine
yards.

This is a usual summer day in uptown Butte. It is hot today, and
mothers are getting sick of children being home all Summer. School
starts up again in a couple weeks but not soon enough for the moms
in the neighborhood.

Don't worry though, I love to play outside. Today, I think I will follow my brothers Mart and Bill. Mart is beginning to take a liking to pretty girls, and I hear him talking about one in particular, Doris Diller. I must say, Doris is a good-looking gal in her own way. I mean, if he ever did marry her, he would be well enough off.

I see my brothers going toward the mine yard, so I follow like a cat silently and sneakily close behind. The mine we live by is the Bellmont.

There are dangerous mine dumps all around town and that is where kids in the neighborhood get some good things to build with. Our mine dump is about a block away.

I see Mart and Bill digging a hole by our mine dump. In Butte that is what we do, dig. Before they got to the dump, I saw them stealing some rugs from the house across the street, taking them directly off the copper wire clothesline.

Then, they find some cardboard and scraps from the mine dump and in the neighborhood trash. After that, they pick up some metal sheeting which they will use for the roof and the used cardboard for the walls. Finally, they go to work building their "castle" that they will invite girls to go into.

Yes, I've seen this rundown all before with boys this age.

I know that if they see me following them, they will tell me to skat, so I am discreet—carefully watching all my steps as I watch this life-like movie taking place right before my almost immature eyes.

I watch them all morning work on their hole. They get it all dressed up pretty good before they begin to cat call some passer-bye pretty girls over to it. Those girls know what is going on, and they purposefully go past the mine yards to get some attention. They get to choose the pick of the litter, and they know it.

None of those girls is Doris though. She must not be around today, because I can tell she likes Mart too.

She purposely comes around the house, and you can see the body language going on between her and Mart. I am getting older, so I know now about body language when it comes to a pretty girl and a handsome boy courting. I am learning many things about romantic love—you must learn on your own by paying attention because grown-ups don't like to tell you a darn thing about it.

Well, it doesn't seem like my brothers are having much success. None of the pretty girls are going over to their castle, so I am getting extremely bored with my not so exciting movie. I begin laughing so hard because no girls have accepted their offer, and I don't care if they see me now. In fact, I want them to know I know about their failures, and when they hear me, they angrily chase me toward home.

I don't go home though. After I get a good distance ahead of them, I head to the playground below the Grant School.

There are two playgrounds by my house, one above the school, and one below it. There is no grass though. You only get to play on grass at the Columbia Gardens.

I'll tell you later all about the magnificent Columbia Gardens, but right now is not the time or the place, because I see some kids from school playing at the playground, and they say, "Come join us, Mary. We are playing Kick the Can."

"Okay," I reply, and after I arrive, we begin our game.

There are five of us. Three boys and two girls. If you have never played "Kick the Can" I will tell you how to play.

First, you gather cans together. They could be any type of cans you like. Next, you stack them on top of each other—making sure they don't fall over. After that, you choose a finder and hiders. When the finder of the hider sees the hider hiding in a hiding spot, they run over to the cans, touch them without the cans falling down and say, "I see 'this person' hiding in 'this spot.'" If the hider thinks the finder sees them, they will attempt to reach the cans before the finder, so they can be free.

Finally, if the cans don't fall, the hider, who the finder found, must go to jail, but if the cans fall, the hider gets to find another hiding spot.

I play with my friends for about an hour, and after playing "Kick the Can" we run through the neighborhood knocking on doors and then running away after we knock. Such a fun morning. I love playing outside.

Big Butte, as they call it, is on Zarelda Street, and it is about three blocks away from our house. Big Butte is where all these activities take place. Mom don't worry about me going all over town, because I always check in at lunch time—being hungry from all the playing. She always knows where I am, but after lunch, I go out again.

Everyone on the East Side knows each other, and most of us get along fine.

After lunch, me and my friends decide to play in the gulch by the mine yard.

Mom says she doesn't want us playing around the mine yards, but that is everyone's favorite spot. I mean, we are a mining community after all.

She says, "Those mine yards are dangerous."

But that is where we are going right now, despite her warnings.

I suppose I can see what Mom is saying about mine yards not being safe, but they sure are fun.

When we arrive at the dusty, old mine yard, there is already a group of kids there hanging from long ropes tied off the gallows of the Bellmont. They are climbing the Bellmont Gallows too.

I cautiously climb a few feet up the towering gallows, but some brave kids go about ten to twenty feet. Others go all the way up. Mart says that the Bellmont Gallows is about sixty to seventy feet high. I don't know how they go up that high without falling.

The desperate boys just show off in front of those pretty girls. They are hoping they impress the girls good enough so that the girls will go back to their holes with them. The holes that they prettied all up earlier in the early morning. That won't work on me when I am that age though. I won't be that easy.

Then, there are the metal train tracks. Now, I have heard of kids getting killed along train tracks, but mostly in the night. I love to walk along the metal tracks, and so do so many other kids, and when a fast-speeding train does come, everyone scatters. There are others who hang off the train trestles with a heavy rope swinging back and forth. I just like to walk the tracks though.

After watching the kids hang off the steep metal train trestle, we slowly walk over to some old mine shafts. It is so much fun throwing rocks down the steep shafts. A little scary too. I guess the scary also makes the activity more fun.

The shafts have coverings on them and a small opening to throw rocks into. There is water at the bottom of the shafts, and you know when the water splashes, the rock has hit the bottom.

A shaft is a vertical opening that goes underground—sort of looking like a well, but it is purposely sunk from the top surface going downward to a depth somewhat below the deepest planned mining horizon. This is why they are so dangerous, but it doesn't stop us kids from throwing rocks in them. (Britannica.com)

These mine shafts can be a little scary. I don't know how deep they are, but when I cannot see the bottom of something, then that seems scary to me, but it is also exciting.

I am surprised we don't hear of kids falling in, because it would be so easy to fall into one of those things. I guess we are all experts on knowing how not to.

There are injuries, like what happened to Irene. The paper reports quite often about accidents with kids getting hurt playing all these types of games—some even dying.

"Well, the day was fun," I say to my friends, "But it is over now, and I am going home for supper."

We part our separate ways, and I run home.

CHAPTER 32

Stop Eating Cats (October 1939)

THERE are endless rumors of a bloody war starting with Germany and the rest of the world. Some guy named Adolf Hitler, it seems, is deliberately attempting to take over the entire world, and he is starting by getting rid of the Jews in Germany, or so the people who are spreading the rumors say. I hope they get the guy because who knows if he will come for us next.

There are many nationalities in Butte, like I told you before. There are the Italians, the Fins, the Mexicans, the Chinese, the Swedish, and the Germans. I think there are some others, but I am not sure which ones.

I have heard that Butte, Montana has more nationalities living here than anywhere in the entire world. That is what people say anyways. Many rumors are spread in Butte.

We moved from the grocery store on 27 Gaylord Street. We are now living on 250 East Mercury Street. We are moving right now.

As I walk into the house on Mercury Street, I'm not especially impressed. To get in the partly underground house we must climb ten steps down from the sidewalk, and when we are in the house, we can look out the window in the kitchen and see everyone's busy feet walking by.

The kitchen is small, and there is no refrigerator, just an ice-box—one of those wooden ones that you lift the lid up on and put in a chunk of ice and open the front door and it keeps things cool till the ice melts. We have never had an icebox, so this is the best thing about this house so far.

The paint peeling bathroom does have indoor plumbing—thank goodness. The white, stained toilet has a long straight handle to turn, and a couple of old rotten boards are missing from the bottom, and when you look down below the bottom of the toilet, murky water surrounds the base.

There is no bathtub or shower—just an old tin tub. The tin tub will have to be filled with water to take a bath. That's what we have always done—except in Red Lodge. Three of us usually must use the same bathing water, so we will only be getting, maybe, one bath a week if we are lucky.

The cheap, fading yellow marble sink is just a bowl on the counter that must be filled up with hot water from the kitchen faucet.

The bathroom is pretty much just a hole in the wall, and there is only three bedrooms. One bedroom for the girls, one for the boys, and one for the parents. There are only three beds too. Looks like I'll have to share a bed with my sister's. I don't even think I want to sleep on that bed, it is so dusty and dirty, and there are obvious rusty, red blood stains from bed bugs residing there.

I despise bed bugs. There weren't any in Whitehall or Red Lodge, but since we have lived in in Butte, they follow us everywhere we go. We can't seem to rid ourselves of the pesky parasites. Parasites is another new word I learned this week.

Looks like we'll be scrubbing the dirty walls and sticky floors just to make this place livable. I can see if it were all cleaned up, it might be a pleasant place to live.

I look around the main room and notice three cement columns in the middle, and when I walk over to the cracked, faded, white trimmed window, I see there is a four-foot ditch running through the two-lot property. On the side of the house where my bedroom is facing West, there is a Chinese Laundry.

"Mom," I ask, "Why is there a place called the Chinese Laundry?"

Mom tells me, "People all over town bring their dirty laundry to the Chinese Laundry and pay the Chinese to wash their clothes and things."

"I would not want to do that for a job," I'm thinking out loud to myself. "I hate washing laundry."

There are twelve other log cabins in this area that surround this house. This is the cabbage patch area. We keep moving closer to the cabbage patch every time we move.

I came to find out that the cabbage patch is where the poorest of poor live. I see that in this neighborhood most of the houses are rented by the Chinese and a couple by the Mexicans.

I know who the Mexicans are. There were some Mexicans in Whitehall and Red Lodge and the boy who lives in Butte that I met at the beginning of Summer, who was the reason Mom sent me away for two whole months.

Mexicans have darker skin than my family, and I am thinking Mom doesn't like their darker skin, which might be the reason she sent me away. Maybe, she thought I would fall in love and have dark skinned babies. Sometimes, dark skinned kids have a more difficult life here in Butte than even us white trash.

I know what the Indians look like too; when we lived with Grandpa, we would go traveling and visit my great grandma in Lodge Grass. Great Grandma lived a little way off the Indian reservation, but we would still see the Indians.

The colorfully dressed Indians would come down around her small neighborhood with their colorful feathery top hats and patchwork blankets closely wrapped around their wide shoulders, and

Great Grandma would sit on her front porch and say, "There goes them darn gone Indians past my house again."

When we traveled up the hill, we would see their fancy, decorated T-pees. It was so fascinating to see them lengthy T-pees and to see the way those Indians lived out there in the wild. It was like they were always camping out, and I loved how their dark, black braided hair hung down past their backs. Being at my great grandma's was like playing a part as a bystander in an old western war movie.

Well, our new house is directly next to the government building. The place where we sometimes must get food when we are getting low on money. We always use the red, rusty wagon to carry the free food as we pull it to the government building, and after we present ourselves, the government people fill up our wagon, and we wheel it home.

School started last month. Mart is seventeen, Irene is fifteen and in the ninth grade, Bill is thirteen and in the seventh grade, I am eleven and am in the fifth grade, and Kay is eight and started the first grade this year. She is so excited.

Kay can be lots of fun, but the older she gets, the more she looks like a boy instead of a girl. She is not too happy about wearing dresses to school every day. I must say though, when she gets all dressed up, she looks so pretty. Like a beautiful, little, blooming flower.

Today, is Wednesday, and I'm so excited to tell you that this morning we found out that Penny is going to have puppies.

We don't know when Penny went and got babies in her now protruding belly, but Mom has seen this before and said this morning, "It looks like Penny has about thirty days left."

Penny had to have gotten pregnant at the end of Summer, since I think dogs are pregnant for ninety days.

This is something exciting to look forward too. If Penny has adorable, little babies in about thirty days, the tiny babies will be born in the middle of November, since it is now October and getting close to Halloween again—a holiday I truly enjoy. Free candy. I don't know if Halloween is an official holiday. I'll have to ask Mart if he knows.

In November, it will be getting freezing cold again, so having puppies in the house will be something fun to look forward too when we can't go outside too much and play.

Thinking about Halloween makes me think of cats. The saying is "If a black cat crosses your path, you'll have bad luck."

Well, in my run-down neighborhood, we don't have to worry much about black cats, yellow cats, white cats, or any color cats crossing our path.

Why? You might wonder.

Last year when a boy in my class blurted out that the Chinese in my neighborhood eat cats, I wasn't sure if I should believe him, but I started to notice that in my cabbage patch neighborhood, where I also found out that you could only grow cabbage, also doesn't have many cats.

All the other neighborhoods in town have a bunch of cats hanging around, so I put two and two together and decided that, that boy in my class that blurted out, "Those Chinese eat cats," was right.

There are a lot of Chinese that live on the East Side where I live.

It took me a little while to figure out that they eat cats, but I figured it out sure enough. I was afraid to ask anybody if it was true, because I was afraid of the answer. Deep down though, I knew the inevitable answer.

Those Chinese sure are nice people, and they treat our family real good, and I have a few Chinese friends, but I must say, I am also deathly scared of them. Well, mostly the adults. I'm sure the children don't eat cats, or maybe, they do. Maybe, the parents just don't tell them that cat meat is in their food.

If Chinese kids have been eating cats for food since they were little babies, they wouldn't even know the difference now, would they?

Parents can be pretty cruel and heartless sometimes about what they tell us kids we're eating. Mom tells me were eating a certain kind of food, but when I take a look down at what is on my plate, I know she must be making up fantasy stories, because it won't look anything like what she says it is.

Like when she says we are eating potato soup, it doesn't look like potatoes. It doesn't even taste like potatoes, and I've eaten good tasting potatoes.

Those Chinese also eat things that are rotten. I see my old man selling them eggs. They are not all chicken eggs either. Sometimes, they're quail eggs or other kinds of bird eggs. He finds them eggs all around town, but mostly in stinky garbage cans that are outside grocery stores. The grocery stores throw out eggs that are old, and he takes them and sells them. The Chinese will give him twenty-five cents for two dozen of those eggs—even if they are rotten.

Well, back to the Chinese eating cats. I am afraid that if they eat cats that they might just as easily come and chop my head off and eat me too.

I've never seen a people use sharp knives like they do.

You see, when school started this year, I found a secret door from my house that led to the Chinese laundry. You must remember that my room is right next to their laundry, and all the buildings are mostly connected together. There is a little 4-foot round tunnel that directly connects the two small doors. Part of my house is underground you see.

I don't know what they are saying to each other, but I love listening to them, so I go through the trap door and through the part dirt, round, cool tunnel, and as I do, loose dirt falls directly in my face. From the tunnel, there is another door that opens to the laundry. I don't open their trap door, but I sit right next to it and listen to them speaking.

They will chatter on all night. You must admit that their language sounds a bit entertaining—almost like watching a foreign film. The thing is—those Chinese talk so speedy fast. I think they talk so fast so we white people won't have a chance of understanding what they are saying.

You know, I must make sure to keep myself safe. If they start plotting and planning on eating little children, then they're probably going to start in the cabbage patch, and I live right next to the cabbage patch, so just do the math and you'll understand what I am talking about.

I figure, if I begin to understand a little bit of their language, then I will know what they are saying. Then, I'll know when they're coming for me, and I'll be prepared. If I come down here next to this underground trap door and listen to them often enough, I'm bound to understand what they are all saying, and then I'll be able to properly protect my people.

Maybe, even be a hero. Yes, I am sure, I will be a hero—a super-hero.

It's been longer than a month that I've been listening to those Chinese, and I still ain't getting a lick of what they're all saying. I feel like telling them to talk a little slower, but then I'd be giving myself away.

Maybe, that's why those Chinese are all so nice to us. Because they plan on cutting off our heads in the middle of the night, or the middle of the day; it probably makes no difference to them. If I keep praying, I know I'll be safe though—because remember—I was baptized, and the Lord is going to protect me.

Lord, please protect me from the Chinese, but still let us be friends.

CHAPTER 33

They're Here, They're Here (November 1939)

AS I said before, our house is partly underneath the ground, that's why we can see all the people's feet from our kitchen window; and you know there's a large hole underneath the grey sidewalk.

Last week, my old man went and got a couple, large, wire rabbit pens and a few rabbits. He placed the pens and the rabbits in the hole that is underneath the sidewalk.

He told us, "These rabbits are our pets."

But I know better, he's hoping that those rabbits have babies so he can sell them to the butcher shop on Park Street. I don't think, I'll get too attached to those rabbits. They sure are cute and fluffy though, and they're all different colors: black, brown, white, and some with spots.

Today, I am sure Penny is going to give birth to her little puppies. She's acting all funny and breathing hard. It's just after Thanksgiving.

I found out a couple weeks ago that dogs only are pregnant for about sixty days, not ninety days like I thought. You might ask how I found out this information.

∞

WELL, when Principal Kelly was giving me my teaspoon of cod liver oil, I say to her, "Penny's going to have puppies Principal Kelly."

Mrs. Kelly knows who penny is, because I talk to her about Penny quite often.

I say, "Dogs have puppies in their bellies for about ninety days, so Penny must have gotten pregnant at the end of summer."

Mrs. Kelly says to me, "Mary, dogs are only pregnant for about sixty days."

"Really. If that's true, Penny must have gotten pregnant in September."

"That's right, Mary."

∞

SINCE I found out this information, I have been taking a good look at all the other male dogs in the neighborhood, and when Penny has her puppies, I'm going to take a good look at those puppies to see if they look like any of the male dogs in our neighborhood.

See, it has to be a male dog that gets a female dog pregnant. A female dog can't have puppies on her own. A male dog is a boy, and a female dog is a girl. You can only have babies if a male and female dog get together; there's no other way puppies can come about. I learned that from Mrs. Kelly too.

∞

AFTER Mrs. Kelly tells me all the informative knowledge about puppies and their birthing process, I ask, "Mrs. Kelly, is that how it works with people too?"

She says, "Yes, Mary. That's the only way people can have babies too."

As I sit thinking about it, I guess that's the reason I have a man for a daddy and a girl for a mommy.

"Mary, haven't you gone to church and learned about Adam and Eve and them having children."

"I don't remember that sermon. But I do remember the sermon about Hell and how I know I'm free of it now. We only go to church when we are in Red Lodge, and we haven't been there for a little while. Maybe, I'll go to the church a few blocks away and ask the preacher to tell me that sermon of Adam and Eve."

"Yes, you should—he'll explain it to you much better than I would."

"Thank you, Mrs. Kelly, for all your good and helpful information. Whenever I ask grown-ups about the serious issues in life, they always tell me they'll tell me when I'm older. But every year I get older and still no one tells me."

"Anytime you need information, Mary, you can come ask me."

I give Mrs. Kelly a hug and begin to walk away when she commands, "Mary, come back here."

When Mrs. Kelly tells me to do something, I listen, so I go back to where she is.

"Mary, you don't have any warm stockings on your legs."

I look down at my bare, cold looking legs and then at my red feet and say, "I know, Mrs. Kelly."

"It's so cold outside, you must have some warm stockings."

She looks me right in my almost teary eyes and says, "I tell you what—I'll bring some for you tomorrow."

"I don't have any money to give you, Mrs. Kelly."

"It will be a gift from me. I enjoy so much our conversations that I want you to look warm next time I see you."

MRS. Kelly must be an angel, especially, since the next day I saw her, she gave me a box and told me to open it. I opened that pretty pink box, and inside of it was a pearly white pair of stockings with garters made out of rubber bands. They were so beautiful. I just began crying and gave her a big bear hug.

A bear hug is what they call hugs that are extra special, and Mrs. Kelly deserved an extra special hug from me. I sure do love her.

She said, "Now go in the back room and put them on before you go on to class."

I went and did what she told me to do, and I must say after I put them on, I had a good confidence about me all that day.

I know I got off the topic of Penny, but I told you that I do that sometimes. I have so much to say, and I don't want to forget what my thoughts are thinking.

So, back to Penny.

It's the weekend, and Mom says, "I think Penny's puppies are coming today."

Everyone is getting excited.

"Go on and get a big box from the corner food store," Mom tells Mart.

Mart quickly runs out the door, forgetting to even put his shoes on.

"Mary, find an old blanket," says Mom.

We don't have many blankets in the house—mostly just the ones we use. I took the sheet off the girls' bed and figured I'd try to wash it later.

Mart just came back and hands the box to Mom.

Mom places the box in the kitchen and takes the blanket from me folding it all nice like in the box. Kay leads Penny into the 4x4x3 foot box, then we anxiously wait.

THE wait is finally over. Penny begins panting hard. She is standing on the blanket with her legs shaking as I pet her head attempting to comfort her. Suddenly, she lies down like a sack of bricks and begins to grunt and push. She seems very calm.

We see the first one. I know sometimes, well, more often than not, there is more than one puppy, so we keep waiting and expecting to see more.

Oh, my, how amazing! That little puppy is so small and cute. Right away Penny begins to clean her small puppy. She is licking all the icky stuff that is all over it.

"Mom, what is all that stuff on the puppy?" I ask.

"It is blood and fluid from being in Penny's belly."

"Is it a boy or a girl?"

"We won't know for a little while, Mary. The puppy has to get a little bigger."

It seems like every fifteen minutes a new puppy is coming out of Penny's belly. A black one, a white one, and a black and white one—even a brown one.

"Good girl, Penny," I tell her as I gently rub her sweaty, furry head.

One good thing about today is—I'm getting a good lesson about the birthing process. I don't understand it completely, but no one wants to say much around this house how a boy and girl get the babies in the girl's belly. Maybe, it is by magic.

Maybe, the boy and the girl just must agree and make a contract with each other. That seems the most reasonable.

Every time I ask an adult about this subject, or Mart, they just say, "You'll find out one day."

I wonder when one day is. Kids at school seem to think that a big, white bird called a stork comes and drops babies down from the air and the baby plops down in a crib.

I was believing that story about the stork until I saw Penny get a big belly and then I saw those puppies come out from somewhere. The way Penny is laying, I can't really see how the puppies are coming out, I just know that they are, and it isn't by a big, white bird either.

I suppose I will just have to wait for "one day" to come around.

CHAPTER 34

Popcorn Balls, And Buster (1939)

IT is harsh and frigid cold outside, and Christmas is soon to be coming. Mrs. Kelly has put up the big Christmas tree that sits in the enormous hallway at school. The tree must be about twenty to twenty-five feet high this year and perfectly shaped too. In my opinion, it is the biggest and prettiest one yet. Since, I have been going to school here anyways.

You must go up the stairs of the school to see the Christmas tree. The fancy and colorful green, white, and red decorations have already been made and put on the tree by us kids. It is always fun when we get to put the confetti on the tree. I love looking at that tree. What a beautiful sight.

Every year, the local paper takes a real nice-looking picture of the school Christmas tree and puts it on the front page. The school should put Mrs. Kelly's picture on the top of the tree instead of the angel, or put her face on the angel, because she is sent directly from heaven—I am sure of it. She is the one that makes all the magic happen at school.

God must have thought Mrs. Kelly was capable of changing things here in Butte when He sent her to us. She loves us for sure, and in order to have a love like that, you must be an angel sent from God.

Mind you, I don't know much about heavenly angels, but I do see them in all the handsome churches, and most people say they are good as can be.

When I get older, I am going to have a pretty tree. We can't afford to have a tree in our home, so I must be content at looking around town at all the pretty trees in the busy streets or in the store frosted windows of the shops and in people's homes.

Some of those rich folks have beautiful, grand trees displayed. Especially, the homes on the West Side. I don't talk about the West Side much, because I live on the East Side. The rich live on the West side and have bright lights, sparkly tinsel, and shiny ornaments all over their trees. Some of those pretty ornaments must be specially ordered—I am sure, because I haven't seen any in the stores like some of the rich have in their homes.

Speaking of the rich. They like popcorn balls around Christmas time. I mean, who doesn't like popcorn balls? Well, everyone I think, but me, because I must go around town selling them.

Everyone knows who the poor are in town, especially, Miss Prissy at my school. Of course, that is not her real name, but that is what I call her, because ever since I have lived here and gone to school at the Grant School, she teases me unmercifully. She is rich, and she's always teasing me about being poor and dirty, and she always calls me nasty, old names.

Mom says to ignore her, but I know I can take her. She's as skinny as a rail and as cold as one in negative forty-degree weather at that. But I keep my cool—usually.

Miss Prissy is a whole other story that I must inform you about later. Right now, I must get back to the popcorn balls.

A year ago, our old man had gotten an idea to sell popcorn balls at Christmas time.

He says to us, "We can charge a nickel a piece."

That is what we do. We make sticky, red and green popcorn balls and sell them at Christmas time. Mom makes tubs of popcorn from a tin, copper tub. She places the yellow kernels in it when the lard gets hot enough, and quickly enough—popcorn is overflowing the tub and all over the counter. She makes them popcorn balls night after night—forming balls, then wrapping them in wax paper.

Our old man tells us, "Go, and sell those balls."

We hate it.

"I don't want to sell any popcorn this year, and I am not going to," I say to Mom.

She replies, "Mary, you are going out to sell them, and that is that."

Once Mom says, "That is that" I guess it is.

IRENE, Bill, Kay, and I are walking the streets selling gooey pop-corn. I'm trying to duck between the houses attempting to throw mine away, but my sister Katherine is a little snoop and is watching everything I do.

Katherine is eight now and is sometimes a pest. I'm not saying I don't love her, because I do; she is getting so darn cute, but she doesn't like to wear dresses like Irene and me. She likes to wear them overalls whenever she gets the chance. She doesn't much like curls in her hair either. You could say she is like one of them "Tom Boys."

I decide that I better get knocking on doors and selling the stupid things, since my attempts at throwing them away fell through.

The night is cold, and the streets are clear.

We knock on the door of a classmate of mine. Bill and Irene are in front of me, and I try to stay hidden behind them, but he sees me, because Katherine says in a loud voice, "Isn't that boy in your class, Mary?"

She goes to the Grant School now, so she sees people I know and knows people I know.

I am so embarrassed. It is a boy in my class! He looks at me and smiles.

The boy asks his parents, "Can we have four popcorn balls?"

"We will take two," they say.

At least, it was one of my boy classmates—I usually don't have trouble with them. They smile at me a lot and try to kiss me when we play kissing tag at school. For some reason they all want to run after me, which surprises me, because I don't look as nice as the other girls.

I am faster than most of those boys though, and I can usually outrun them. So other than Walter Jap, I don't get any kisses, and I don't want any, mind you.

Boys always chasing me seems to make the girls in my class all mad, especially, Miss Prissy, but I remember what Mom said about her being jealous, so I don't let her bother me much.

I am almost twelve. I will be in May anyways of next year, and it's almost 1940.

As we walk around the town knocking on doors, I think to myself, well; I guess we really need the money, and every nickel helps. After thinking so hard about the money we need, and because I got a smile from a boy in my class, I figure it isn't so bad selling these popcorn balls tonight. After all, it is the depression, and even though the depression doesn't seem to affect me much, I hear people talking about it all the time and it is real upsetting to them, even the rich folks.

We have always been poor, barley scraping by, so it is like my whole life I have lived the depression.

IT'S Christmas day, and Mom is making soup from a soup bone that I got at the butchers a couple days ago.

The butcher shop is just around the corner and has dusty, yellow sawdust on the floor. The yellow sawdust is used to soak up all the red and pink blood that escapes from the raw meat, at least that is why I think it is on the floor. No one has actually told me that is why the sawdust is on the floor, but I can reason myself you know. Mom always tells me I have a brain that needs to be used, so I guess today, I am using it real good.

There is a great big barrel in the butcher shop that has sour, green pickles in it—which cost two cents a pickle. The butcher also has those big, round, yellow and white cheeses, and every time I go in there, he cuts me off a big, cheesy slice.

I love cheese, but I don't get it too often, so I gladly volunteer to go to the butcher shop when Mom needs something knowing that the kind butcher will give me a nice thick slice of soft cheese.

The grocery store is not far from the butcher shop, and there are four saloons in this area too. The butcher usually gives me a frankfurter. He is an old, fluffy, bald Irish man. I love the way he talks. I come here usually twice a week.

I say to him, "Do you have any tasty bones?"

Dog bones are free. They aren't actually dog bones from a dog, they are for a dog.

"Yes, I do, little miss," he replies.

Then, he gives me a whole bag full of them. He gives me the ones that still have quite a bit of meat on them, because he knows soup will be our Christmas dinner.

He gives me my frankfurter and a couple of potatoes too.

"I have extra," he says.

I give him a hearty thank you and leave to go home. That butcher is always kind to us.

∞

YESTERDAY, we had a very unfortunate accident which makes Christmas day a little less happy and joyful. I know, or at least have heard, that Christmas is really about Jesus Christ. I am trying to get to know Jesus, but I don't go to church enough to really get to know Him. I'm just guessing that I know how to pray correctly.

I talk to the Lord most days, but I don't always know if I am doing it right. People say that God and Jesus and the Holy Ghost are one being and that they aren't human, but that doesn't make practical sense to me.

People also say that God is not a person like us. That doesn't make much sense either, considering when I talk to Him, I feel like He is like me, knowing me inside and out, and how could He know me that well if He wasn't like me or if I wasn't like Him?

After all, when I see pictures or statues of Him on that mean, old cross, He looks like me, and He must have had a body like me, or I wouldn't be able to see all that blood coming out of His side and from His hands and feet. It amazes me that someone so good could be treated so bad.

Well, I asked Him for a ham for Christmas, but all I got was soup. I know that most people probably ask Santa Claus for things, especially around Christmas, but I really don't think he is real. Some kids say at school that he is a made-up story. Others, say he is a real story, but he is now dead, and they just carry on his traditions.

But all the churches say God is real, so I think I will depend on Him more than Santa. God didn't deliver any ham this year, and when I plead with Him to save our puppies, He must have been busy answering someone else's prayer.

Mind you, this doesn't make me think He isn't real or that He doesn't listen to me, I just think He is awful busy answering other personal prayers that are probably more important.

I guess sometimes, we might have to suffer a little bit. I mean, the preacher says Jesus suffered, and He was better than us all, so I guess to ease His burden, I don't mind taking some suffering from

Him. I'll do anything to make Him feel better, because even when puppies die, I can feel Him comforting me, and sometimes that is all I need. He knows how to make me feel better when others just can't.

So, back to yesterday. Penny's puppies died. Well, not all of them. One was saved. So maybe, the Lord was listening and heard part of my prayer. It must be difficult to listen to all those prayers people send up to heaven every day.

I will tell you the story.

Yesterday, was Christmas Eve, and us kids and our friends met up at the snow hill behind our house. We were sledding down the 50-foot hill with our brown toboggans and some old, narrow skis that we found in the trash.

After we got so cold, we couldn't stand it any longer, we headed home, and when we walked through the door of the bathroom there was a terrible, awful sight that I won't soon forget.

Penny was sorrowfully hovering over the toilet crying like a dog that has just lost her favorite bone, except in this case, her favorite puppies.

WE look down and see that all her puppies have drowned in the exposed water. The boards are missing, and they all fell in the pool of water below the base of the toilet. But we don't see all of them. There is one missing.

We look everywhere around the house for the missing puppy. We find him at the foot of the girl's bed shivering like a cold horse out in a negative 50-degree snowstorm. Penny likes to climb up on our bed. She even started bringing the puppies with her. She firmly parks herself on the foot of the bed and sleeps with us girls all night. I don't know how she finds the room in the bed, but she always makes me feel safe. She even finds room when our friends come over.

Mom never knows sometimes how many kids are sleeping at our

house. We have friends coming in and out all the time. Bill and Mart have their friends over too, and if their friends can't find room in the bed, they will end up sleeping on the floor.

Our toilet is old and to flush it you must pull a long handle, and boards are missing from the bottom, so water is all exposed. It is not quite sanitary, no, but at least it is indoor plumbing. I mean, how sanitary are outhouses? Not very!!

The bad part about penny losing her precious little puppies is that penny's puppies are gone, and she went through so much work to have them. She must be so sad.

In an attempt to comfort Penny, I give her a bear hug, because that is the kind of special hug she needs today. Bill takes the dead pups outside. The only place he can bury them is in the snow, because the ground is frozen. I am thinking he might have to rebury them when the snow melts, and that won't be a pretty sight.

The puppy that lived—his name is Buster—and we made sure the same fate did not come to him. We covered the opening by the toilet as much as we could so he would be safe.

Buster is a faithful dog, and he comes into my story again later. Much later.

CHAPTER 35

The Radio (1940)

THIS winter has been long, but it is almost my birthday. It is now March, and last month our old man found a cool radio.

In January, my teacher asked everyone in class, "Who has a radio?"

All, except four hands went up, which included mine. I didn't know how wonderful a radio was until we got one in our home. Our radio is a wooden stand. It has an oval top with a straight base and is about sixteen inches high and nine inches wide. It is a dark, mahogany color with yellow speakers. It has three black buttons in the front and is one of the greatest inventions in the whole world—in my opinion.

As soon as we figured out how to use the radio, we would sit around it as a family listening to it almost daily. It is an amazing invention and came at the perfect time—the season being Winter and so cold outside. One of my favorite programs that are on it is "The Shadow, Only the Shadow Knows" which has become famous talk around the entire school. Before I had a radio, I didn't know what the other kids were talking about, but now I do.

Other shows are: *The Squeaking Door, The Lone Ranger, and Dick Tracy.*

Since it was cold outside, we would just sit around it hour after hour listening to everything that came on. Besides the telephone and moving pictures, the radio is the most amazing creation I have ever seen.

Mart says that it first came to Butte in 1929. He said he was seven, but he didn't see much of it because it was expensive to buy. I did not live in Butte when I was three and when Mart was seven. We lived in Red Lodge.

I love the radio.

CHAPTER 36

Get Out Of Our Way (1940)

SINCE the root beer idea fell through, our old man decided to sell gas. Last week, he bought a few bulky gas tanks and is storing them in the backyard of the house.

He said, "I am going to buy gas and sell it from the backyard."

Is this really my life? Uuugghh! O, well, it is what it is.

Mom and us girls are going to the thrift store today. Winter is over, and next month school starts. Mart will be 18. He is still working in the mines. He bought a brown horse with black spots so he could get to work. He really loves that sturdy, faithful horse. I have noticed lately that Doris Diller has been around a lot more lately too.

Irene will be in the tenth grade and will soon be sixteen. Bill is in the eighth grade and is fourteen. I am going into the sixth grade and am twelve. Kay will be nine and will be starting the second grade.

I know Mom doesn't have much money to buy anything really nice for school, but we might find something at the thrift store today.

The Old Man brought home a bunch of high heel shoes a few days ago and told us girls, "You can use these to wear to school this year."

I am too young to wear high heel shoes, so from the smallest pair he tore off the heels. The shoes don't quite fit. I am going to have to put some sort of stuffing in them so I can actually walk without them falling off. I don't even look forward to going to school this year wearing these overgrown, lopsided, ugly shoes.

I also don't look forward to going to the thrift store today, and not because I don't want to find something nice for school, but because I don't like the way people look at Mom when we go shopping. We don't go shopping much together mind you, but Mom says that we must go today.

I know I have told you before that my mom uses bulky crutches. She also has a great big silver metal brace around her leg, and it is made of steel and iron. She had to have a special shoe made because of it.

Whenever I see someone around town that has troubles or is handicapped in any way, I just look away, because I wish people would look away when they see my mom. If they were just looking at us like they look at everyone else, it wouldn't matter so much, but they always look at her bad leg and shake their heads shamefully.

These kinds of ignorant people don't even know how special Mom is. She has always provided shelter for us, and she never has abandoned us—even when times are harder than usual, and even when we drive her crazy which happens plenty let me tell you.

Mom has always been good at getting some kind of food on the table, even if it isn't good food. I mean, Mom knows how to cook, she just isn't given the proper materials to do it well.

My favorite food is pasta, and I would eat it once a week if I could. Not every day though, because I would probably get sick of eating it like I am sick of pink bologna. Oh man, even saying that word, bologna, makes me want to hurl my lunch.

I know I got off the topic, but I am going to get back on it right now.

The thrift store isn't too far away, so we are just going to walk there. The weather is nice and has been all Summer. Sometimes, it snows in July, but snow didn't visit us this July. By the way, it is July 1940. Going to the Grant School this year will be Bill, me, and Katherine.

Why do Mom's crutches have to make so much noise?

Well, we are in the thrift store, and there are lots of people with their kids. Another name for "thrift store" is *The Salvation Army* or the "dime store"—because things don't cost much more than a dime.

Most the kids I see in here are from the East Side. The kids on the East Side have a reputation of being tough. We must be. No one will usually mess with a poor kid on the East Side, because we have been taught through experience to just survive, and we aren't pampered like the kids on the West Side.

Those rich kids live, they don't know what it means to survive. The longer this depression goes on though, the more people I see in the thrift stores that I never thought I would ever see. You can tell they are ashamed to be in here, because they hold their heads down hoping that no one notices them, but I notice, and I purposefully look them straight in the eyes.

"What do you think of this coat, Mary?" asks Mom.

Mom is asking me what I think of this pretty black coat. A coat is what she is going to be concerned about me having the most, because the winter will be cold when it comes again.

"I have never had a coat like that before, and I think that it is real nice."

It is black and looks sort of like a fur coat. I know it must be fake fur, but it is nice and soft.

"Wow, I like that one Mom." I reply excitedly.

"It is a little long, but I could trim it."

"I would sure be happy to have it."

Mom takes it off the rack and puts it in our take home basket.

Just as we are going to look at some dresses, a lady suddenly passes by us. She is looking down at my mom's leg. I am getting mad and can feel the red, hot fire coming up to change the color in my face from pale to crimson.

Then, the most unspeakable thing happens, the lady that is looking at my mom's leg stops and asks, "Why, you poor thing, what happened to your leg?"

Well, that was the spark that turned to fire which sent lava spuing out of my mouth. Lava comes out of mountains that are full of fire inside. I learned that in school.

I tell you right at this moment, I am feeling like one of those mountains full of fire, so I say to the woman, "You get away from her, and you just go on walking a different direction, you busy body old hag."

That woman quickly moves out of our way and says while leaving, "Well, I never in my life."

Mom isn't too happy about what I had gone and done though. After we pay for our stuff and are leaving the store she says, "Mary, we don't treat other people that way."

"But she was mean and looking at you like you are different."

"I am different, Mary."

"Well, that doesn't mean you should be treated bad because you are."

"No, it doesn't."

"And who knows," I say as we walk home. "Maybe, in God's eyes, you are the normal one, and we are the ones that are different. Maybe, what happened to you is for us 'normal people' to learn lessons on how to be kinder."

CHAPTER 37

Columbia Gardens And The Trolley (Summer 1940)

MOM spends her time taking care of us kids, but she doesn't spend time entertaining us. How could she, she is always trying to make money for us to live.

She says, "I clean and cook, and you are going to have to entertain yourselves."

Sometimes, when she wants personal time, she gets rid of us all. How does she do that?

She sends us off to the best place in the whole entire world. Well, I don't know too much about the whole world yet. In school we are learning about the world, but even the teachers don't have all the information about the entire world.

I would like to visit the world someday. I know about places like Paris, Germany, and Italy. I know about Germany because of my old man and his stories of it, and it seems from what the radio says there are some things going on in Germany that are not so good right now. People are getting all worried about what is going on there. Hitler, some crazy leader, is trying to take over the world or something like that, and some are saying that a war could even happen here in the states.

I know all about World War I, because it is the war that caused the depression that everyone is dealing with.

And Paris, what I know about Paris is—they call it the city of love. That is what the radio says too. And Italy is where romance happens. I would like to go to those places one day. I don't travel much, but I know deep down in my imaginative soul, I would be a traveler if I had the money for it. Just another thing to wish for and dream about.

I won't stop dreaming. Living like I do that is all I have to do. If we don't dream, or rather if I don't keep dreaming, I will be living this way my whole life, and I have different plans for myself than the way I am living now.

That is why I love books so much.

I love to go to the public library and read books. I stay there sometimes reading on the floor pillows until they kick me out. In Winter, I would like to sleep there if they allowed it, because it is a lot warmer than our house. I usually check out eight or nine books before they do kick me out.

I like reading books, because I can escape to different worlds and travel to different, exciting, adventurous places. My favorite books are loving romance and scary mystery, and if you can get them both together; well, then I am a happy camper.

Well, back to having fun. Yes, Mom sends us off to the best place in the whole world, and it is always on Thursday's.

The Columbia Gardens, or Garden's for short, is where she sends us.

Why—on Thursday's, you are probably wondering?

I will tell you. Thursday's is children's day which means many things are free. The rides are not free, but the trolley is. The rides are five cents apiece, and I love the free trolley rides.

That is where we are going now—to get on the trolley. I have enough money for one ride, but there are so many other activities to do there that will keep me occupied that it doesn't matter how much money I have to bring to the Gardens. Just being at the Gardens' is magical and makes a person feel special.

The trolley car has no doors, and here it comes now.

Mart, Bill, me, and the rest of the kids are getting on it, and the conductor is telling all the kids, "Sit down while the trolley is moving."

He says that because we all love to hang our heads out of the trolley car. Why, that is the best part of the ride. The trolley doesn't have windows—just open squares that you can stick your head and arms out to feel the warm breeze when it's moving.

The Trolley car is bright red with a sun yellow strip down both the sides. And on the inside are bench seats that fit three people, depending of course, on how large a person you are. There are ten bench seats occupying each side of the car, and there are three steps you must walk up to get on the trolly. The back of the trolley is open too and has no door, that's how Mart and Bill escape every time the trolley stops.

Mart and Bill are getting out and running alongside the trolley when it slows down to pick up more kids. All my friends are on the trolley now, and I know I might get in trouble by the conductor, but I really want to stick my small head and body out of the side of the trolley car. So that is what I do.

Oh, my, I love to feel the warm, soft breeze on my pale face and my unruly hair blowing in the wind. I feel like I am in a moving picture, and I am the beautiful actress waving goodbye to her love as she goes back to where she came from.

"Mary, get yourself back in your seat."

Yes, that was the conductor. He knows my name because he keeps telling me that if I keep getting out of my seat an' hanging out the side, I won't get to ride the trolley anymore. He lets Mart and Bill because they are older and bigger.

See, I am not so big, and I make the conductor nervous. I know he won't keep me from going on the trolley though, because this is like the millionth time he has told me to not stick myself out of the car. So, I stick my head and body out again when he is not looking, and I dream the same romantic setting as I did before.

This ... is heaven.

We finally are at the Garden's. As you enter the Garden's, you see a big, long pavilion, and as soon as you walk in the gate, there is a red and yellow popcorn stand. I don't have money for the buttery popcorn, so my friend Ronald Rolando and I run to where the fishpond is.

Mind you, there are not real fish in the pond—it is a game. We get to fish for prizes. I don't have money for that either, but it looks like fun, and is fun to watch kids get neat prizes. The prizes are generally small, but occasionally, someone snatches up something big.

Ronald Rolando met me here. We are going to play together today.

As we walk a little longer, we see the ice cream parlor. Ice cream is expensive, and I don't have money to pay for it. It is not easy to keep things cold. You must have a nice refrigerator to keep things cold for a long time.

We have an ice box but no refrigerator. They are expensive. It sure would be nice to have one though. You can store a lot of food in a big refrigerator. Not that we ever have a lot of food to store anyways, so I guess I shouldn't want something we can't use so much.

Anyways, we are heading to the top of the hill where the flying planes are. These planes are wonderful to look at. I have not ridden on them yet, and they look kind of scary. If I were to imagine I had enough money to ride on the planes, this is what I would imagine.

I would imagine I was in the air with a pilot—a very handsome one of course. He would fly me up and over the perfect, fluffy, white clouds, then he would lean over and ...

"Come on, Mary," says Ron, "Come on with me."

There goes Ron disturbing my dreams.

Ron is my friend, who I go to the Gardens with the most. His name is Ronald, but I call him Ron for short. Ron is a good friend, and he is a boy, but I don't think of him the way girls and boys think of each other when they are getting all romantic like. We never do any of that kissing and hugging stuff.

Ron has a bad eye—it is pretty much gone, and he can't see out of it. He lives on the curve of the street going to Meaderville. Meaderville is the place that is in the middle of town. We have Walkerville, Meaderville, the East side, the West side, and we have the flat area below up-town. And you can't forget the cabbage patch.

One dreadful night, some irresponsible drunk was drinking and driving, and he hit Ron's house when Ron was a little younger. Ron's mother was killed, and even though Ron didn't die, his eye got all messed up.

I did get distracted telling you about Ron, but now I am back to dreaming. I don't want you to get confused, but I think Ron's information is important.

I am thinking today is the day that I am going on this ride. The planes go around in a circle, and while they are spinning around, they go up and down. I am not quite sure how they make that ride work, but it sure is wonderful.

"Okay," I say to Ron, and I get in the plane.

I am by myself, and the plane seems too big for me, but I have never heard of anyone falling out, and I see kids my age riding in these planes all the time.

The conductor is saying to the kids, "All aboard!!"

The last kid gets in the plane and the engine, or whatever starts the planes, is running.

The red plane I am flying in is going around slowly at first, and gradually it picks up speed. This seems just fine. Then, the plane goes up, and then down, and then up and down while it is spinning around fast. I am thinking, I might lose my lunch, but the fun of it makes up for the feeling sick part.

I get brave and stick my hands in the air and scream, "AAAHHH!"

Everyone is screaming and making a fuss, so I suppose it is okay. We go on it a few more times before we head over to the carousel.

The plane ride does seem fun, doesn't it? Sometimes, maybe, the dreaming is better than the actual ride—or maybe, not.

The horse carousel is my favorite ride to watch. I love the horses and their colors. I already know which one I would ride on if I had the money. It is the one I ride on most the time, in my imagination, when I come here.

As Ron and I are watching the carousel go round and round, we see Miss Prissy. Oh great, I was having such a good day until she came along. She is in line to ride the carousel, and she doesn't see me. I can just imagine what I would say to her if I was in front of her in line.

She and her friend would get in line right behind Ron and I, and she would say, "Well, Mary, what horse do you want to ride on?"

I would just ignore her—thinking she is not going to ruin my fun today. And because that is what my mom tells me to do.

It would almost be time for the ride to stop and for us to get on. We would be waiting, because there are people on the ride right now.

I would say to Prissy, "I want to ride on the horse that is farthest away from you, after all the smell that is coming from you isn't so pleasant, and I want to enjoy my ride."

Ron would lean over and sniff where Prissy was standing, plug his nose and grimace his face, and then we would start to laugh so hard that maybe I might just almost pee my pants. Miss prissy wouldn't be too happy though.

She would say, "How dare you! I am not the one that lives on the East Side—right next to the stinky, poor cabbage patch."

Then, she would say, "I think I will get a seat on that horse."

She would point to my horse, and I would think to myself, "There is no way she is getting my horse."

She would say, "Isn't that the one you usually ride on, Mary? The cowboy horse with the beautiful maiden and runaway outlaw."

Now the words of Mom would come into my head, "Behave Mary, remember she is just jealous."

I would in my imaginary world try to listen to Mom and behave. So being a good girl, I would just ignore Miss Prissy.

The conductor would then say to the kids, "All aboard," and we would all run scrambling to the horse we want. Prissy would try to get my horse, but she is not as fast as me. Remember, even the boys can't catch me, so there is no way that Prissy ever will.

She would give me a dirty look, and she would ride on a horse that was opposite Ron and me.

The horse I picked does have the beautiful maiden and runaway outlaw.

The ride would begin, and I would close my eyes, feeling the light, warm wind blow my long, brown hair back. I would continue to imagine that I was riding a real horse on a hundred-acre plot of land that I owned. I would be riding away from my heartbreak, or rather the handsome outlaw who broke my tender heart—and of course—he would ride after me, attempting to reclaim his prize—which is me.

Of course, I am going to take him back if he works hard enough and says enough nice things to me, and if he gives me a rose—a big, red one.

As soon as he catches up to me, the ride stops. I guess the next time I take an imaginary ride on the carousel, I will have to finish my imagination.

I would pat my horse, and say, "Good girl, you rode well."

There is so much detail in every wooden horse, it amazes me. I love my imagination—it can take me so many places. One day though, I will not have to imagine.

Back to reality.

Miss Prissy never does see me and Ron, and we go the other way.

It has been a fun day. Many families are having picnics in the blazing fire pits. There are white picnic tables all around, and people pick their favorite spots to eat their lunches. I don't have picnics with my family here though. We come here together sometimes—well, not usually, but we do go off with our own friends.

I can't feel bad though, there are lots of families like me in Butte. I don't mind so much. I don't get to feeling bad about my life. I won't live this way when I am older and grown, but I also don't feel sorry for myself. There is no time to feel sorry for yourself when other people are also suffering. I am just happy, and no matter what my life is, I can see so much joy. Like today—how could I not have joy today?

Even Prissy could not ruin my day. Well, my imaginations of Miss Prissy. Why would I let someone else ruin my happy times?

Ron and I are walking past the rollercoaster. Even though we are not going to ride on it, it is so much fun to watch. We are heading to the playground to play on the slides and the cowboy swings. Yes, the kids are having fun on the rollercoaster.

The white roller coaster dips down three times and the ride goes around in an oval twice. I will wait awhile before I take an imaginary ride on the rollercoaster—I had my fill on the airplane today.

"Let's ride on the red cowboy swing," Ron says excitedly.

The cowboy swings are different colors. There are red ones, blue ones, and yellow ones. They have a three-foot seat on each end. There is a bar attached to the front of each seat that you hold onto, and the pole in the middle helps you go back and forth. You must push and pull and push and pull against the other person until you are high in the sky.

We are getting extremely high, and then my imagination takes over again. I feel like I am in a plane flying high in the sky. No, I am a bird. An eagle. A bald eagle.

I learned in school that bald eagles are strong and can fly the greatest height of any bird. That is me—a bald eagle. I can feel the wind ruffling my feathers as I sour through the giant, blue sky. Then, I see my prey—in the water—a nice big salmon.

I have good eyesight and can see long distances.

I fix my sights on him, or her. I fly down at an angle as I scoop up the wet, slippery fish with my sharp tentacles. I have achieved my goal.

I am going home now to my babies that are on the highest cliff.

Right before I could make it back to my eagle babies, Ron says, "Mary, let's ride on the swinging bar."

I leave my imagination, and Ron and I walk over to the swing bar. At least that is what we call it. I really don't know its name, but it is a round metal silver circle that is attached to a pole by chains, and you grab onto the round part. You can fit about fifteen people on it and swing around. People are always pushing each other off and then trying to get back on when they are pushed off. People also try to make you hit the pole in the middle. It is so much fun to watch but kind of crazy at the same time.

Ron and I have spent most of the day playing in the playground. We stop to see the animals at the zoo and check out the arcade. Now it is almost dark, and I am going to have to meet up with my family soon.

Before I get back on the trolley though, I absolutely must pick some pretty pansies.

Picking pansies is another fun thing to do at the Garden's. On children's day, we get to pick a handful of pansies and bring them home or whatever we want to do with them.

I hear that some of the miners that have wives pick those pansies for their wives. I think that is so romantic. Romantic, I get that word from all the books I read. Did you notice how I don't get too distracted when I am at the Gardens. I do a lot of dreaming, but I really focus on the fun that goes on here.

Anyways—about the greenhouses. There are huge greenhouses in the park that grow pansies. The people that work at the Garden's put the pansies out every week for the people to come and pick them.

The Anaconda Company owns the Gardens. Anaconda is a town close to Butte, about 30 miles away, and they own the mines here too. They carry on the traditions of the original owner.

The original owner of the Gardens—William Clark, died in 1928 which was the year I was born, so I never did get the opportunity to thank him for all the good work he did here at the Gardens. He was the one who made Thursday's children days. I tell you—he must be an angel like Mrs. Kelly to build such a beautiful place for us. Everyone says what a good man he was.

He made up the idea of the pansy picking. The Gardens are special because of all the flowers they have here. There are many flower gardens here, but the pansy gardens are specially made to be picked.

One of the flower gardens is in the shape of a butterfly and the other in the shape of a musical instrument. I can never remember the name of it though. I will have to ask Mom when I get home what it is called.

The Gardens must be at least fifty acres big, and the grass is so green—like emeralds—which means something in Butte. There is not much grass in Butte, or rather in people's yards. With so much mining, the town of Butte mostly consists of dirt yards—especially, the poorer neighborhoods.

Some of the rich people have yards with grass, but not much in the way of flowers growing in them which is one of the reasons the Gardens are so special. I can take my shoes off and feel the cool, green grass poking between my tiny toes. I absolutely love to sit in the pansy garden and pick pansies.

There is a blue lake close by the Gardens, and I pretend I am the owner of the pansy garden and that the lake is also mine on some property I have in Italy or Paris. The pansy garden is so much bigger in my dreams, maybe, an acre big, and my true love and I spend hours just taking in the pansies' aroma while laying together in the summer sun, and occasionally, taking a dip in the fancy blue lake.

My thoughts get the best of me when I am around flowers. Being around flowers just makes me happier somehow. It's amazing how something so beautiful can grow from just a tiny seed. I wonder if that is the way babies grow. I wonder if the mom and dad plant a seed inside the mom. Maybe, that is it. And the little seed grows as the mom gives the seed love and care from the outside of her body. That would explain how her tummy gets big gradually and not all at once.

There are many other activities that go on at the Garden's and things that are free—like *Miners Union Day*. There is a parade, and after the parade, everyone goes to the Gardens and they have miner games, such as: the mucking contest, the drilling contest, and the shoveling contest. It is mine against mine, and the families and friends from that certain mine will cheer them on.

They have sack races and free ice cream. A lot of stuff is free on *Miners Union Day*. The entire town comes on those days. They also come, at least the older kids and adults, to the dances that are held here. There is a place in the gardens made just for dancing, and big-name bands come and play.

I have never been to a dance, but Mart and Irene have. I am still too young to be dancing. At the Garden's, men play football, and baseball too. There are so many activities that go on at the here. Today, I shared some of my favorites.

Well, enough daydreaming for one day. I must get back on the trolley. Darkness is covering the Gardens, and Mom is expecting me. Maybe, I will give my handful of pansies to her for all the work she does for me.

The trolley ride home is just as good as it was there. I did not see Mart and Irene, but Bill is coming home on my trolley. Even though I am tired, and it is getting a little chilly outside, I put my happy head and body out of the side of the trolley, enjoying the wind blowing carelessly in my thick, brown hair.

It is dark, so the conductor does not see me.

I didn't spend any of my money today. I usually save my money to go to the movies. The movies are my favorite. We have many movie theaters in Butte. I'll tell you about them later.

I am so tired as I walk through the door of our house that I just walk to my room and plop down on my bed. Before I fall asleep though, I ask Mom, "Mom, what is the other flower garden in the shape of? There is the butterfly, and what is the other one?"

She says, "A harp, Mary."

O, yes, now I remember. I am thinking now of Jack and the beanstalk and how the giant had a golden harp, and he forced the harp to play for him so he could go to sleep. I will always think of that story next time I go to the pansy garden, so I can remember the name of the shape. Thinking of the harp putting the giant to sleep puts me to sleep, and I forget to give Mom my pansies.

CHAPTER 38

Let Me At Her (1940)

I must tell you what happened to me and Miss Prissy today.

It is October, and the school is getting ready for Halloween again. Mrs. Kelly is telling the school about the Halloween parade coming up in a couple weeks. I love the Halloween Parade at school. It is so interesting—all those costumes people dress up in. I really never do dress up, because I don't have any costume to dress up in, but that fact doesn't take the fun out of the parade or Halloween.

Some kids dress up as princes and princesses. Some of those boys dress up like miners or members of the Italian mob. The girls dress up like brides and mothers. A few even dress up like those ladies from the Red-Light District—mostly the seventh and eighth graders though.

I hear that the ladies that live at the Red-Light District, which is just a few blocks from my house, get paid to dress that way. Maybe, the girls in school think someone will pay them money for dressing that way in the parade. It seems like an easy way to get money.

Mom says that what they do for money is not morale. I am not sure what morale means. I suppose it has something to do with dressing appropriately.

Some of the women around town say that the Red-Light District ladies are going to go to hell. I decided to stay away from that place because I got baptized, and I don't want to mess up my standing with God; after all, I already had to be cleansed once. I don't want to have to go through the cleansing process all over again.

The ladies from the Red-Light District are not the only ones going around making money the wrong way. A few boys have said that they are going to be dressing up like bank robbers because of what happened in 1935 with the bank robbery in Whitehall. Remember, I told you the story, and bank robbing is not something God wants people to be participating in.

As I think about it, even though it was five years ago, I hope I don't get punished by the Lord for taking those coins. If I hadn't of taken them, some other kid would have, right?

I will not worry about it, especially, since I already spent the money, and since I went to the preacher to be cleansed.

I heard the preacher say once that God forgives us right away, but sometimes it takes longer for us to forgive ourselves and that the Devil wants us to not forgive ourselves, so he purposely attempts to bring those sins back to our memory to make us feel guilty.

I would say then that the Devil is bringing up this bank robbing memory to make me feel guilty, so I will just push the Devil out of my head. The preacher says we are stronger than the Devil, so I won't think about it anymore, because I know I am already forgiven and am stronger than the Devil.

But today, I need to say a special prayer to God, "Lord please keep me forgiven, and while I am here talking to you, forgive me for what I am about to do today."

I better get back to my story about Miss Prissy and what the Lord needs to forgive me for.

I was thinking today about all the different languages that kids speak at school and how amazing the teachers are at trying to figure out what we are all saying. Most days, they are patient, but some days they just can't take it. I'm surprised with everyone speaking so different that we all get along as well as we do.

I am not saying there's no fighting, because there is plenty of that. Like I said before, there's even a few gangs formed around town.

My speech is pretty good since I decided to talk right so long ago, and the teachers can understand what I say, so I don't get into too much trouble that way, but there are ways I do get into trouble. Today, is one of those days. I must sadly admit that I might have been following the Devil instead of God today. But I said a prayer earlier, and I am sure God was listening—knowing what I did today had to be done.

It is getting cold outside, so I had to wear my new-old coat that I got at the thrift store. Miss Prissy has already been teasing me, this year, about my high heel broken off shoes, but I obeyed Mom in keeping my cool—except for today. Today, was just too much.

What happened I would never live down unless I did something about it—the embarrassment was just too much this time.

"Mary, Mary, quite contrary dresses like a canary."

Then I hear, "Halloween is not today, Mary, it is in a couple weeks, but I see you dressed up for it today."

My back is turned, but I would recognize that squeaky voice anywhere. It is Miss Prissy. Now, I know that contrary means unfavorable because we learned about it in school last year. As far as knowing what canary means, I don't, but I know it can't be anything good if Miss Prissy is saying it.

I am fed up and have had enough of her making fun of me about the way I dress and about how poor I am, so I stand up and I say with boldness in my voice to Miss Prissy, "I dare you to say that again to me, Miss Prissy."

"Mary, Mary quite contrary dresses like a canary. Halloween is not today, Mary. It is in a couple weeks, but I see you dressed up for it today."

Then she adds, "Mary must sell popcorn at Christmas because she is so poor and dirty."

I must admit, I am surprised she said it again and then went and added more dialog to it.

I get right up in her face and say to her, "You might be rich Miss Prissy, but I know I can whoop you in a fight."

She suddenly looks small and scared, but she doesn't back down. If she did back down, she knew all would be lost. She was probably counting on me just ignoring her like I usually do.

She quickly stands up and says, "When and where?"

She is acting extremely brave, but I can see the fear in her small, blue, ice water eyes.

I say, "After school. After the last bell—in the mine dump behind the school."

Oh ya, I was ready for this. I know there is no way that skinny armed Miss Prissy can take me. I would be surprised if she shows up. Her pride will make her go though.

Now, I know what I am going to do is wrong, and I am going to get into so much trouble over it by Mom, and God, but you know I have my pride too.

I am trying to remember what Mom says about the girl just being jealous, but I made a commitment, and I must keep it. God says we need to keep our commitments, so I think keeping my commitment is more important than what I am going to do to Miss Prissy.

The news of a fight has gone through the entire school, and kids from all grades are meeting at the mine dump after the last bell.

I arrive at the scene of the soon to be crime, and I can't believe the crowd; especially, since it is two small girls like ourselves.

I must say, it is kind of exciting, even though I am sort of scared at the same time.

Don't get me wrong, I know I am going to win this fight; I mean, I am from the East Side.

I am pushing my way through the huge crowd until I get to the fighting destination. There is brown, dusty dirt everywhere, so this is not going to be a clean fight.

Miss Prissy is here with her clan who are prepping her up. Becky is in my corner.

The crowd of kids are yelling. The boys are mostly yelling in my favor, and the rest of the boys, and most of the girls—except for the poor ones—are yelling in Miss Prissy's favor.

I see a few kids taking bets.

I say to Miss Prissy, "Are we going to do this or not?"

She quickly whips her curly, blonde hair around and says, "Yes we are."

"We begin dancing around each other a few times, and then I go in for the kill. I reach for her skinny weak arms so I can drag her down on the ground and level her. I get them, and she grabs my hair.

Such a girl thing to do.

But I overpower her and get her down on the ground. I straddle her with my stronger not as skinny legs and grab her now dirty hair and start banging her head on the hard cement.

She is screaming, "Get her off me, get her off!"

I say, "Are you done, Miss Prissy!? Are you done making fun of me?!"

She screams weakly, "Yes!"

Tears are in her swollen, red, puffy eyes and crimson blood is flowing out from her now bloody head.

Then, I hear the ambulance coming.

"Wwwwrrrrr!"

And the police.

School is out, so one of the neighbors must have called the ambulance and the police.

Miss Prissy and I are suddenly being torn apart. She is going in the ambulance, and I am going in the police car.

I hear someone say before I get into the police car, "She has a big cut in her head and will need stitches."

I guess since I am not bleeding, and I was on top, the police figure I am just fine.

The policeman is asking me, "Where do you live, Miss."

I tell him shyly, and we head in the direction I say.

When we arrive home, and I get out of the police car, I see Mom talking to the police. I head straight for underneath the bed, because I know I am going to get a beating with her crutch.

CHAPTER 39

Bill Is Okay (1941)

1941 has been an extremely harsh winter. Food from the government trucks has become the norm for most people on the East side and even some well-to-do folks on the West Side.

You might say that the depression is even affecting the poorest of the rich. Our trusty, old, red wagon is still good for hauling the food we need, like flour and potatoes, which is what we receive most often.

The red, double story, brick government building is close to our house—just a couple blocks away.

We get free food because when Franklin Roosevelt was president, he wanted to help the poor get relief, so in May of 1933, he made the Federal Emergency Relief Act.

I am told that on December 28, 1937, Eleanor Roosevelt, Franklin Roosevelt's wife, stopped off in Butte. I was in Red Lodge when this famous event took place, but people talk about it, thinking it was a real special event. Many people were unemployed after WWI, and a lot of the distressed where kids.

In 1935, *The Eye Opener*, Butte's pro –labor newspaper, said, "Butte is a poor city atop the richest hill on earth."

Weird, right? We are the richest place but also the poorest. How can that possibly be?

It seems like we will be having another WW. WWII. Everyone thinks we will be joining in on the current war. Germany has been invading many countries, and I hear Adolph Hitler is responsible.

Tomorrow, is my birthday. I will be thirteen, and the weather is finally getting warmer.

January through March, I spent some of my time at the Holland Skating rink. There are a few ice-skating rinks in town, but the Holland is the biggest. It even has a beautiful pavilion. Most the kids go there.

There is a nice ice-rink at the Clarks Park, but the Holland is closer to my home and is more fun. The Clarks Park also has a ball field that the boys like to play at, and there are grown up games there too. I don't go there much, because I must walk wherever I go, and that seems far away from where I live. It is located on the flats.

Well, the Holland fills up with water, and the water freezes. That is what I am learning about ice. Interesting how that works. To form ice, water has to be at a certain temperature, and in Butte the winter temperature is just right for making ice.

The kids in Butte love to ice-skate. There are even some that take it so seriously they do a lot of competing. I see some of those girls and boys skating, and they remind me of heavenly angels gliding smoothly along the ice—kind of like I imagine how angels would glide smoothly in the heavens.

There are a couple of kids in my class who are real good ice skaters. I am okay on the ice but nothing like some of those kids.

One bit of information about the kids that live in Butte—they are tough. When I go to visit other places, like Red Lodge or Bozeman, the kids seem a bit tamer. I think it has to do with mining. Butte is big in population too, close to 100,000 people. It seems like people here know a lot about survival.

Bill is getting better. He has been real sick for a couple months. He went to a log cabin in the mountains with a friend this winter and contracted pneumonia. He never seemed to be able to warm up for the whole two months afterwards.

Dr. Monahan has been taking care of him and trying to get him back into good shape. We were all worried there for a while. Mom couldn't afford to go to the hospital, and we don't have medical insurance, so we did a lot of sincere praying.

Not together, mind you. I don't ever remember praying with my family, but this was something we needed to be praying about.

All Winter, mom would put a blanket around Bill and keep him by our old coal stove.

After a lot of prayer, Dr. Monahan told Mom about an experimental drug that people were using for infections.

"It is called, penicillin," he said.

He told us that he had acquired some and knew we didn't have the money to pay for it, but because he didn't want Bill to die, he gave him some doses of it. Right away, Bill began feeling better.

It is a miracle drug, some people say.

Dr. Monahan says, "It is an antibiotic and is therapeutic."

I guess a man named Alexander Fleming from the United Kingdom found out about the miracle drug, and the medicine is sort of like a kind of mold. I am not real sure what mold is, but it sounds like something awful, although, it can't be awful, if it saved Bill's life.

He now seems to almost be back to his old teasing self.

Bill loves to tease. He is fifteen now.

The good and gracious Lord answered my prayer about Bill, because he is now recovered. But that is an important prayer. Someone's life is important, and I know that the Lord was listening.

Bill will be graduating from the Grant School this May. Mart is eighteen now. Irene is sixteen, and Kay is nine.

It is my birthday today, but I am not getting any special presents, and for dinner, we are eating ordinary beans and real potato soup.

CHAPTER 40

Let Us Go To The Movies (July 1941)

MY old man works at the Belmont Mine, and he walks to work, because the Belmont Mine is close to our home, which I did mention before, but I'm just reminding you again. Mom always packs a black lunch bucket, full of food, for him to take to work. All the miners take black buckets, or lunches, down in the mines. They are down underground for the entire day and need something filling to eat.

To work in underground mining, you don't need training or a high school diploma, but you must be fifteen or sixteen to work there. Some kids go to work there right out of the eighth grade.

My old man goes to work at eight in the morning, and we sometimes don' t see him until the next day. After work, he spends all his time in the bars, especially, after pay day. After payday, he is sometimes gone for days at a time.

I really don't know how Mom gets food on the table. I really don't! We would give anything to just have a good breakfast. A good breakfast would have even been good to have for dinner.

It is common though for all the miners in Butte to go to the bars, especially, after payday.

After payday, you will see angry women sending their kids to the bars to encourage their fathers to come home. Most the time, the women will send the kids before it gets too late. The later the drunken men are at the bars, the more money from their paychecks they spend. They like to be generous and buy drinks for the other men too.

That is where Bill and I are heading now. We are here, and we see him. He is loud and sitting in the same familiar place he always sits. Men like their same seats, or stools rather.

Before we say anything, he sees us and says in our direction, "Get ta lotta out of here, or else."

We know he is going to say that because that is what he always says.

For some reason, Mom still sends us here, and we go because we love her. I think she sends us, even though the same exact outcome occurs, because maybe, deep down, she still has hope—hope that he will change. Maybe, that is why she still stays married to him and why she has stayed for so long.

It is good to have hope, and Mom does all she can to help him. But sometimes, all you can do is not enough, and it is likely that change will never take place, because he doesn't know how to help himself. He has been doing the same things for so long that he might not want to change himself, because that might be too hard and require that he accepts that he is not being good, and him not seeing or recognizing he has a problem, and well, that has nothing to do with her.

I think he will always be this way, because he doesn't know any other way. But that doesn't mean that Mom must keep putting up with it. One day, I have the feeling, when she realizes that his not changing will affect her mental, emotional, and physical health to the point of her no return to normal sanity, she won't keep staying.

Well, we get out of there fast after he tells us to leave, and we don't see him until this morning. It is Saturday morning and that means the movies.

After he came home and fell sound asleep, Katherine and I do what we always do the day after his drunk fest payday. Steal his change. Don't get me totally wrong. I don't think we are really stealing, because he is our dad, and he is required to support us. It is his responsibility you know.

We sneakily tiptoe to the front room and see that he is completely passed out on the green ripped sofa. Even though Mom doesn't like him coming home drunk, it works to our advantage the day after payday. He has pockets full of heavy change, and Kay and I take all we can handle in our small hands. Then, we swiftly head out the blue front door before Mom wakes up.

We had told Mom early yesterday that we had some money saved up from the last couple of weeks and told her we were going to the movies today. She told us yesterday we could go—but to come home after the first show—thinking we only had the money we saved.

Saturday at the movies is a special place for me and all the kids in Butte. To get into one movie, it costs a dime. Sometimes, if you get lucky, you can get in for free by the alley way. The ticket holders will let you in if you are short on change. If you get in free you can use your money for a sack of popcorn or candy. Most the money I get is spent on going to the movies, but because I took my old man's change early this morning, I have plenty for popcorn and candy.

The movie theatres are close to where I live, so we do not have far to walk. I am going to meet Ron and Becky there. To get to the movie theater, Kay and I must walk by the Red-Light District. I know I have mentioned this unusual and curious location before, but I did not explain myself fully on what it is.

Yes, the Red-Light District has red lights and is located in a narrow alley on Galena Street. To see what might go on in the mysterious building, you must climb a six-foot high green fence that runs around the entire building. I have always wondered why the fence is so high.

Today, we are going to peek in to see what kind of activities go on in there. We always do this on our way to the movies or whenever we are walking past. We are still kind of short, so we must climb on each other's shoulders to get a decent look.

I don't know why we care so much about what is going on in here. I guess because of the mystery of it all and the fact that it is forbidden. When you are a curious, inquisitive, kid, like myself—finding out the mysteries about these mysterious and forbidden facts and places make life more interesting.

I see Ron walking down to meet us before we reach the theater, and I yell, "Hi, Ron!"

"Hi, Mary and Kay," he says back.

"Come over here, Ron, so I can get on your shoulders. Kay is too small for me to get on her shoulders."

"Mary, why do you want to get on my shoulders?"

"Because I want to see what is going on behind this big, green, faded fence."

"What does it matter anyways?"

"Are you going to help me or what?"

Reluctantly, Ron walks directly over to me and allows me to instantly climb up onto his small, narrow, boney shoulders.

While on top of Ron's not so sturdy shoulders, I can see apartments and ladies walking back and forth and back and forth. They are dressed different then what I am used to seeing women dress like. If you can say they are dressed at all—as so much skin is showing.

Now, the girls that dress up like them ladies for Halloween are dressed in more clothes at school. I can't imagine their mothers would let them go out of the house the way these ladies dress. I wonder, if the girls at school have ever seen the way these ladies dress or if they just hear about it and try to copy them.

"Ron, these ladies don't have many clothes on. One of them is wearing a green feather in her red hair and bulky costume jewelry is covering her entire naked neck and arms. She even has a slit in her crimson red, pink flowered dress that is traveling all the way up to her thigh."

None of the kids my age knows what is going on, really. The older kids seem to know. But no one tells you. Mom won't tell me and either will Mart and Bill. They do say what goes on there is not proper.

I asked Mart once, "Have you ever been past the green fence?"

He says to me, "Mary, don't ask men those kinds of questions."

I say, "Why not? Are you a man now?"

"Yes, I am a man," he replies.

But he never did give me a straight answer. O, well.

"I know what goes on in there," says Ron.

"What?!?" I say in surprise.

Just as I look at Ron and am about to lose my balance, one of those half-dressed ladies takes notice of me, and she is attempting to chase me off yelling, "Get off that fence you sneaky girl."

They chase you off real quick when they see you poking your eyes over the forbidden fence. The men that are in there with those ladies are screaming at us too. Of course, you don't see who those men are very often, they seem to stay inside most of the time and pull their top hats over their eyes. It is like they don't want to be seen. Those unproper ladies though, they seem to want to be seen, not by us kids mind you, but by the men.

We quickly begin running away from the Red-Light District and start walking to the movie theater.

"What do you mean, Ron, when you say you know what goes on there?" I ask curious like. "How do you know what goes on there?"

"I'm a guy, Mary. All the guys know what goes on there," he replies matter of fact.

"Well, then, tell me," I command. "I want to know."

"I'm not going to tell you, Mary, because you're sweet and

innocent, and a sweet, innocent young girl like you don't need to worry about such things right now."

I was mad at Ron for knowing and not telling me, and he knew I was mad, but it didn't' destroy our time at the movies. Nothing can destroy my time at the movies.

Many movies we go to are westerns that are featuring Harry Carey, Hoot Gibson, or Tom Mix. Just last year, Harry Carey was nominated for an acting award. He is good in all the silent movies, especially, the one called Mr. Smith goes to Washington. He's not so handsome, but he has a way about him.

Hoot Gibson isn't much of a looker either.

Tom Mix, on the other hand, is so strikingly handsome. His dark, brown hair and tantalizing eyes as he wears that wide-rim, brown cowboy hat could just bring a young girl to her boney knees in forever happy tears.

I love sitting through these shows. The shows I never get enough of are the ones with Shirly Temple. Why, everyone knows who Shirly Temple is. She is a young actress, who has been acting since she was just a young three-year-old girl. Her hair is full of tight, light brown curls, and she always wears it in a bob to her shoulders. Her latest film, the one we are seeing today, is called, The Little Princess. One of my favorites though is, The Blue Bird. Boy, can she sing.

A famous Butte movie, because of the actress, Marguerite Clark, who played Eve, is famous in these parts because they say she lived in Butte for a while. The movie is about slave trading. Slaves were all black folks in those days, and they tend to like to make movies out of their horrific stories.

There are no more slaves now, but there are many movies that like to portray what happened in the slave days and how the slaves were freed. This movie was before my time, but I have seen it, because in the movie theaters they have days that they play all the old favorites. I like the old silent movies—they are fun to watch.

There are ten theatres in Butte.

1. Ansonia Theatre, located on West Park Street, costs a dime.
2. Elysium Theatre.
3. Liberty Theatre, located on West Broadway, cost a nickel.
4. Rialto Theatre. This is the theatre Bill often drags me around to when he meets the Meaderville Club, which meets just under the Rialto Theatre.
5. Orpheum Theatre.
6. Grande Theatre. This theatre produces movies that are apparently morally wrong.
7. American Theatre which is located on Park Street.
8. Harrison Avenue Theatre which is located on the flats.
9. Lyric Theatre, located on the East Side, is located by the East Side Opera House.
10. Park Theatre, which has movies for 5 cents every Saturday.

We are at the Park Theater, because it is Saturday, and we only want to pay 5 cents per movie. At only five cents, we can go to more movies. You see, most the time, I go and watch the double features and stay there half the day. That is what I am going to do. I got enough money for a sack of popcorn and candy. Today is the height of my childhood amusement.

The theater is wonderful with their soft, pull-down, red velvet seats. Being at the movies makes you feel like you are in a different kind of land, and for once, maybe, a little rich. Because at the theater it doesn't matter your standing or how much money you have, this is where the imagination and magic happens and takes you away to all the possibilities life has to offer.

The first movie is over, and I am trying to convince Kay to stay longer. She is tired, but if she goes home before I do, Mom will know I took money from our old man's pants. Kay usually goes home early, because she doesn't want to get into trouble. Mom thinks she is such a goody two shoes. Kay does as much trouble making as me, she just doesn't get caught.

I know, I will get a beating when I get home if I stay too long. Mom will be waiting with the fire shovel, and of course, she will use her metal crutch on my backside or whatever side she can reach. When I get home, I'm heading for underneath my bed which means I have decided to stay for another fantastic show.

Kay goes home after one show because that is what Mom told her to do, and she doesn't want such a beating, but I don't care. I am going to stay all day watching movies and eating candy bars and popcorn until my tummy hurts, and I feel like hurling.

I love the movies because you can escape and go to a different world, places you have never been to before. I need to escape sometimes. I mean, I have a positive attitude considering my situation, but I need to escape from it occasionally.

At home, I have a small like dresser with a drawer that I can put a few personal items in, so when I get my hands on a newspaper or magazine that has a picture of an actor or actress that I love, I mix up flour and water until I get a good paste going, and then I cut one of those pictures out and paste it with my paste that I made on the dresser.

It is decorated real nice now. I have almost the whole drawer covered with fancy pictures of actresses and actors. I am going to be in a movie one day. I have been preparing myself for it. People say I am a looker, and when you are a looker, you should be in the movies.

Mom has ponds face cream that she puts on her face every day, and when she is not looking, I sneak into her room and put some on my own face. If I am going to be in a movie, I want my skin looking good, and Mom has nice skin, so I figure, it must be working for her, so why wouldn't it work for me too. I need to be beautiful and have smooth skin, so I can look good in the movie I will be staring in.

The last movie is over, and it is time to go home. Ron and Becky went home a long time ago. Becky met us later; she had some chores to do earlier in the day. No one stays as long as I do.

I see my dark house as the bright, brilliant moon shines down on it all silvery like.

After I carefully walk up the three narrow steps and reach the wiggly doorknob, placing my hand quietly on the door handle, and as I am trying to be as quiet as a scurrying mouse avoiding a sleeping cat, so Mom doesn't see me—I almost accomplish my task when Kay sees me and blurts out, "Mary's home from the movies."

She didn't get into trouble, because she came home after the first show. That tattle tale. I think she wanted me to get into trouble. Darn her!

It really doesn't matter much if I get into trouble, because it is all worth it. As I run and slide under the bed, and while Mom is telling me to get out using the fire shovel, all I can think about is what movie I will see the next weekend when my old man passes out on the dirty couch again, and what worlds I will explore next.

CHAPTER 41

Don't Kill My Brother (September 1941)

SCHOOL has started again, and Mart is gone. He sold his trusty horse and left town yesterday, saying to us all, "I am going on an exciting adventure."

While on his way, he said, "I'll write. I promise."

He bought a horse while he was working at the mines, and he took that horse to the mines with him almost every day. He kept it in our backyard. He sold it yesterday, because he knew he would need some money, and he couldn't take the horse with him, so he might as well just sell it.

He even said goodbye to Doris. She was in heartache tears as he was leaving the train station.

You must know the reason he is leaving. You won't believe it either after I tell you the tale. Well, after all the things you know about our old man, maybe, you will believe it.

Four short days ago, Mart and The Old man were made partners in the mine at the Belmont. They were going to work together. This is what Mart told us yesterday.

"I was working and coming up the manway," he said.

Manways are holes that are between the levels underground.

He continued, "I come to the manway and see a light at the top of the manway. I think that I better get out of the way, because I suddenly notice tiny trickles of sharp rock coming down it. No sooner had I stepped out of the way, when here comes a large round boulder about as big as my head, and after the boulder falls to the ground, I look up at the top of the manway and looking down is none other than our old man."

I know that he does some awful, unspeakable things—but to attempt to kill your own son—why would he do that?

As Mart continued, I found out why.

Mart said, "A couple days, before today, he asked me to sign over my insurance to him—the insurance was for $1800.00 for a death. I had refused to sign it over to him. I had to sign it over to someone, so I signed it over to you, Mom, just in case something did happen to me.

He kept pestering me, continually asking me the last couple of days over and over to sign it over to him, but he knew I signed it over to you. Mom, I think he tried to kill me today. Maybe, he still thought he would get the money from you. Mom, I can't stay here any longer."

Mom shook her head as if to say, "I understand, you need to go."

"Mom, I have saved some money, and I am going to sell my horse, buy a car, and take a trip to California. I have always heard what a beautiful land California is and that it is a land of opportunity. I am leaving tonight."

Mart left alright. He is gone, and I am happy for him. He gets to go on an exciting adventure. I wish I could have gone with him.

Well, school started, and I have been helping my mom with the paper route. With Mart in California and the rest of us kids helping with the paper route, we are getting one of those nice refrigerators soon.

I forgot to tell you that there is a big housing project in the Cabbage Patch, and so the Cabbage Patch is torn down. I think that the kids at school won't be teasing people any more about living in the Cabbage Patch, because it no longer exists.

I finally found out why everyone in town thinks the cabbage patch is so bad. The cabbage patch was full of small cabins with no paint, shacks that are broken down, and shanties that were full of rotten wood. Of course, I knew this information, but I never thought it was bad. I am used to seeing it.

Some of the shack cabins were even built out of cardboard and grocery boxes. Some miners slept in those cabins, bootleggers too, and criminals.

There was just a bed in some of the cabins and mostly just men who lived in them. Police or anyone, didn't like to go there, because criminals operate their businesses there, and many people have gotten shot or stabbed throughout the years.

There was also no plumbing. People say that the Cabbage Patch was unsafe because of the open sewage. They say it was making people sick, and it was on an old mining claim. I think it was called, Mahoney's Lode.

Lots of people thought that they owned the land, and because of it no one really knew who to pay for rent, so the people who were renting the places on the claim ended up not paying at all.

This was the first part of Butte that went up in the late 1800's. The Cabbage Patch was the part of town that was always known to be poor.

Judgments and ideas should be different now with the new buildings being built. I must say, the buildings are nice, and the neighborhood does look better.

The first move in to the new apartments was on May 9th, a little bit before my birthday.

There is now a fire station right above the new apartments, so if anything goes wrong, they can help.

CHAPTER 42

I'm Dying (Pearl Harbor—
December 1941)

IT is almost Christmas, and it is extremely cold outside. Maybe, the coldest Winter ever. Mom must work the paper route, and it is difficult for her to climb our narrow steps in the new house. I have been attempting to contribute in small ways by getting a few odd jobs here and there and helping her with the paper route.

In six months, I will be turning fourteen. I started the seventh grade. Bill is not going to school—he says he would like to join the army, but he is too young yet. Irene is in the eleventh grade, and Mart is in California. Kay and I are the only ones going to the Grant School at the present time, and it seems kind of lonely with everyone gone.

Everyone is growing up, and I am not ready to grow up. Today, I had to grow up—I had no choice, or at least that is what my neighbor, Mrs. Bailey, told me. Before I get to that story, I must tell you about the war.

Thinking about the war, makes me ponder about death, so I must tell you before I forget that on November 15th four miners died because of dead air in the St. Lawrence Mine. The whole town is in mourning.

Sorry, I will get back to the war and then my story.

It is official. The war started, and everything is starting to prosper pretty good in Butte. Butte mines gold and copper, and the war needs both. That is why there was such a depression in Butte after WWI, because when there is war the war needs copper. During the depression, we lost a few people living here in Butte because the demand for copper was not as in demand.

On December 7th, the Japanese bombed Pearl Harbor, and the next day, the States declared war on Japan.

On December 11th, Germany and Italy declared war on the States, and we in turn declared war on them.

This war will bring business to Butte, because the military will be in need of copper.

I must tell you that WWII is not the only war going on. There is one going on inside my body. I have been cleaning this kind, old woman's house, Mrs. Bailey, for money lately.

Like I said, I am trying to help Mom out, and Mrs. Bailey gives me ten cents every day I clean. Something terrible happened while I was working today.

I was washing dishes in Mrs. Bailey's sink, and I was almost done when I noticed something running down my thin, pale leg—something like water.

Before I get to that I must tell you about this old lady's house. Her name is Mrs. Bailey. She lives in an apartment building on 234 and 234 ½ Mercury Street. It is a two-story house, and the house is made of white brick. She hires me to wash her dirty dishes and clean up her dusty house. I get paid a nickel every time I wash her dishes.

Mrs. Bailey is a nice enough lady. She is in her thirties and has a few young kids. The only bad thing about this place, is the bugs. Not only are there bed bugs, but there are cockroaches and big ones. Of course, everyone in the neighborhood has bug problems, but this house seems to have the worst bug problems around.

Bugs are always coming out of every crack and crevasse, and there are a more than a few cracks and crevasses in this broken-down house. The black rodents are almost as big as a serving spoon, and you can see their antennas moving in all directions like they are searching for their next victim—which sometimes, I am sure is me.

They run up the wide, white walls and onto the high ceiling and drop right down in front of me, and land sometimes on my unexpecting head.

I don't think I can work here too much longer, because I just can't take all these creepy, crawlies. I am trying to help with bringing money into the home, but the bugs might just be too much for me to handle.

Next to Mrs. Bailey's is the Gaetoano house. Irene has a friend that lives there. They are the same age. They are talking about going to Jamestown, North Dakota to learn how to telegraph. Since the war is going on, there will be some jobs in Montana for telegraphers. Irene is talking about quitting school to go.

Irene's friend lives with her grandmother and her grandmother chews brown snuff. You often see her chewing that stuff and spitting it out. Not the womanliest thing to do, I must say. But in this neighborhood, this behavior is not unusual to see.

Next to the Gaetoano house is our house. Across the street from our house, on 222 Mercury Street, is where my friend Facincani lives. Further down the street on the corner is a grocery store. That grocery store is where we get our lunchmeat for school.

Well, back to what was running down my leg. It was red, slimy blood. Different than blood that comes pouring out of your arm when you get a sharp cut.

Blood is all over, everywhere. I do not know what to do. I knew this day would come. God is punishing me for all my sins that I have not repented of. Probably, especially for beating up Miss Prissy. I am going to die. I have tried to be good lately. I have even been helping Mom more, but I can see that it is not good enough.

I am not ready to die an untimely death. I have so many wonderful and exciting dreams yet to fulfill and that need to come true. I haven't even met my prince charming yet.

"Why God? Why do I have to die?"

Well, I had to face the music, so I went out and found Mrs. Bailey.

I say, "I am so sorry, Mrs. Bailey, I will not be able to work for you anymore."

Mrs. Bailey curiously asks, "Well, why not Mary?"

"I am dying."

"Why are you dying?"

"Because I am full of sin, and God is punishing me!"

"Now, that is not true, what is wrong, dear? Tell me."

"I was washing your dirty dishes, and I noticed that I had slimy, red blood running down my bare legs. I could feel the slippery blood, and when I looked down on my leg, it was there staining my shorts."

Then, I show her what I mean. She could see with her own eyes that I was a mess. I started to cry, and Mrs. Bailey began to laugh.

I think to myself—boy, I thought Mrs. Bailey was a sweet lady, but here she is laughing at me when my life is going to end.

After a short while, Mrs. Bailey stops laughing and takes my trembling, sweaty hands in her big lap and says, "You are not dying, Mary dear, you just started your period."

"My period," I say questionably. "A period is at the end of a sentence. A period never starts it just finishes."

She could tell I was confused, so she says, "Women have babies."

I say, "Yes, I am only thirteen, but I know women have babies, Mrs. Baily. I had this talk with Mrs. Kelly when Penny was having puppies. I know women have babies, Miss Kelly, my principle, explained it to me a long time ago."

Some of the high school girls get sent away because they are going to have a baby. Just down our street, there was a girl whose tummy was starting to show, and a week later she was gone.

I questioned Irene, "Why is she gone?"

Irene said, "Because she got pregnant, and her family is embarrassed, so they sent her away."

I asked, "To where?"

She said, "I don't know, but when the baby is born, she will give it up and then come back and her family will tell everyone that she was visiting a relative. But by then everyone will know the truth."

I thought to myself, what an awful thing it would be to have to give up your child. I just can't imagine the awful situation. I still don't know how you get pregnant, but I do know that a man must help. I just don't know how, no one ever wants to tell me, until today.

Mrs. Bailey reveals the answer to my long-awaited question and informs me, "In order to have babies Mary, women need to have a period. A period is when you bleed in a place that the baby will be born out of. It is the only way to have children. It is nature."

I think to myself—why do I have to be a part of nature?

I say, "It seems a cruel thing for God to make women this way. I can't imagine why He would do it."

Mrs. Bailey says, "You get this period once a month, and it last for a week."

"A WEEK!" I say, "Are you crazy?"

She says with a laugh, "No, I am not crazy. Hasn't your mom ever talked to you about this?"

"No."

"You have an older sister; doesn't she have one?"

Then, I think about how sometimes I see blood after Irene has been in the bathroom, and I say, "Sometimes, I notice blood in the sink, but I thought she was getting bloody noses."

Bloody noses are common in Butte, because the altitude is so high.

Mrs. Bailey says, "Well, that is because she is washing out her bloody rag."

I must have had a look of horror on my face, because Mrs. Bailey is laughing again.

She finally stops laughing and says, "Mary, most people, especially those that don't have a lot of money, use rags and wash them out."

She showed me what we do with the rags and how to wash them out.

"You need a few of them and you have to change them often, so you don't soil your clothes. Go home, and tell your mother that you started your monthly, and she will give you a rag and some pins."

"Pins? What do I need pins for?"

"You need safety pins to keep the rag in place; otherwise, it will fall out."

AS I am making my way home, I think of how nice it was of Mrs. Bailey to tell me about this whole period pandemic.

I am home and say, "Mom, I started my period."

And just as Mrs. Baily said, Mom gives me torn rags, a couple of pins, and tells me, "You will need to wash them out."

And that was that. She never mentioned anything else to me. She just started giving me a teaspoon of Lydia Pinkham when I was on my monthly, and boy, that stuff tastes rotten. I must force it down my throat every time I take it.

When I asked the girls at school about Lydia Pinkham, they said, "I think it is supposed to stop you from getting pregnant."

Well, I don't like taking the rotten stuff, but I don't want to get pregnant either, so I will keep taking it. I don't want to go away from home, have a cute, adorable, little baby, and then give it up. I will probably just stay away from boys while I am at it. They seem to cause the problem too.

How grateful I am to Mrs. Bailey for giving me some more detailed information.

CHAPTER 43

Butte Legends, And A New Refrigerator (1942)

IT has been a long Winter; a real cold one. Talking about the cold makes me think of our new, white refrigerator.

Mom has been delivering the paper. She goes up to the post office in Walkerville to get the papers, and I have been helping her since Mart left.

Walkerville is on the uttermost top of the Butte hill, and in the winter, it is very icy. We must travel up the long, steep, icy hill, but like I said, Mom is not afraid of those things. And if she is, I don't notice. If she is, I am glad she purposely hides it, because I don't know what I would feel like if I knew for sure that she was in pain every time she went to get those inky papers.

Before school starts, we travel to Walkerville early in the morning. I must help her carry the heavy sacks full of newspapers. I haul the hefty sacks into the post office, and the workers there fill them up. Then, I haul the papers out and help Mom deliver them. I hold the sacks while she delivers.

She makes $50.00 a month and she said, "We are going to get a refrigerator with this money!"

Bill helps with the mail too and does other odd jobs. Irene babysits and helps too.

I try to help, but I am having trouble keeping a job, except for helping Mom with the newspapers. I had to stop working at Mrs. Bailey's house because the bugs were just too overwhelming to handle, and I had gotten a job at the Gamers last week, but it was not meant to be.

Gamers is a fancy restaurant. It has small tables and long booths to sit in, and after you walk past the wide entrance, there is a four-foot island with black swiveling highchairs to sit in, and behind the counter is ice cream.

While I was working there, some of my friends came in and ordered pasties. I gave the pasties to them, but after they ate, I did not charge them for the food. The manager found out and told me I was fired.

I don't think I am cut out for the kind of work where I am in a position to give things away. My friends don't have much, and if I am surrounded by nice things to give them, I will probably give those things to them.

Before Gamers, I got me a sewing job at a place on Galena Street, but as soon as they saw I could not sew things up fancy like, they went and fired me.

The Boss asked, "Why did you apply for a sewing job, if you don't know how to sew?"

I really didn't have an answer, so I just left.

We were able to buy a refrigerator with everyone pitching in a little.

It is 1942, and I am now fourteen. Mart is nineteen, Irene is seventeen, Bill is sixteen, and Kay is ten.

The snow is beginning to melt except for in the mountains, and many boys in the neighborhood are shining shoes. Boys who can't work in the mines earn money by shining shoes.

Those eager young boys build two-by-two-foot cedar boxes to put their shoeshine stuff in, and then they yell, "Shoeshine, come get your shoes shined for ten cents!"

There are young-boy-shoe shines everywhere, all between the ages of 7 and 15.

There are also many dirty bums and poor beggars on the street trying to get money. There is this particular guy, we call him, the pencil guy, and he is in a wheelchair, and a one-legged man pushes him all over town, wherever he wants to go. They also have a brown, ragged dog that is with them. I wonder if they got injured in the war and that is how they lost their limbs. Nobody seems to know, or at least, nobody that I am familiar with knows.

Among the beggars, was a woman named Shoestring Annie. I was just six years old when she died, but people still talk about her today.

They say she was a hefty, drab looking woman, and she came here with her husband in 1914. I guess her husband was completely blind. They say she would guide him around Butte for years while he sold brooms.

Apparently, he died before her, so she took over his business and eventually sold shoestrings. The miners started calling her, "Shoestring Annie," and said she carried quite a whollop. They say she weighed over 200 pounds and that she was a strong woman with a vicious tongue.

The story goes like this; as the miners would come out and get their pay at the Anaconda Company building, she was known to hold out her cigar box and shout, "Buy a pair of shoelaces, you cheapskate!!"

They say, if a miner refused her command, she would call him every name in the book. I am not sure what book they mean, but I am not sure if I want to see that book.

She would also hit the miner with her crutch if he did not buy a shoestring from her. It is said that the miners usually gave in to her and bought the shoestrings, and legend has it, that the miners even paid for her lonely funeral.

I guess her real name was Rose Herron, and she was said to have died on October 25, 1934. (Montana Standard September 2014)

I always laugh when I think of the story of Shoestring Annie.

Nickel Annie was another legend, but I don't know much about her.

There are also some famous people that were known to live here and pass through, like Mary MacLane. She was a famous author. People refer to her as the "Wild Women of Butte."

Why you might be asking?

It is because she wrote unfavorable stories about Butte. She was born in Canada but came to Butte and even Graduated from Butte High. In 1902 she wrote her first book "The Story of Mary MacLane." Butte disliked her book so much that her book was banned from being sold here. She supposedly died in Chicago at age 48 in 1929.

I love hearing about these legendary Butte folks. These stories and folktales make walking the busy Butte streets so much more interesting when you have such deep, enthralling legends lurking around. It sometimes seems like Butte has ghosts that like to come back and visit.

CHAPTER 44

Mart's Adventures

I begin my eighth-grade year at the Grant School this September. It is August 1942, and my parents are getting a divorce. I will talk about that later, but first, I want to talk about Mart.

Mart sent enough money home to help Mom buy the refrigerator. Mart seems to be doing quite well on his adventures. He is at Lake Tahoe, which is on the border of Nevada and California, and he is coming back to Montana. He is going to join the Navy.

These are the letters we have gotten from him.

Dear Family,

I had forty-one dollars when I left. When I arrived in California the papers were full of jobs. You could find a job anyplace you wanted. In the Butte mines, we were only making $3.25 a day, not an hour, but a day.

The first job I got in California paid me $11.00 a day.

Man was I floating in money. I had money to burn. I got a second job working for a produce rancher while I was down there.

These were all Italian people that I worked for, and they are beautiful, beautiful people. If they liked you, they took you in, and they treated you good.

While working for this produce man, I took his big truck of produce down to the market every morning, at 1:00 am in the morning, and he paid me $16.00 for the one trip.

After that, I was making $11.00 a day working for a sash and door mill. Boy, did I have it made there—I tell you. I had payments paid ahead on my car and bought beautiful clothes down there.

While I was there, I stayed with an Italian couple, the Italian men you know don't stay with their wives. They are the biggest cat hounds you ever saw in your life, always out with some other woman.

I stayed with this one woman and man and their two little kids for about six months. They treated me like I was royalty. They liked me, and I really had a good time in this, Walkeen Valley, they called it. Nothing but a great, big produce place where they raised all this produce.

While I was still in California, I started cooking out of the Greek restaurants as a fry cook, because they needed them so desperately. I worked with an elderly woman. She was, well to me she was like a grandmother, but she taught me so much. She took me into this one Greek restaurant and working alongside of her, I learned how to become an excellent fry cook.

I must thank you mom for always allowing me into the kitchen at home. It gave me good experience to work as a cook in these parts. You are always such a good mother, and I appreciate you.

Any place I went in San Francisco, they called for me. Called me out to work for them. So, I just said, "Well, I'm going to move off again."

I left San Francisco and went to Los Angeles, and that didn't satisfy me, so I took a trip over to Reno, Nevada, and I got a job over there.

The Job I got over in Reno was packing chutes, you know chutes that guys jump out of airplanes in the army with. They didn't tell me too much about it though, but they were willing to pay me every two weeks; $350.00 in wages.

Can you just imagine?

I worked for them for about six weeks, and one day the foreman came to me and said, "Marty, we never told you what the contract consisted of, "After you learn the full trade of packing these chutes, you must take one of them up in the plane, and you have got to jump in one of them before you get your ticket to be a chute packer."

O, boy, that scared the living pants off me.

I said, "No more of this for me."

I walked off the job that afternoon, and I didn't look back.

I went to another cooking job in Reno. I worked there as a cook. I was making $12.00 a day which is good wages.

While in Reno, I heard of a place called Lake Tahoe. A great big lake. I thought I would take a trip down there and see what they had to offer. I went there and got a job as a salad maker.

I'm telling you, the people teaching me were so beautiful. They started from the bottom teaching me how to make salads and from there how to cook roast beef, pork, gravy's, sauces, and all that stuff.

I say, I have learned so much on my little bit of travels. I am glad that I had the guts to do it to. These experiences are ones that I will always remember.

I know I have moved and moved, but I just wanted to learn everything there was to learn.

I am in Lake Tahoe now, but I am coming back to Montana. I thought that I might go back into the mines again. Then, I thought, no, the war has started, and I think I am going to join the Navy. They will probably draft me anyways.

I am letting you know that I am going to Helena, Montana, and I'm going to enlist in the Navy.

I found this letter on my travels, and it was so funny that I wanted to share it with you.

It is a letter from a North Dakota mother writing to her son. I hope you enjoy it as much as I do.

Dear Son,

Just a few lines to let you know, I'm still alive. I'm writing this letter slowly, because I know you cannot read fast. You won't know the house when you get home. We've MOVED.

But your father has a lovely job. He has fifteen hundred men working under him. He is cutting grass at the cemetery.

There was a washing machine in the new house when we moved in, but it isn't working too good. Last week, I put fourteen shirts into it, pulled the chain, and haven't seen the shirts since.

Your sister had a baby this morning. I haven't found out whether it is a boy or a girl. They don't know whether you are an aunt or an uncle.

Your Uncle Dick drowned last week in a vat of whiskey at Bismarck Brewery, and some of his workmates dived in to save him. He fought them off bravely. They cremated his body, and it took three days to put out the fire.

I went to the doctor on Thursday, and your father went with me. The doctor put a small tube in my mouth and told me not to open it for ten minutes. Your father offered to buy it from him.

It only rained twice last week, first three days, and then four days.

Monday, it was so windy, one of our chickens laid the same egg four times.

We received a letter yesterday from the undertaker. He said if the last installment wasn't paid within seven days, up he comes.

Your loving mother,

P.S. I was going to send you ten dollars, but I already sealed the envelope.

Well, if Irene does go to North Dakota, I hope she doesn't run into that woman. She seems strange.

Love Mart

CHAPTER 45

The Divorce (1942)

OUR old man stopped trying to sell gas. It is hard to sell gas when you don't have any gas to sell, so he decided to make and store chili instead.

Talking about gas makes me think of my friend Joe. Last month my old man chased him off our property with a sharp hatchet the size of a baseball bat. My old man was in his white underwear boxers, and he was running after poor Joe like a crazed madman. He chased Joe two blocks before he realized that he could not outrun him.

Why you ask, was he chasing my friend Joe down the street. I will explain.

Joe, and a few of our friends, have all been hanging out this past year and sometimes, mostly just this summer, we would go out after dark when my old man was asleep.

Joe has a black Coupe, and it is so old that it has a rumble seat in the back. Well, Joe never has any gas, so all Summer we would wait for my old man to fall asleep, then we would siphon the gas out of his car.

When he realized all his gas was gone, he would get up in the morning and scream, "There are thieves stealing my gas."

Of course, I never said one word, but if you think about the irony of it all, karma always comes back to us. I mean, the old man has been stealing from people for years, and he's mad because someone is stealing from him.

I'm not real sure if you can say Joe is really stealing. I mean, I live under the same roof as my old man, and he is my father, and he should be giving me money for having fun. Instead, he is always spending money on himself.

Last month, he caught on to who was siphoning his gas, and he must have been waiting for Joe the night he found out, because I never even got out the door to meet him before he started the speed chase. I haven't seen Joe since. I must say though, the whole thing is kind of interesting, and I don't suppose, I will be forgetting about it any time soon. He never did catch up to Joe.

Back to the chili. The idea of making chili didn't last long, because my old man began doing something entirely different before he could even get the chili idea off on any kind of good foot.

Mom heard a couple weeks ago that he was going to some meetings in town that concerned the war. He is from Germany, or so he says, and he is always telling us that Germans are the dominant race. I guess that is what the psychopath Hitler thinks too.

A couple weeks ago, Mom decided to follow him to one of those meetings. These "secret" meetings are supposed to be for those who are for Hitler. I thought I would follow along. I am part of the family, and I need to know what is going on.

Many of his native people have settled in Meaderville. Meaderville is close to where the Columbia Gardens are. He associates with the people in Meaderville and speaks the language. He also has a cousin that lives in Baltimore, Maryland, who writes him letters. He takes those letters to Meaderville and has the people there read them to him. He can speak his own language, but he can't read his own language. I don't think he even went to school.

He used to use that excuse in a lot of his schemes that he dreamt up. That he didn't know how to read and write—trying to get people to feel sorry for him.

We think that Joe Miller is his real name because he has cousins in Great Falls and Dillon, Montana, but we are not always sure.

Anyways, that night a couple weeks ago, Mom caught him going to those meetings. I saw the whole thing go down, and after she saw where he was going, she went right home and called the police.

It has been a couple weeks since then, and the word around town is that those meetings have stopped. The police broke into the place they were meeting, and the people there never knew who called it in.

Then, just last week, Mom also found out that he has a girlfriend. Kay followed him one night—thinking he was going to the German meetings again in some other spot, when she found out he was going to this gal's house. Her name is Annie.

Well, Kay sure is a busybody snoop, but in this case, it wasn't such an awful thing. Kay came home right away and told Mom all about what she had seen.

This is why—today—Mom is telling him to leave.

"I'm getting rid of you this time for good!" she tells him. "Between trying to get insurance money on Mart, going to the German meetings, and cheating—I'm just fed up with you."

The divorce wasn't nearly as hard to get as it was when Grandma got hers.

Now Mom is free. She gave it all she had. I do believe that she did, and probably much more than was required of her to give.

CHAPTER 46

A New Man
(December 1942)

MART is now in the Navy. He enlisted in Butte, then went to Helena, Montana to get his final papers in September.

From Helena, they shipped him over to the top of the mountain here to a troupe train. Mom, The Old Man, Kay, and I met him at the troupe train.

Mom told Mart, "Your dad and I are divorced."

Mart says to Mom, "After twenty years you got a divorce? Finally, got rid of the old goat, did you?"

Mom says, "After what happened with you in the mines, the German meetings, and the cheating, I couldn't stay married to him any longer. I have had enough of his beatings and schemes too."

Mart is getting on the troop train with about seven hundred other young, strong men who are ready to fight for our freedom and for other people's freedoms. He is so brave and courageous. He is going to Seattle, and from Seattle, he will be traveling to San Diego, California.

Mart tells us, "It will take about a week for the whole trip."

MART is gone. It is December, and Mom got married.

You see, Irene was slightly interested or rather good friends with John Zebley—paratrooper from Helena, Montana. John would come to the house Irene was living in while staying in Helena, and he would take her out on dates.

Irene decided to go to Jamestown, North Dakota at the beginning of Summer. After school got out, she never enrolled in the twelfth grade, because she saw an ad in the paper for telegraphers and just decided to go. Her friend went with her.

Since the war started, our country is in desperate need of telegraphers. She went with her friend that lives next to us, the one I was talking about before. She was hoping that they would get a telegraphing job located in Elliston, Montana, and they did. Elliston is a small town next to Helena, Montana. Helena is about 60 miles from Butte. Well, she heard that they were looking for telegraphers, so she took the first opportunity

While living in Elliston, she met John Zebley. She didn't like John in a romantic sort of way and told him that nothing was going to happen with them. This knowledge didn't stop John from taking Irene on dates. He was going to war soon and would be stationed out of the country, and instead of getting together with Irene, he ended up marrying Mom. He doesn't have any other family, so he decided to marry Mom, placing all his life insurance in her name; in case he dies in the war.

John is quite a bit younger than my mom, but he is very kind and seems to care about her.

It is strange, Mom marrying again, but I never see John since he is gone now. He left right after they got married, so it just seems like she is not even married. Mom is happier since she left my old man, and so is Grandpa.

I think John cares about my mom, but I also know he is in love with Irene. I think, he just married Mom to stay close to Irene, and I have a suspicion that he feels he might just possibly die in this war. Sometimes, we just feel things in our soul that tells us what steps we need to take in life.

If John knows he is going to die, or at least feels there might be a possible chance, then that would be kind of him wanting to leave his small fortune to my mom. I don't know him, but he seems like a real good guy, and I am happy for Mom.

CHAPTER 47

I'm Walking The Plank In My New Dress (May 1943)

IT is 1943—Graduation Day. I am fifteen now, and my generous brother, Bill, bought me my first new dress.

He says, "Mary, you should have a new dress for such a monumental occasion as this."

It all happened when I came home today. It is a Thursday night, and after I came home, I saw lying on my bed a beautiful, pale, brown dress. It has two pieces, a top and a skirt. The brown skirt is pleated, and the light, brown top has green with a flower design spreading down the right shoulder.

I look at the tag and it reads $7.00. I am so excited that I go screaming through the house asking whoever will listen, "Is this my dress!? Is this my dress!?"

Then, I see wonderful Bill, and he is holding a pair of green high heels and says, "Here are the 2-inch heels to go with it."

My now watery eyes begin to flow like waterfalls. I don't cry too often, because I am no baby, but this was one of those historic, memorable moments that deserved a few tears streaming speedily down my face.

I cannot stop the waterworks coming even if I tried; so, I give him a bear hug so tight he says as he laughs, "My eyeballs might fall out if you hug me any tighter."

I tightly wrap my arms around his neck and hug him tighter than I have ever hugged anyone.

"That was a lot of money," I say to him, "And it is so extremely kind of you Bill. I love you so much, brother. I've never had a new dress and this one is beautiful."

Both my big brothers are so kind and generous to me. Bill loves to tease me, but he's always been a good older brother. We never argue or fight with each other.

I quickly go into my cramped room with the faded, green curtains and try the fairytale dress on. It is just my perfect size. I have never had anything that was just my perfect size. Even the shoes fit. I can't help but continue to stare in amazement at myself as I look in our splotchy mirror and wonder to myself, when did I get so pretty?

I pull back my long, brown hair which lines the middle of my back now into a high beautiful bun as I twirl around pretending I am one of those ladies in the movies who always gets the handsome stranger that comes into town unannounced, and I smile as if he is directly in the room with me. But instead of being in this worn-out room, we are on the beach, and he is about to propose marriage, and all the girls in town are extremely jealous and leave in a huff when I answer excitedly, "Yes, of course, I'll marry you—my one true love."

Then, we kiss passionately as the golden sun fades into the dark, blue ocean distant horizon.

Yes, I have been thinking a little bit about kissing lately. I'm sure, I will be kissing sometime soon. It will be a dark, handsome stranger—I am sure of it. Wearing this designer dress could get me noticed by any famous movie star.

I never realized that clothes could make someone extraordinarily beautiful. Irene always looks beautiful, because she has nice clothes, but with these magnificent clothes, I think I am just as pretty. People say I'm a looker without the fancy clothes, so designer clothes could make me a movie star—I am sure of it.

Becky is graduating too. We are not close anymore. We were best friends before I suddenly moved to Mercury Street. Even though she still lives on the East Side, she stopped being my best friend.

Her mother thought I was far beneath them after I moved and said, "Becky, you can't play with Mary anymore, she is no longer one of us."

We used to walk to Grant school together every day when we lived directly next door. Right now, we live six blocks away. She lives on the corner of Galena and Idaho.

Her mother teaches kids about the Bible at church, and I never go to church, so maybe, she thought I was following the Devil not going to church and all. I would go to church if someone took me, but no one does, so I don't go.

Next door to Becky's house is a lady that teaches music. I remember listening to the piano playing as the students she taught played. I loved just hearing the piano's sweet melody.

Next to the music lady's house, is a couple who are married, and the wife is white, and the husband is colored. Colored means black. With all the nationalities living around Butte, you would think they would be accepted, but this is not the case. I think it still has something to do with all that slavery that happened many years ago. They have four or five kids, and no one will have anything to do with their family. People even say that one of their sons is mentally ill.

To be honest, I think they are interesting people, and their children have a nice brown color that is becoming.

Thinking about graduating brings me back to my early childhood as I remember the activities I used to participate in with good friends and special neighbors.

Recently, my best friend that lived down the street moved away. She had three brothers, and they already died in the war. Her mother went a little crazy over it all, so they moved to California. My friend's name was Nita Josavich.

These boys and my brothers, and most everyone on this part of the East Side is known as the East Side Gang. The Markovich's, the Asabeto's, the Josavich's, Bill and Bob Jenkins, and Talbert Adams. These are all of Bill's friends. No one wants to bother with the East Side Gang. There are too many of us.

So, Mart was not the only one who went to California.

These experiences are now faded memories.

I must be more grown up now that I am done with the eighth grade and will be going on to high school. I must put away childish things and begin thinking about my immediate and far distant future. It seems like so many things are swiftly changing, and I'm not sure how ready I am for all the changes.

Well, back to graduation.

There is a tradition at the Grant school. When the eighth-grade class graduates, we write our names on the stage curtain. It is an enormous dark blue curtain. I suppose it is made from cotton and velvet, and each graduate embroiders their name on it with yellow thread. Mart has done it, Irene has done it, Bill has done it, and now it is my turn to do it. I suspect in the future Kay will also get the chance to write her name on this beautiful cloth.

As I embroider my name in yellow, my life seems to flash quickly before my eyes, and I feel like this is a sign of maturity that I am growing up and moving on.

Today is the magical day, and my amazing dress—Oh, what a dress! I have never felt so magnificent. I just wish I had a bra. I just feel like my upper body is viciously shaking everywhere when I walk.

The more I mature, the worse the shaking gets. Sometimes, I will be minding my own business, walking down some narrow street, and all the men go an' whistle at me. At first, I didn't know why they are whistling. I thought, maybe, it was because I was growing into being a woman which is probably partly true, but I soon realized that was not the only reason.

We don't have money to buy bras. We barely have enough to get undergarments, and we need those because of the whole period thing, which I am getting used to. I don't like it mind you, but I am becoming accustomed to it being a part of my womanly life. Something embarrassing happened just a couple of months ago concerning the whole period thing.

I was quietly sitting at my brown, faded desk in school, and I had gone and leaked through my undergarments. I had to wait till the whole class left, and when they did, I got up and walked out the door. I had to tightly tie my blue sweater around my petite waist to cover up the evidence, and by the end of the day, everything down there was as hard as a rock. At home, I had to wash the rag and myself with cold water.

You always know when girls have their periods, because the teacher always makes them sit in the back corner, so you don't have to take in the odor of it all. Boy, is there an unspeakable, foul odor.

I am now carefully walking directly across the pale, cedar wood stage, and I see many people staring at me. I am trying hard to walk correctly in these magnificent green two-inch heels that Bill so graciously bought for me, but I am not used to heels that actually have heels on them. I make it to the stage well enough though.

Principal Kelly gives me my diploma and says, "Good job, Mary, and good luck."

I stop and take my diploma, but don't keep walking across the stage until I give her a huge hug full of love, because she is just one of my favorite people.

She hugs me back and tells me, "You look beautiful."

As I try not to tear up like waterfalls again, I give her an appreciative smile and say, "I love you, Mrs. Kelly."

I must say, it does feel good having this graduating diploma securely in my hand. I don't much like school, in fact, I absolutely despise it, but I have learned a lot of information and am glad I finished.

The festivities are now over, and I begin my walk home. As I think about the wonderful day I had—feeling extremely proud and pretty, a man suddenly reaches out and deliberately places his sneaky arms around my arms and waist. I didn't see him, because I was day-dreaming. He is attempting to pull me immediately away with him. I suddenly realize I must break away before he accomplishes his desire, but he is so strong and much bigger than I am. I am almost home too.

He says, "Stop fighting me!"

The only option I have at this critical time is to scream as loud as my lungs can holler, so that is what I do.

"AAHHH!!!" I bellow.

I keep attempting to get away, when at this moment I see Bill. Thank goodness, he heard me.

Bill quickly comes from the house running and is yelling at the same time, screaming to the man, "Let go of her immediately, if you know what is good for you!"

The man sees Bill, lets go of me instantly, and takes off in the opposite direction.

"Are you alright?" Bill asks me as he puts his arms around me to walk me home.

"Yes, I am. Just a little shook up. Bill, thank goodness you came out when you did," I say.

I turn towards Bill lovingly and say, "Bill you made so many things good happen for me today, and plus, you saved my life. It's almost like the time that Rascal saved Irene from that drunk in Washington. I appreciate you so much."

That is all I am going to say, because we don't say, I love you in our house so often. I mean, we know we love each other, but I don't often hear those words spoken. I could tell Bill wasn't going to say it either. But you know, it doesn't need to be said. We show each other all the time, and that is how we know.

I know I said that a stranger was going to take me away someday, but I meant one that I loved.

CHAPTER 48

School Memories

I am at home now, and I comfortably sit down on the tattered green sofa as I read all the memories in my graduation book. These are some of the memories.

Graduates of the Grant School
Class of May 28, 1943

- Avad, Adelmo
- Boucher, Frank
- Burns, Shirly
- Elich, Helen
- Faroni, Harry
- Griffen, Dick
- Hicks, Helen
- Holling, Jean
- Jaaskela, Kenneth
- Johnson, Wilbur
- Jolly, Shirley

- Kingsbury, Dan
- Kramarich, Charles
- Kranitz, Ione
- Lahti, June
- Lundstrom, Evelyn
- Mattson, Leo
- Michaely, Denise
- Miller, Mary
- Moodry, Robert
- Niemi, Bernard
- Opack, Ruby
- Radulovich, Rose Marie
- Reynolds, Donald
- Schlickenmeyer, Raymond
- Simonich, Willie
- Tauson, Steve
- Wattula, Lee
- Wills, Jo Ellen

Class Song Tune
There's A Star-Spangled Banner Waving Somewhere

We've assembled here today for graduation
From Grant School, and all our friends we must depart.
Fond mem'ries of these years of preparation
Will forever linger deep down in this heart.
It is said, "There is no royal road to learning"
Each must strive to do his very best
And so, He'll attain his distant goal in this great nation
So, now, class of 1943 – Let's Go!!!

Dedication

We, the members of the class of 1943, in saying goodbye to friends and teachers of the Grant School, wish to express our thanks and appreciation to all.

We are especially thankful to you, Principal Kelly, for your patience and kindly advice so unselfishly extended to us all the time. It gives us great pleasure to present a copy of our graduation book to you, to whom we have fondly dedicated it.

Class History

Our class at present numbers is thirteen girls and sixteen boys. Of this group only five have spent all their school days in the Grant school. We call these "one-hundred per cent Grantites."

They are: Harry Faroni, Helen Elich, Shirley Jolly, Leo Mattson, and Donald Reynolds.

Dan Kingsbury and Adelmo Avad started their school days here at the Grant in the second grade – just missed being "one-hundred per cent Granites."

We welcomed in the third grade, Willie Simonich, **Mary Miller** and Lee Wattula.

Steve Tauson spent the first two years in the Grant, leaving at the beginning of the third, but returned before the year was finished. He's been with us ever since.

Helen Hicks came in the fourth, but left for a few weeks in the fifth, returned and joined us for the rest of her school days here.

In the fifth grade Bob Moodry, Jean Holling, and Wilbur Johnson added three more to our class.

Kenneth Jaaskela came to the Grant in the sixth grade.

Frank Boucher started his first and second years in the Grant but left and did not return until he was in the sixth. We did not let him leave again.

Ruby Opack joined our class in the sixth, although, she had spent the first, second, and third grades here.

When we had become seventh graders, our class was increased by five pupils who came to us from the Jefferson – Shirley Burns, Ione Kranitz, Dick Griffin, Charles Kramarich, and Jo Ellen Willis. June Lahti, coming from the Lincoln, added one more to our class.

Bernard Niemi returned to the class also in the seventh. He had started here in the fourth but left us in the fifth grade.

We didn't become acquainted with Rose Marie Radulovich or Denise Michaely until this last year. They joined us in the eighth grade.

Our newest member, Raymond Schlickenmeyer, has been a member of our class only for a few months, coming here from the Franklin School.

Sporting Achievements

Some of the members of our class have figured prominently in athletics.

Shirley Jolly was a member of the Girls' Champion Bowling Team.

In 1941, our school's football team won the City Championship. Three members of that team are in this class: Bob Moodry, Lee Wattula, and Wilbur Johnson.

Last year, the Grant School boys piled up a record of 113 points, an all-time record in the city track meet. Two athletes of that team are members of our class: Harry Faroni and Wilbur Johnson.

Harry Faroni was also awarded a medal three years ago for being a member of the runner-up team in Baseball.

Kenneth Jaaskela, won a special award for football passing while attending school in Arizona.

Ione Kranitz and Shirley Burns, won medals for Girls' Relay Ice

Skating. These girls also won awards for ice skating, as did Dick Griffen and Jo Ellen Wills.

Wilbur Johnson designed the cover for our class book.

The Grant School retained its championship for track Friday, May 14th, by piling up a score of 56-2/3 points. Seven members of our class were on the team: Bob Moodry, Adelmo Avad, Wilbur Johnson, Donald Reynolds, Steve Tauson, Bernard Niemi, and Harry Faroni.

Adelmo Avad won second place in the middleweight class with 12 ½ points. Wilbur Johnson won second place in the lightweight class with 14 points. He was first in the high jump and missed beating the lightweight high jump record by only one-half inch. Bob Moodry scored nine points for his team.

Hall of Fame

Each year at graduation, it is customary to elect the member of the class, because of certain outstanding characteristics, to the Hall of Fame.

We, therefore, take this opportunity to nominate the following students:

1. ADELMO AVAD
   Because of his unfailing courtesy at all times.
2. FRANK BOUCHER
   Because of his happy disposition. He always comes up smiling
3. SHIRLEY BURNS
   Because of her fine cooperation in all school activities.
4. HELEN ELICH
   Because we believe she is the world's fastest talker.
5. JEAN HOLLING
   Because of her beautiful penmanship.
6. DICK GRIFFEN
   Because of his artistic talent, and his ability to get things done.

7. HELEN HICKS
Because college won't worry her a bit. Romance is in the air.
8. HARRY FARONI
Because of his personal neatness and spick-and-span appearance.
9. KENNETH JAASKELA
Because of his great proficiency in his favorite sport, teasing the girls.
10. WILBUR JOHNSON
Because of his outstanding record of athletics.
11. SHIRLEY JOLLY
Because of her activity in all girl sports.
12. DAN KINGSBURY
Because of his uncompilable indifference to everything.
13. CHARLES KRAMARICH
Because he's the best of the "I-Can't-Be-Worried-Group."
14. IONE KRANITZ
Because of those two unusually beautiful dimples.
15. BERNARD NIEMI
Because of three dimples, as well as being the class Romeo.
16. JANE LAHTI
Because she's the "brain box" of the class.
17. EVELYN LUNDSTROM
Because of her originality in writing perfect paragraphs in English.
18. LEO MATTSON
Because he is a fine example of "Early to bed, and early to rise, makes eighth grade boys healthy, with shiny bright eyes."
19. DENISE MICHAELY
Because of her attractive appearance and glamorous personality.
20. **MARY MILLER**
Because no other student in all this world could ever waste so much time.

21. ROBERT MOODRY

Because we feel that he is a potential movie star and expect Hollywood to pick him up soon.

22. RUBY OPACK

Because no matter the weather, it's always bright and sunny around Ruby.

23. DONALD REYNOLDS

Because his cute little smile can never be erased from his face.

24. ROSE MARIE RADULOVICH

Because she's the champion giggler – her favorite pastime.

25. WILLIE SIMONICH

Because he's a real "Lone Wolf" and a dreamer we little understand.

26. RAYMOND SCHLICKENMEYER

Because he has the longest name of any Grant student –S-C-H-L-I-C-K-E-N-M-E-Y-E-R.

27. STEVE TAUSON

Because he never gives the same alibi twice, yet he never seems at a loss to give one.

28. LEE WATTULA

Because he tells corny jokes and enjoys a good laugh. We enjoy him, too.

29. JO ELLEN WILLS

Because she's the beauty of the class.

Class Prophecy

One day, a great Princess of Egyptian ancestry came to the United States, not only to escape from the many terrors of the war, but to raise funds for her country. She brought with her an odd circular instrument, which she claimed to have originally belonged to Amad, famous crystal gazer of Egypt.

The day after the Princess' arrival, I received an invitation, as did many others to be present at a reception held in her honor. Because we were so very curious about the strange apparatus in her possession, the Princess kindly consented to explain the mechanism to us.

We were asked to face the setting sun while looking steadily into the instrument, then we could ask to see into the future. Naturally, I expressed a wish to see my classmates ten years from today. A picture appeared, and I saw our old classmate, HELEN ELICH, busily assisting and mixing paints for DICK GRIFFEN, the Walt Disney of 1953.

The scene changed and became a great ice rink where IONE KRANITZ, was cleverly dancing on skates, accompanied by HARRY FARONI, recently acclaimed Olympic fancy skating champion. Seated nearby, and intensely interested, were two well-known people, BOB MOODRY—the handsome Argentinean Ambassador, accompanied, as always by his indispensable secretary—DENISE MICHAELY.

Now, a man stands at a microphone—a master of ceremonies, it seems. On closer inspection, I recognize KENNETH JAASKELA. Nearby is a lovely lady waiting her turn to sing—it is another member of our class, SHIRLEY JOLLY.

The comedienne on KENNETH'S show is none other than RUBY OPACK. The announcer, DAN KINGDBURY, starts to speak, "And so we say goodnight and remind you again to start the day right with a bowl of WATTULA'S Wonder Wittles, put out exclusively by the LEE WATTULA's Wonder Wheat Craft Company."

Again, the scene changes.

Now, I see the City Hall of Butte, and there occupying the mayor's chair sits that prominent WAAC of the recent war, JEAN HOLLING, now the Mayor of Butte. Consulting with her is that very active and newly elected sheriff of Silver Bow County, WILBUR JOHNSON.

They are trying to solve the theft of a $4,000 ermine cloak belonging to the wife of Butte's millionaire mining executive, DONALD

REYNOLDS. Due to the great shortage of men, we see in the mayor's office, the present Chief-of-Police, JUNE LAHTI.

Now, after a slight pause, a great ocean liner moves into view. The captain, I recognize as STEVE TAUSON. Seated on the foredeck, like a queen on her throne, is HELEN HICKS, lazily sunning herself, and she is surrounded by a group of beautiful girls. They are a group of New York City actresses who are to appear before the Royal Family of England.

Before me now, is a brightly lighted sign "The Hoot Owl Night Club" the proprietor of which is a former classmate, BERNARD NIEMI. Scheduled to appear twice nightly was the world's famous slight of hand magician, ADELMO AVAD. He now calls for someone in the audience to take part in his act. As a beautifully gowned woman steps to the stage, I recognize the United States Beauty Queen of 1953—JO ELLEN WILLS.

The picture again changes, and before us in a great hospital built by the noted DR. FRANK BOUCHER, and under the management of our dear old pal, ROSE MARIE RADULOVICH, is famous Red Cross Nurse of the Second World War.

LEO MATTSON, known as the 1943 vitamin boy of our class, is seen in his laboratory working out new type of vitamin pills containing all the fundaments of education—swallow a pill and you have it. No study. No homework. WILLIE SIMONICH, his assistant, smiles as he thinks what this idea would have done for all the class of 1943.

MARY MILLER, a student chemist, seems only interested in examining the many bottles of red, pink, and purple on a bench before her. Now, I begin to understand. When better cosmetics are made, **MARY MILLER** is determined she'll make them.

Now a great plane lands and out steps the intrepid pilot, CHARLES KRAMORICH, who makes a trip daily to Germany just to check up. With him, is his trusted navigator, RAYMOND SCHLICKENMEYER.

Only one of the class remained to be seen, and again the scene changed. It seems to be a courtroom—it is! And rapping for order is a person whose face could be none other than that of SHIRLEY BURNS, now Judge of the Supreme Court.

Now only a gleaming light showed. I couldn't make out anything more. I was quite anxious to learn my fate, too. I turned to the Princess and asked why I couldn't see my future, too. She opened her mouth to speak— "Get up now. It's getting late."

I opened my eyes and the bright sun shining in my eyes awakened me in a hurry. As I dressed, I thought of the fun I'd had telling what I'd seen in my dream of the future.

The girl who woke up, without finding out what was in store for her, was none other than EVELYN LUNDSTOM—the girl who wrote the class prophecy.

Class Will

We, the class of May 1943, being of very sound body and doubtless of considerable sound mind, feel that since we are soon to leave this building, we should draw up a will by which the members of the seventh grade may legally fall heir to the following:

1. Since the mortifying expose' of Bob Moodry's torn pants, he has always carried a needle and thread. These he leaves to Merle Holmes, and hopes he takes time to sew down that shirt tail.
2. Shirley Jolly leaves her endless line of chatter to Violet Lasell.
3. Ruby Opack requests that Bud Mirich collect all the gum, new and old, now reposing in her desk and turn it over to William Jeffers, the Rubber Administrator.
4. To Lois McLennon, Frank Boucher leaves his thunderous shoes, which frighten us all when he treks across the hall. He does help to wake up some of the sleepers, however.

5. Dan Kingsbury could start a fair-sized library with all the funny books he has collected. Since he's afraid to take them to high school, he wishes his brother, Earnest, to put them with his fine collection for future use.

6. June Lahti always has the right answers. She'd like to show James Persling how "He can get that way", too.

7. Kenneth Jaaskela, always has been depended upon to amuse the girls at recess. Since he must leave, he requests Fred Webster to take over for him.

8. Dick Griffin, will leave his favorite seat in the corner of the room to John Henderson. This seat is man sized, with plenty of room for long legged boys.

9. Raymond Schlickenmeyer, intends to have a jolly time in high school, so he wants to leave his sober thoughts and serious expression to Charles Twardus.

10. Rose Marie Radulovich, will present her recipe for spreading sunshine and happiness to all the fearful sixth graders, who, even yet, are not at home in the upper department.

11. Steve Tauson, transfers his long list of alibis to Teresa Booth, who, no doubt, can use them as often as he did.

12. Adelmo Avad, has a book called "Good Manners Pay Big Dividends." He wants to leave it to Jack Boucher.

13. Wilbur Johnson, leaves his outstanding record in athletics as a high mark for the Grant School Athletes to shoot at.

14. Jean Holling, goes about her business depending on no one. This admirable trait she hopes Donald Scott will acquire.

15. Shirley Burns, will give six lessons in tap dancing to Billy Bennetts, 'cause "He doesn't get around much"—period.

16. Lee's, happy disposition is a joy to all. We want him to take it along to high school.

17. Leo, our vitamin boy, must know all the rules for keeping "fit." We'd like him to give some pointers to Ellen Bowers.

18. No boy should ever possess three dimples. Even Bernard thinks it's too many. He'd be glad to leave all three someplace, if he could.

19. Jo Ellen and Denise, have been very faithful in caring for the teachers' lunchroom. This task they leave to Martha Yelenich and Ramona Wudel.

20. Charles Kramarich, is one of the most popular boys of the class. Wouldn't all the pupils like to know how he does it? See him after graduation.

21. Evelyn Lundstrom's, quiet and lady-like conduct is a good example of how girls should act. Will the future Eighth Grade girls please take note?

22. Donald Reynold's popularity with all the teachers has never waned. He, we know, leaves pleasant memories with them all.

23. **Mary Miller's good looks will be missed on our stage in the auditorium. Eileen Markovich is asked to be her stand in.**

24. Ione Kranitz and Harry Faroni, feel that their studies in high school may not allow time for skating, so they will donate their skates to the Chavez Brothers.

25. Helen Elich, has a way of whispering that can be heard across the hall. Better leave it, Helen.

26. Willie's dislike for girls is most unusual. He'll probably lose the characteristic in high school. Adolph Otonicar, could try Willie's system next year, and perhaps spend more time on his studies.

27. Helen Hicks hates to go to high school and leave John behind. She wills him to no one but urges him to speed up and catch up in high school.

Principal

Isabel Kelly

Teachers

- Nancy York
- Marie D. Brown
- Mildred Charnison
- Carolyn Sullivan
- Dora O'Brien
- Nellie Mulholland
- Katherine Sullivan
- Agnes Sulhiem?
- Marie Egan
- Catherine Sullivan
- Mildred Whitney
- Mamie Lynch
- Mabel Erickson
- Mary Deeney

CHAPTER 49

Who Died? (August 1943)

IT seems that I am getting more interested in boys,

I have only been out a few times this summer with boys. One was Ron. He ended up getting a job at the funeral parlor, a place where they keep dead people, and when he came to take me out on a date, he would noisily pull up with a big, black, depressing hearse.

Mom would yell at me, "Tell him to get that thing out of here, people are going to think that we run a funeral parlor."

In Butte, they keep the decaying bodies of dead people at home. Well, until the people get buried in the ground of course. Most people just have funerals in their homes. I don't know much about death, but Ron tells me that the families usually have the bodies of the dead done up at their homes. I mean at the homes of the dead's family.

He says, "They have the funeral in a family room, and the people that want to pay their respects come in and pay their respects. People that know the person and the family bring all sorts of good food. Then, they get really drunk after it is all over."

On the day of the funeral, Fat Jack, the undertaker, will drive the hearse.

I must say, I haven't seen anyone dead before, and I hope I don't anytime too soon.

Well, back to my dating boys. I never did go out on dates too often this summer, and Ron is not a boyfriend—just a friend. Irene has been gone, and Kay is only eleven, so I can't go on double dates with them.

Often, boys will come around the house and talk to me and my friends, or we will go for long walks.

We have this high, dark brown, wooden fence along my house on the sidewalk, and the boys will come and park along the fence—usually every night. They will sit on the fence, and we will play games on the sidewalk. They never go to many movies, because no one seems to have much money this summer. Life seems different now that I am not in grade school. Everyone is changing in ways I don't completely understand.

Mom seems much happier since she divorced my old man and married John. He still comes around though. Sometimes, he sits and watches our house for hours checking on Mom and seeing what she is up to. It makes me wonder if he really loved her, or if he just wanted to control her.

I am in Elliston now, a town outside of Helena. It is September 1943. Irene is working in Elliston, Montana as a telegrapher—like I told you before.

When she was in Jamestown, she met a guy. He was in the army stationed there. She has been writing him often since she came back. She thinks he is the one.

I am here, because my mom sent me here. I walked into Butte High School the first day and walked right back on out. I figure that I am not made for school, so Mom thought it might do me some good to help Irene and keep her company, so she wouldn't be alone.

I'm not sure if Mom sent me to Elliston to keep Irene company or out of trouble.

Usually, I am the one in trouble, not Irene. Maybe, she is trying to keep me out of trouble, thinking Irene will be a good influence on me.

Bill and Kay are staying in Butte with Mom.

CHAPTER 50

Mister Italian
(December 17, 1943)

THE last few months have been extremely exciting, and the most exciting part was meeting an Italian prisoner of war—Bruno Roggia. He had been living in Missoula, Montana—a town a couple of hours outside of Butte, and is now in Elliston, Montana.

Bruno came to America on an Italian cargo ship which was delivering goods to America. The ship he was on, plus five other Italian ships, were docked in North Fork, Virginia.

As the men on these six ships were unloading goods, news of Benito Mussolini, the Prime Minister of Italy who founded and leads the National Fascist Party in Italy, decided to join Adolf Hitler—a German Politician and leader of the Nazi Party who rose to power as the German Fuhrer in the war with Germany—which rang through the streets of America.

This sudden news forced the American government to take immediate custody of the Italian men on the ships docked in North Fork and bring them to Fort Missoula—a prisoner of war camp. The Japanese prisoners of war were also living in this camp.

Bruno, and the Italian men who were in Missoula with him, are considered civilian prisoners of war. They lived in Missoula for almost three years. These men had a decent life in Missoula. They raised vegetable gardens, used their carpentry skills to sell things they had made and even had passes to go to town to enjoy activities.

Because of the war becoming more intense this past year, and because of men constantly dying in the war, the government must draft more men. The draft caused a loss of work on the railroads, so the government decided to use the Italian prisoners of war to work on building the railroads.

Bruno was brought from Fort Missoula to work on the railroad in Helena and Elliston, Montana, and the Italian men are living in railroad cars while they work on the railroad.

My sister, Irene, has a little place in Elliston. She works as a telegrapher when she is needed, and she also delivers mail.

Irene works the night shift. When she is working, I sit with her and often fall asleep on the bench in the train station. We wait at the train station for the mail to arrive. We also wait for any passengers coming off the last train before her shift is over.

Elliston is a quaint, small town. Irene is renting a little, white house. I am not working anywhere right now—other than helping Irene. Elliston has a small post office, grocery store, and bar.

When Irene gets off her night shift, we usually walk home together. No one really bothers us, well, except old Tony when he is feeling up to it.

I must tell you a little bit about Tony. Tony is Italian, and after Irene and I arrive home and get settled, he oftentimes stands next to the window and sings songs to her. He is a real short Italian, not any taller than five-foot-three. It seems to me that Tony is just as wide as he is tall. He does not have much hair on his shiny head—just a bit surrounding the base above his neck. He is not attractive like Bruno. Bruno is much taller than Tony, although, he is not all that tall, maybe, five-foot-seven inches.

Tony thinks he has a chance at Irene's eventual affections.

There are a bunch of Italian men in Elliston, and they are always coming around to Irene's house trying to gain her affections. Danny is an Italian friend of Irene's who also came from Fort Missoula. While Danny was in Fort Missoula, his first job was peeling potatoes. Later, he worked his way up to the chef position. He tells us that he wants to be a chef someday, and he really can cook!

Don is another Italian man that seems to be in love with Irene, but she has Warren. Irene and Warren are even talking about getting married. Warren is not an Italian. He is an American.

Irene is a real beauty. She has dark chestnut hair and deep brown eyes. Her skin is darker than mine. My sister Kay also has the darker skin, but Kay doesn't always look like a girl. Her hair is always short, and she is always wearing bib overalls. She has worn those hillbilly pants most of her young life, except, when she attends church of course. Kay also seems to always have an unruly scarf wrapped around her head, with some kind of hat over it.

I always tease Mom, asking her, "Are you sure you didn't have a visitor?"

She always gives me her dirty look.

I must take after my old man. He has light skin. He came from the southern part of Yugoslavia where people are known to have lighter skin. Most of the Yugoslavians are dark-skinned, but he is not, and his eyes are as blue as the sky. My brother, Bill, and I inherited the sky-blue eyes and snow-white skin.

Talking about my old man makes me think of when I was young. He called me his Mamiska. In German, Mamiska means little Mary. When he called me his Mamiska, I sort of felt close to him—like maybe he was good, and maybe he did have love in his heart. In these moments, I would sit on his lap, and he would rock me. Those days seem so long ago now.

Well, back to Bruno. A few months ago, Irene and I were taking a leisurely walk by the train tracks. Irene has a girlfriend named

Wanda who lives about a mile up the hill from the tracks. She is a rumbunctious redhead, and she is also a telegrapher.

I met Bruno on the night Wanda invited us to her place for supper. This was at the end of September. I will relay the story.

AS we walk to Wanda's, I notice a long line of boxcars less than a fourth of a mile from her house. The Italians live in these rectangular boxcars, and they have just arrived in Elliston. Wanda told us last week about the Italian men who were coming to Elliston to work on the railroad.

Some of the men are standing outside of her house when we arrive.

Wanda says to me and Irene, "Come on, I will introduce you to some of the men."

We walk over to where the men are standing. Wanda introduces Irene and me to them. They want to show us their boxcars, so we begin our walk down the hill to the boxcars. As I am walking with the group, I look over to my left and my eyes connect with the eyes of one of the Italian men. His name is Bruno. I immediately look away, but I get a good enough look at him to see that he is a handsome devil.

As we leisurely walk along the dark railroad tracks, I notice Bruno has a long, grey cigarette holder in his hand. I see him take a long puff of his white cigarette. His black beret, black slacks, and black turtleneck sweater blend into the dark night, and the brightness of the moon creates a handsome silhouette around his perfect face. My heart quickly skips a beat.

I think to myself, "Who is this handsome oddball? I would like to get to know him better."

I can't believe the conversation I am having inside my head. I won't tell you what I am thinking.

I can't seem take my eyes off Bruno. I keep turning my head his way to catch quick glances of him. I think he notices me looking at him. I think he is looking back.

Irene, Wanda, and I look at some of the boxcars. The Italian men have decorated the boxcars to look just like a home.

As I catch another glance in Bruno's direction, I see him, with the swift wave of his right-hand motion for me to come over to him. Dumb me, I go over to where he is standing. Irene is busy with Wanda, so she doesn't notice I leave.

Standing next to Bruno I say, "What do you want?"

The perplexed look on his face tells me he has no idea what I am saying. I am assuming he can't speak English, but what he wanted to do had nothing to do with speaking.

Suddenly, I feel his right hand take a grip on my left hand, and our fingers intertwine. I think to myself that he must have experience in handholding because he is not shy in grabbing mine.

While holding my hand, he motions with his left hand for me to follow him. I think he wants to show me something in his boxcar.

I think to myself, "Should I go?"

I stand firmly in my place, like a tree's roots stuck in the ground as I try to decide whether I should go with him.

I realize Irene is still close by, so I feel safe enough. After all, I am only fifteen.

I still cannot get over the fact that I am holding hands with an Italian man. I have never held hands with a boy, and I must tell you, Bruno is not a boy.

I think to myself, "He must be almost thirty years old."

I wonder what my mom would think about me holding hands with a strange thirty-year-old Italian prisoner of war?

Holding Bruno's hand is frightening, but at the same time, it seems to be the most exciting and romantic thing I can imagine doing at this exact moment. I give up the semi-permanent roots I have planted firmly in the ground and decide to leave the group and follow him.

My heart is pounding like a thousand wild horses racing through the plains, and I can feel the flush of red blood warm my bewildered face. I am so close to him. I think, he must be able to hear the beating of my heart. In this moment, I feel a bit childish because of my inexperience.

Bruno slides open the door to one of the boxcars. I think this boxcar is his. The boxcar is simply decorated but has a good aura about it. Suddenly, Bruno is facing me. I feel his arms wrap around my waist. He pulls me close to his chest. His eyes lock on to mine, and I can't look away.

As he stares deeply into my eyes, I think that he might be able to see what I am thinking in this very moment. I do not want him to know what I am thinking, or maybe, I do. My head feels dizzy, and I think that I must be dreaming.

I say to myself, "Wake up, Mary."

I realize, as I try to keep my composure that Bruno is about to passionately kiss me, and what is happening to me is not a dream or my imagination.

With his warm hands now on my petite waist, he slowly and carefully pulls me into his boxcar. He leans his face in closer to mine, and our pink lips touch slightly. His thin lips softly caress mine, and then they press down on mine with such passion. He is kissing me like crazy, mumbling in Italian this and that. His anxious hands move upward to the middle of my narrow back, and he softly presses our bodies closer together. I am not sure—I might be doing some of the pressing.

I think to myself, "What a crazy man!"

I realize that I must be even crazier, because I don't want him to stop.

I don't know how long we have been kissing, but I feel lost to the real world, and find that I am enjoying my present predicament. I find myself easily kissing him back with just as much determination and force. My able hands seem to find their way up to and then over his wide shoulders. My wanting fingers slowly find their way through his thick, black, wavy hair

As he pulls me deeper into his boxcar, at this moment, I realize that Bruno might be some nut wanting to take advantage of me. I am a lady after all, and I can't go around letting strange men, much less a thirty-year-old Italian prisoner of war, go on kissing me in such a passionate way

As soon as I can catch a breadth, I start screaming, "Help! Help! Help! This crazy man has me."

Irene comes running, yelling with wonder in her voice, "What's going on? What's going on?"

I must have scared Bruno because he let's go of me in an instant, and I am able to get away.

I run to meet Irene and say to her, "There is some nut in that boxcar, and he just started kissing on me. I don't know what kind of lady he thinks I am, but we have got to get out of here."

I take one last look back, and I feel my heart flutter.

CHAPTER 51

Is It Love?
(December 1943)

BRUNO, has been coming over to the house almost daily when he is not working. I let him come, because Wanda said, "He is harmless."

She could not stop laughing when I told her the story of him kissing me in his boxcar.

I found out that Bruno is thirty-one. Well, today December 16, 1943, he will be turning thirty-two. I haven't told Mom about him yet. I am not sure what it all means.

Bruno has a car. He bought it when he arrived in Elliston. It is pale yellow, and it is in pretty good shape. He is still just learning to drive and has a long way to go in getting good at it, but Irene and I get into the car even if it can be a bit scary at times. The brakes and gears are always screeching when he drives, and people look as we pass, like the car might fall apart. You know how it is when you're just learning how to drive. Sometimes, when we are supposed to go forwards, we go backwards, and when we are supposed to go backwards, we go forward.

We are going to Helena today to celebrate Bruno's birthday.

Don, Danny, and Wanda are coming with us. Danny has a girlfriend in Helena. Danny liked Irene, but Irene is taken. Danny is good looking. Very dark and very well built. I must say it is a joy to look at him. Bruno doesn't like when I look at him, so I only do it when he isn't looking.

We are all piled on top of one another in the car. We only have one car, so we must sit on laps sometimes if we all want to go. Bruno is not in the right gear as we attempt to leave, so until he figures it out, we just buck along. Irene knows how to drive better than Bruno, but she never says anything, because she doesn't want to unintentionally insult him.

He eventually gets the right gear, and now we are off.

We are planning to go roller-skating and then to the movies, or maybe dancing. We will decide when we get there. Helena has a huge roller-skating rink.

To get to Helena, you must travel over the McDonald Pass, and today it is snowing exceptionally hard. We are in the beginning of Winter.

We are almost to Helena, but it is not an easy ride. Not only do we have to deal with Bruno driving, but the snow is falling down so much that Danny has to stand on the running boards to inform Bruno if he is on the highway, all the while giving him directions. Don must now get on the hood right before town so they can get a better view of the road and make sure we do not pass Helena. This does not bother any of us. We are having so much fun that we just keep going merrily on our way.

We are having a great time in Elliston—those Italians are so nice to all of us. If the law knew Bruno was dating me, being fifteen, and him being a prisoner of war, he would be in prison for a long time.

I think Irene finally told Mom about me and Bruno, and Mom said, "I am coming to see you."

Usually, she just writes, but she is now coming and bringing Bill and Kay. I better enjoy today if Mom is coming soon, because she will probably ruin all my fun.

I am having fun too. So much fun. I have never been so happy in all my life. The Italians don't let us pay for things when we go to Helena. They pay for the roller skating and the movies. They save money on gas though. I will tell you how.

Bruno made himself a key by imprinting one of his boss's keys in malleable soap. Then, he cut out a key from the soap to go to the gas tank of his bosses' car that they used for the railroad.

After cutting the key, the Italian guys use it to steal the gas after dark and fill the tank of Bruno's car—that's how we go to Helena so often; otherwise, we would not be able to go so often. The gas costs, plus miles adds up.

Now, you must realize, I am not the one stealing gas, so God can't be upset with me. I just know about it, and I don't know the boss of the railroad, so I am still in good standing with God. I don't even speak their language, so how would I tell them to stop stealing gas.

Danny and Don speak a little bit of English, and Bruno speaks almost none. He is learning, but he isn't that good yet. He carries an Italian-English dictionary around whenever we are together, otherwise, we point at things, and he learns from being around Americans.

In the Missoula Prison, almost all prisoners were Italian, well, except for the Japanese that were there, so he never had to learn too much English, but now he does, because I am his girlfriend. Well, not officially. I mean, he hasn't asked me yet, but we are always together when we can be, and I have learned one Italian word—Caramia. This is what he calls me now. I am not sure what it means though. He won't tell me.

We quickly learned how to communicate though. Of course, Bruno likes to communicate through a lot of intense kissing, which I must say, I don't mind; he is extremely good at it, and every time he kisses me, I feel instant heat quickly rush throughout my trembling body. It is an amazing feeling—one I have never felt before.

I think, I am in love, but I am not going to tell him that I am. I have learned if a man thinks he has you, then he won't try so hard to keep your affections, so even with the kissing I must set limits. I just wish I did not enjoy it so much, because setting limits means I am also limiting myself.

CHAPTER 52

Mart's Army Letters
(January 1944)

WE heard from Mart last week. This is his letter.

Hi family,

Thought I would write a note to let you all know what I am doing.

When I got to San Diego, I was beat; the whole crew was. That train was miserable, but at every stop, the girls that work on the train would give us sandwiches—everything to keep us going. At some stops, they would offer whisky and beer. I never took any though.

I began my training—six weeks in boot camp in San Diego. We were supposed to stay there six weeks, but they needed men so badly that they rushed us through in four weeks. I was already a partial cook at the time. My experience in California and Reno, cooking and baking, has sure paid off here.

They sent me to a prison where Al Capone served his time—they call it Terminal Island. I spent two months up there cooking for the Navy. Army prisoners were there too.

Then, after two months, officers came and said, "We are looking for two good sailors."

Me, trying to be big and brave sticking my nose in where it shouldn't of been, said, "I will go."

So, they picked me and sent me to San Francisco. They put me out on the docks. The officer told me, "This is your ship, and this is where you are going to spend the rest of your Naval career."

I climbed on that ship and got myself a place to sleep, got myself something to eat, and got myself all squared away.

The next day we took off, and we were out to sea for six days. I was seasick five of the days. I don't know where we went, I was so sick, but I found myself back in San Francisco after the six days.

Then, we had orders that we were going to Hawaii, and boy was I excited. I always wanted to go to Hawaii. I always wanted to see that part of that world.

The next day we headed out to sea, but we were not headed to Hawaii. Plans had changed overnight. We were going to Alaska. There are wars in the Allusion Islands. The Japanese are moving in there and taking over all the islands. I guess they are scared Alaska will be next.

So, that is where I am now. I don't know how long I will be here. I hope all is well in Elliston and Butte. Sounds like you are all having a time.

Mart

CHAPTER 53

Poor John Zebley
(February 1944)

MOM received a letter from the War Department. This is what it said.

John Zebley: Wounded February 3, 1944

Dear Mrs. Zebley: I have just had word from the War Department that your husband, John has been wounded in the Mediterranean Area and am very sorry to learn this. Mrs. Wheeler joins me in extending our sympathy and hope that he has good care and a speedy recovery.

If there is ever any way in which I can be of service to you, here in Washington, please do not hesitate to let me know.

With best wishes,

I am Sincerely yours, B. K. Wheeler

Yes, Mom is in Elliston now. She arrived in the middle of January.

Mom got suspicious that we were having such a good time that her, my brother Bill, and my sister Katherine decided to move to Elliston—to keep us company which ruined all our good times.

We are still having a good time, but we are now indirectly monitored.

I can't tell how Mom is taking the news about John. Sometimes, Mom is hard to read.

Life is going good for Bruno and me, despite Mom being here. Maybe, it is better now that my mom is here, because he is trying to impress her, and he knows that he needs her permission to date me.

Bruno is always trying to kiss me. I like it, and I am letting him do it more often. Every chance he gets off work, he immediately comes around.

It is a good thing I look like I am older when we are together, and that he looks younger, because otherwise, he would get arrested for kissing me so much. He always tries to get something more from me, but I am not that kind of girl, plus, if you give a guy something more, they just leave. I think I am pretty smart at what I am doing.

Mom is okay with us dating. She keeps a close eye, but she seems to be accepting of Bruno. He is always asking me if I am a virgin.

He says, "If you are not a virgin, I am not staying around."

I never give him a straight answer though, because he don't need to know what I do and don't do. Until he decides to stay for sure than I am not giving him any information. He will have to go back to Italy soon. The war is not going to last forever, so he will have to decide what he is going to do about me.

Bruno has been speaking English much more clearly lately, and he is always telling me how nice my body is built. I act like I don't care, but every time he says sexy things like that to me, I just melt down like a marshmallow roasting in hot, flaming campfire.

My hair is light brown now, but it has gotten a little red sparkly in it as of late and is quite long—down past the middle of my slender back.

Bruno keeps telling me that I don't even need to wear a bra—I am built so good— but I do because it is the lady like thing to do, and I don't like to be flopping around all the time.

I think, he might just say that because he wants to take advantage of me, and he thinks it might be easier if I am not wearing a bra. And I think, he wants to see me flopping around all the time, because men like that sort of thing.

I finally was able to get one. When Mom came to Elliston, she noticed I was in need of it and bought me one. My first bra. It sure is nice.

Right before Mom came to live with us, Tony, on a particular warm night, began singing outside Irene's window. Irene and I were sleeping, and we heard him singing love songs outside the window. This happens at least once a week.

Until that day, everywhere we went, it seemed like he was around the corner. I think he was really harmless, but he did think he was in love with Irene. Well, the singing all stopped on that night because of what Tony left at the door. A package. I noticed it the next morning, and I opened it. Inside were a pair of black, sleek, lacey underwear.

The next day Irene gave them back to him straight away, and when I told Bruno what happened, he had a few words with Tony too, so he doesn't come around anymore. Too bad, he did have a nice singing voice.

Before Mom came to Elliston to live, we took a ride to Butte so she could meet Bruno. On that night, we were driving to Butte from Elliston, and Bruno fell asleep. I was driving, and I missed the turn to go to Butte, and we almost ended up in Canada.

Gas is rationed, and if it wasn't for the gas station attendant at the gas station, Bruno probably would have gotten arrested for taking a minor into Canada. Irene was there with us, but she was asleep too.

There always seems to be someone around Bruno and I. Either Irene and now Mom and Kay. Kay is always sneaking behind us following us everywhere we go, putting her poky nose into our personal business.

Danny has been developing such a crush on Irene, and he asked her to marry him, but she was writing to her future husband Warren Younglove. She told Danny that she met him while she was studying in South Dakota to be a telegrapher. She said she was in love with him. Warren is in the Army and is a navigator on one of those huge airplanes that drops bombs.

CHAPTER 54

The Break-Up
(April 1944)

MOM is real nice to all the Italian guys. She likes the ones that know good English, because she can talk to them. Bruno is getting pretty good at it too. She lets them listen to the radio about the war. It has been frigid cold, so we have been sitting around the radio a lot lately.

Anyway, it is April, and today, I found out that Bruno has a couple other girlfriends besides me. It seems, when I think he is going to work, walking past our house, he is really going over to see the boss's daughter. His boss, the railroad boss, and she lives down our street.

So, today I got so spitting mad, and I guess I was exceedingly jealous. I saw him drive to her house and normally, I would just think he was innocently talking to his railroad boss or working, but now, I know what is going on. I know that the boss is not home.

I follow him to the house, and when he is out of sight, I hop in his yellow Model A and quietly start the engine.

I have a plan mind you. My plan is to drive into her dirty outhouse while she is in it.

Speaking of dirty, old outhouses, I must tell you about Kay.

Kay is the worst pest I have ever seen in my life. She always has her nose in everybody's business, teasing them and arguing with them. Not arguing in a bad sort of mean way, but in a way just to irritate us.

Katherine waits in those stinky outhouses, waiting for someone to come out and do their business. Well, when you go out into it, she opens the wooden door and jumps at you, and she likes to do it in the nighttime when it is hard to see. You never know when she is going to surprisingly pop out at you. She also likes to jump at you when you get out of it, then she yells and hollers after you.

The worst thing she has ever done, is put a dead snake outside the door. I don't know how she gets those snakes or where she keeps them, but when she does that, we all chase her around the block like crazy.

O, what an intentional pest she can be, and we always must take her around town with us, but she doesn't get to go to Helena with us—thank goodness. I would never have any fun if she went there. I love Kay. She will always have a special place in my heart, because she is my little sister, and I saw her right after she was born, but that doesn't take away the reality that she is, and probably always will be, a pest.

Kay is not just always into mischief—she is ornery on top of it. Mom doesn't seem to worry about her much though. It is always me she seems to think is going to get into trouble.

Well, back to the Boss's daughter's outhouse. I thought that I needed a better plan, since I might run her over and kill her and then God would really punish me.

I thought the next best thing would to be just run over her outhouse. I begin revving the engine, so he knows I am in his car and outside the house. Then, I begin honking the obnoxious horn. I place the car into gear, and just as I am about to run it into the outhouse, he comes out and sees me wondering what all the crazy commotion is.

He begins yelling at me in Italian, and I cannot understand what he is saying.

He is shaking his fists at me telling me, "Stop! Stop!"

I stop the car right in front of the outhouse and begin laughing widely in his face through the open window.

I think to myself—this is so funny, and I cannot stop laughing. Salty tears stream directly from my angry eyes, down my face, and over my flushed cheeks, and my vibrating tummy is aching.

Bruno opens the car door, grabs me, takes me out of the car, and says, "What you doing?"

I say, "I found out that you were dating her and another girl in Helena. You better make up your mind! You are not going to be kissing on me and two other girls."

He didn't know what to say, because he knew he was caught red handed.

About a month ago, a young boy my age moved into town, and after he moved to town, he kept coming by the house—asking me to go out with him, but I would always tell him that I had a boyfriend.

"I have other options you know, and I no longer consider you my boyfriend," I say to Bruno, and I turn around hastily and run back home.

My eyes fill up with sad, angry tears as I run, but I don't let him see.

THE last couple weeks, ever since the outhouse incident, I decided to become friends with the boy I have been ignoring, and I make sure Bruno sees me with him.

This handsome boy has been taking me up the hill and teaching me how to shoot a gun properly. The first time I tried it, the gun knocked me on my backside and left a nasty black bruise on my right shoulder. This kind boy comforts me by putting his arms around me and bringing me back home. Bruno sees the whole thing.

It has been a while since I talked to Bruno. A couple weeks. He keeps coming over, and I continually send Kay to the door when he does—and Buster.

Buster came with Mom too. Buster is Penny's son. He has short hair, white and brown spots, and black circles around his eyes. He has short little legs and is about three feet long. I love Buster.

When I see Bruno coming down the walk, I will go out the back door with Buster and sit by the outhouse, and sometimes when I see Bruno get out of his car, I will send Buster after him. Buster starts barking widely when I let him at him, and he will meet Bruno at the metal gate. He growls angerly when he meets Bruno at the gate, and when Bruno doesn't stop coming, he sinks his sharp, saliving teeth into Bruno 's pants and shakes him like crazy.

Bruno always tries to kick Buster off his leg, but Buster don't care—he survived a pool of water when he was a baby, so he can survive a few direct kicks in his direction. I laugh so hard as I hide behind the outhouse.

Afterwards, I always give Buster a treat and say, "Good Dog."

Mom always goes out and rescues Bruno.

Bruno will ask her, "Where is she?"

Mom won't tell him where I am.

He asks, "Is she with that other guy?"

Mom doesn't say a word, and he leaves trying to find me.

The last time he came over, Kay went up to Bruno holding a hammer in her hand, and she had gone and hit him right in the foot with it. He called her a lot of names in Italian, and Mom told her, "Go away from him."

It was nice of Kay to stand up for me like that. She is a warrior sometimes.

Well tonight, he came over, and I was not expecting it.

He is coming through the door uninvited and says to me, "Are you seeing that guy?"

I say to him, "What if I am?"

"I left the boss's daughter, and I am just seeing you."

"What about that girl in Helena?"

"I left her too."

"Well, I guess you can come in then."

CHAPTER 55

Bruno's Life (June 1944)

TODAY, Bruno told me a particular story about his life. His life is like a movie in itself. I marvel at all he has been through and done. The sun shines down warmly approving of us closely cuddling by the narrow, flowing, cool creek close to my house.

I ask, "Bruno, what was life like in Italy."

This is what he tells me as he holds me underneath the weeping, bendy willows.

I was born and raised in Liguria, Italy, and I love my mother dearly. Because my father died at a younger age, I feel the need to take care of my mother. I still send her money, even though I don't live there. I want to please her and want her to be happy.

My mother, Romana Andreani, became a widow in 1922. I did not know this for a long while in my life. I thought my father, Pietro Roggia, died in 1916, shortly after I turned six, because my father was no longer living at home. My father was really in an Italian hospital, Quarto Demille, Genova, due to depression, which was caused by leaving his wife and four children to go to war.

My mother and father fell in love years before his death. My father was from a well-to-do family, and my mother was a peasant from Florence, Italy. They wanted to get married, but my grandparents were against it, because my mother was not an aristocrat. She was considered a peasant.

My parents did eventually marry, and my grandparents, on my father's side, had absolutely nothing to do with either one of them; although, I still had a relationship with my grandparents.

When I was five years old, my uncle showed me his wood carving shop. I loved my uncle. He was good to me. He taught me how to carve and work with wood. I love to build. I also loved to wander about Italy, because I loved what I could discover and create from those discoveries.

When I was twelve, I built a little boat. I was so proud of that boat.

One day, as the golden sun was sneaking up past the peak of the mountain range where I grew up, and the rays started waking up the world around my Italian home, I asked my mother, "Mother, can I take you out in the boat I made?"

Mother was surprised at my request, because she did not know that I had made a boat. I think she must have been a little bit worried since I was only twelve, and here I was asking her to take a boat ride with me on a boat that I had made.

If you can picture Mary, we live close to the Mediterranean Sea, and even though my mother is apprehensive about the look of my boat, she comes with me on the water.

As we walk towards the dock, I can sense the fear in my mother, but I can also sense the love she has for me as she takes her first step into the boat. The boat is stained brown. I had worked hard at sanding it just right so it would be smooth and comfortable to sit in. I had even made a wooden chair for mother to sit in so she would find comfort in my little boat.

After I place myself in the boat, I grab the paddles that I had made and paddle a little way out to sea. The sea is always magical to me, and as the sun shines down upon it this morning, the water seemed to be like a sea of glass with sparkly, rainbow diamonds.

Mother and I sail on the water's surface for a short while. The little sail that I made was helping move the boat as the gentle breeze pushes us where we wanted to go.

My mother, at one point, closes her eyes and breaths in the salty air. I think she is surprised that the little boat is still afloat. The satisfaction I feel watching my mother breathe in the ocean air automatically fills my swelling heart with pure happiness and joy.

I can tell that Bruno must love his mother, because he tells this story with such tenderness, so much so that I could see a small, wet tear trickle down his already pink, flushed cheek. Her going out on that boat with him that beautiful morning meant the world to him.

I guess we all want to be loved and accepted by those who we are closest to. We want to know that what we have built in this life was good, and when we put love into our hard work, we want that work to be recognized

Bruno built a boat and took his mother for more than just a sail. Because his mother took a chance and got rid of her fear, she helped her son not only have faith in that little boat, but that single moment in time helped him have faith in the rest of his life. She shaped her son that day and gave him determination and courage to become the man that he was supposed to become.

CHAPTER 56

More Of Bruno's Life in Italy

BRUNO goes on to say, "My mother had five kids—Emilia, who was the oldest, me, Norma, Rosa, and Natalia. Rosa died of influenza just four days after her fourth birthday.

My Father, Pietro Roggia, was still young, not quite thirty-seven when he went into the mental hospital. He was born in Torino Leaternite, Piedmont, Italy on November 20, 1885, and he died in a rest home on February 21, 1922.

My Mother, Romana Francesca Andreani, was born in Scandicci, Florence, Tuscona, Italy on January 24, 1889, and had to support us kids as we grew up.

My Mother told me that she had heard that when my father's father heard the news that a baby boy was born into the family, he was so excited that his watch fell in the toilet. I guess my grandfather was sitting on the toilet when he heard the news.

He was excited there was a boy to carry on the name. See, my father was their only son. Even though they were happy about my birth, my grandparents still wouldn't have anything to do with my parents.

When my grandparents died, they left all their money to my elderly Aunts and the church. They never supported my mother, my sisters, or me at all, even after death.

I did know my grandparents a little. They lived in Florence, and my grandmother would give me a nickel or dime to go spy on my grandfather. She thought he was cheating and wanted me find out for her if he was having an affair.

I followed him around and could see that he was having an affair, but I would come home and tell grandmother, "No, he is not, he is just drinking with the guys."

I don't know if she believed me. Maybe, she wanted to, and sending me out and giving her that report made her feel better. She could have gone out on her own.

My mother cleaned houses to support the family, and me and my sisters were left home, but neighbors always looked out for us. They would kindly check on us often to see if we were okay.

Emilia was born September 17, 1910, in Lerich, San Terenzo, Liguria, Italy. We were all born there.

I was born on December 16, 1911, Norma on July 13, 1913, Rosa on October 16, 1914, and Natalia on December 22, 1915.

After my father's supposed death in 1916, my aunt suggested, to my mother, that I should study to be a priest. I went to priest school for four horrible years, and it was a hard, torturous life. The punishments the sisters gave us were extremely cruel. They used to beat our small hands all the time with narrow stick-like rulers.

Sometimes, the ornery, bad-tempered sisters would make us kneel on the hard, wooden floor, and we were forced to put beans or other hard objects under our knees while we knelt. They would do this when we got into trouble. This was called penance. It didn't take much for us to get into trouble though, because I think they enjoyed seeing us in pain.

Most of us were good and obeyed, but we all had to go through penance, even if we were good. Sometimes, they would crack our knuckles with a board ten to fifteen times until they bled.

The priests were also mean, so I got out of there and finally got away. Four years was too long being there. I hated that life and could never be a priest and live that kind of life. To be a priest in Italy would be unbearable.

Mother always told me that my father died in the Navy when I was six, but rumors were that he died in a mental hospital from sadness because of the war when I was ten. I never knew the truth until later in life. He would have died about the time I got done with the priest school.

After I got away from the priest school, I went to another school. I was there for a few years. I had to go there before I could go in the Navy, because I was still too young to go into the Navy.

Mother worked at this second school, and we would get fed real good there. This school had their own cows from Switzerland. We ate pork, and there were gardens.

By the school was a mountain that we walked up to pick mushrooms. We would take one piece of bread to eat, and as we walked, we would pick sweet fresh fruit. If you ate too much of the wonderful fruit, you would get a belly ache, but oh, it was so delicious.

My mother would say, "Go on you kids and get to picking."

I would take one extra brown cloth sack and fill it with wooden pinecones for the fire. We cooked with charcoal, but pinecones worked too and saved us some money. We would pick chestnuts too and also figs from the fig trees. Then, mother would dry them.

My mother told us, "Never climb a fig tree because the branches, no matter how thick, will always break. Fig trees cannot hold much weight."

One day, when we were picking fruit in those blue mountains, and I knew my mother wasn't watching, I climbed an unstable fig tree.

I soon learned that I will never do that again. I fell and was badly hurt. I recovered well enough though.

As I went to school, I worked with my uncle learning carpentry skills. I also learned to be a baker.

On December 16, 1921, I turned ten, and my mother wanted me to join the Navy. She knew a man who was a captain in the Merchant Marines, and he pretended that my father died in the Navy and told the crew that I was an orphan. If they would have known he was in a mental hospital, they would not have let me in the Navy.

I worked under Mussolini as a ballela, and before I was permitted to join the Merchant Marines, I had to train with the Fascists youth groups. I fired machine guns.

Mussolini was a good leader. He was intelligent and did good for the poor people. He gave land and built houses for the poor. He had wet swamps drained and made useable highways. Mussolini made the rich people invest their money, and he incorporated new sewers and clean water, so people could have better plumbing.

My Uncle was very kind, and he put my name in to work on one of those Merchant Marine ships. I was about fourteen, almost fifteen, when I finally joined the other men. I was still a child really, but living my kind of life, I had to grow up fast.

At fourteen, in order to get into the Merchant Marines, I had to go to sea six months in a sailboat. I had to go to top sail. Many didn't make it that long and were cut from training.

I made it though. It was hard work to climb in rough sea. Every week, we came ashore, and everyone that didn't go up successfully, was cut from the training.

After I passed my training, I started out as a cabin boy. Then, I was promoted to sailor—until I was given the head steward.

Anywhere I went, I always sent money home to support my sisters and my mother, so they could take care the house. I would come home about every two to three years. It was the only time I could.

My first boat trips were in the Mediterranean. My mother didn't want me to go too far when I was just a cabin boy. When I was a sailor, I did all the things a sailor did. Sailors did not work in the kitchen.

At eighteen, I worked the machinery as an engineer. I was there for thirteen years. While I was there, we went to Canada in 1929, and I was on the cargo boat. The cargo boat went all over the world. Wherever there was cargo.

While in Canada, I was on a boat that was half cargo, half passenger. We would take oranges, grapes, and wine from Sicily and take it over to Canada, and in Canada we would pick up grain.

While stationed in Canada, I made money being a bootlegger—up to four thousand dollars. I would buy stuff in Montreal and sell it to the US citizens. We would carry the booze, and the whiskey, which was against the law—people called it—selling black market, but that's where I got extra money to live on.

One night, when I was docked in Canada, and it was so cold, I was walking on the dock and got too close to the near the side of the ship. I instantly fell into the deep, frigid water. I couldn't breathe after my body was immersed in the water. It was so cold, but I managed to climb back into the ship before hypothermia could set in. I thought I was going to meet my maker then.

Before the Spanish Civil war, my ship sunk. There was an enormous, dangerous storm, and we were close to Algeria. I was in the water for thirteen hours before we were rescued.

During this time, we furnished troops in Africa. I was on a troop ship during the war in Abssyania. It was the depression. The war in Ethiopia made everyone happy.

In 1936, when the Spanish civil war started, I was in Spain getting ready to come to the US. Italy requisitioned the boat for the war. We were right there when it started.

We brought in tanks, troops, and ammunitions. People were burning down churches, hanging priests, and dragging nuns behind their cars. It was the communists who were doing it.

Then Mussolini sent 10,000 troops and the navy. The Italians invaded and then turned the area over to the Phalangist under Franco. He was a general in Spanish Africa. It was Italian troops and Germany Air Force that won that war. The Italians put in 50,000 troops and had 10,000 casualties. Italy wanted a free Mediterranean. That is why Mussolini helped Franco. Then, Italy was strong.

Then, I went back in the merchant marines. We worked for England and anybody that would pay us. We would get triple the money when we were in a war zone. We got paid more than when we were on a passenger ship.

We made machines for the Russians and would drop them off and get grain from them. When we went to the communist's countries, we were not allowed to get off the boat. They would only let you off if you wore working clothes, because they didn't want their people to think the fascists were better off than them.

At that time, they were all starving. You could get any Russian girl for a bar of soap. We used to give them anything: socks, shirts, underwear, coats, ties, and any clothes. Their money was not worth anything.

At Danzig, we saw thousands of planes lined up to bomb Poland. The planes were in boxes and then they were put together, and three days later they bombed Poland.

If we would have stayed there another six hours, we would have been right in the middle of the chaos. I was in Danzig when the Germans attacked. Germans telegraphed Italian ships to get out. I was out to sea, and I could see bombardment. I saw many ships sink. I will never be able to get some images out of my mind. Maybe, that is why my father was said to have gone crazy because of what he witnessed.

Then, I came to America, in North Fork, Virginia, with 5,000 tons of copper for England. The Germans sunk ships in the English Channel then went to Italy with another boat going to the U.S.

That is when the war broke out, and I was on the ship that carried the copper. We had three ships docked in North Fork, Virginia.

Then, Mussolini declared war against America, which is why America seized our ships, and everyone on the ships were considered civilian prisoners of war.

I went three times around the world before I was captured in North Folk, Virginia.

We were brought to the concentration camp in Missoula, because Italy was in war with England, and the US. The British ships were outside the harbor waiting to sink us.

We were in the harbor in 1939-1940. The Germans sank the ships. We just put rocks in our machinery, because it was not an army boat, and that is how we became civilian interns.

Before we left to travel to Missoula, almost all the men died on the ship because the meat we bought from the US was bad. We got deathly ill, and at that time everyone was down with dysentery. We stayed on the ship until we were all well, then we were shipped to Fort Missoula.

While we were recovering from the bad meat, I was chief steward on the ship at the time. The captain was from my hometown. The captain couldn't buy contraband, so he made me chief steward, so I could buy the liquor, and we would split the money.

I was in charge of all the silver and possessions on the boat. We were taken to Philadelphia for a couple of days, then Montana. Everyone on my ship went to Fort Missoula. I stayed in Missoula a few years. From 1940-1943.

In Missoula, I had a garden and sold vegetables. I made wooden trunks and things to sell to merchants. I had passes to work in town, but never did go, because I made good money, making things where I was.

A lot of the guys got married in Missoula, they dated the wardens there and were having a ball.

After being in Missoula, we were placed on the railroads to work. This is why I am in Elliston working as first-class carpenter on the Northern Pacific Railroad—because of the manpower shortage.

I work on the bridge crew as a carpenter now. We currently aren't prisoners of war, we are civilians, and the railroad box cars are nicely equipped with showers and beds.

"Then I met you," he says. "When I met you, you never had shoes or socks, I wondered how you survived the cold weather."

Then, I say, "Well, Bruno Roggia, are you glad you met me?"

He turned his head sideways and softly kissed my lips.

I guess that is a yes.

CHAPTER 57

Bad News
(June 27, 1944)

DEAR Mrs. Zebley:

It is with regret that I am writing to confirm the recent telegram informing you of the death of your husband, Technician Fourth Grade John F. Zebley, 39,379,825, Infantry, who was killed in action on 23 May 1944 in Italy.

I fully understand your desire to learn as much as possible regarding the circumstances leading to his death, and I wish that there was more information available to give you. Unfortunately, reports of this nature contain only the briefest details as they are prepared under battle conditions and the means of transmission are limited.

I know the sorrow this message has brought you, and it is my hope that in time the knowledge of his heroic service to his country, even unto death, may be of sustaining comfort to you.

I extend to you my deepest sympathy.

Sincerely yours,

J. A. ULIO Major General,

The Adjutant General.

John is dead. I am not sure how Mom is taking it, but she will get all the money he left to her. John's inheritance will help her and is a great gift that he gave. She is not always in good circumstances financially, but this money will sustain her for years to come.

CHAPTER 58

Letter From Mart
(July 1944)

DEAR Family,

I finally made it to Hawaii.

I spent six months in Alaska. Some of those days were so cold—sixty and seventy below zero.

We chopped the ice off the ship because it was literally so heavy. We took axes and went out there, and some of us had three and four sets of underwear on, plus heavy-duty weather gear, you know.

We had two invasions while stationed there. Fact of the matter is, we took the guns and boats and troops in to Atou and Kisskin Islands where the Japs were supposed to be. Then, we went to Dutch Harbor. That was another one of the islands where the Japs came and dropped one bomb on us. No one was hurt, but we lost two anchors trying to stay in the harbor.

I tell ya, I have never been so cold and miserable. Even colder than good old Butte, Montana. The wind cuts like ice here.

The only animal I ever saw was those red and white foxes running around the islands.

They call the area, Tundra, because every time you would step on to the stuff, it would shake like jelly.

Those islands were so wet and so damp, being so close to the ocean.

We didn't find many Japs there. We brought two submarines up, brought charges on two subs, brought them up and one of them broke in half on the surface, and you could see the men jumping out of them on to the ice-cold water. As soon as they hit the water, they would be dead.

Oh, I will never forget that part of that trip to Alaska. That part will always be in my memory.

Congratulations to Irene on her engagement.

Best wishes to you Mother concerning John's death. I wish I was there with you all.

Mart

CHAPTER 59

Back To Butte
(September 1944)

IRENE decided to marry Warren. They are going to live in Texas, and we are on our way to Butte to buy her clothes for the wedding.

We are leaving Elliston for good. Bruno can't leave, because he is still working. He told me that he would come as soon as possible, but I am going to miss seeing him so much.

Before we left Elliston, Kay asked me, "Will you run away with me?"

I said, "Yeah, okay."

I was not really going to run away from home. Kay is now thirteen, and she just started the sixth grade. Where does she think she is going to go? She has been such a pest lately that I just told her I would run away so she would be quiet about the whole thing.

Much to my surprise, she had the running away idea more planned out than I had supposed. She came to me last night, before we were to leave Elliston, with her specific plans and how we would live. I must say it was well planned, not easy to do if we were actually going to run away, but feasible.

"Kay, I am not really going to run away. Why would I? I do have a beau, and I don't want to rough it like you have planned. Where are you going to go anyway?"

"Anywhere we want to go."

"You are crazy, and I am not running away. We are going back to Butte and getting Irene ready for her special day."

"Everyone is leaving, and soon you will be leaving too, and I will be the only one with Mom."

"You will meet someone too, then you will leave."

I never ran away with her, and I don't think she is ever going to forgive me for it.

We made it safely back to Butte.

TODAY, Kay started school, and Irene is getting ready to leave.

It is October 10, 1944, and Irene is leaving tomorrow to get married to Warren in Texas. They are getting married in San Marcos on the 18th. We won't be attending the wedding, because Texas is a long trip, and we don't have the money for all of us to travel that lengthy distance.

After arriving in Butte from Elliston, we decided to go to the fancy department store to get cloths for Irene's wedding. Before we left, Irene bought her and I each a new, soft black and white fur coat.

What we don't realize, is what the fluffy fur coats are made from until this frightful night as rain pours ferociously down upon us.

Irene and I were extremely proud of our beautiful waist length fur coats as we danced gayly at the local club on our dates with Bruno and Warren. That is until now. As we are now walking home from the club and are caught in a downpour, we notice a familiar stench. The stench becomes more horrid the more it rains, because the more it rains, the more wet these coats get.

We run faster as the smell becomes unbearable.

Finally, the house is in our view, and as we quickly run in and past the door, we take off our coats. We take a good look at our once thought to be beautiful coats.

SKUNK!

Yes, Bruno comes to Butte almost every weekend to see me. One thing about Bruno that I love is he always has on a nice, dark colored dress hat and well-tailored suit when he comes to visit. He always looks so handsome and groomed. I, on the other hand, always have the same worn-out clothes on. There are so many fancier dressed girls in town that have beautiful clothes—it makes me wonder why Bruno keeps coming to court me instead of them.

Sometimes, when Bruno comes to Butte, we go shopping, and not at the thrift stores—at the fancy department stores. At these shopping trips, he always buys me some cozy, warm cotton socks or a pair of comfortable shoes—clothing items that I need, you know. He doesn't want me to be cold. I won't take any expensive gift from him, because Mom would kill me, and she knows everything.

Kay and I live in the Silver Bow Homes with Mom. I guess we are never going to leave the Cabbage Patch area. I must say, they are nice homes though. We live in a three-bedroom apartment, and there is a nice bathroom and kitchen.

Mind you, non-organized and organized crime still exists in this area, and crime is still more prevalent in this area than other areas around town.

Bill will no longer live in Butte tomorrow. He is going off to fight in the tiresome war, so Bruno will sleep in Bill's bed in the future when he comes to Butte. Tonight, he's sleeping on the sofa.

Bill went with us tonight as his and Irene's last hurrah before leaving Butte. He was the one that desperately wanted to go dancing.

I will miss Irene and Bill so much.

Bruno still has not asked me to marry him. I think he is seeing someone in Helena again, but I cannot be sure.

After we come inside from the pouring rain, waiting for the rain to subside so we can dispose of the smelly skunk culprits, we enjoy telling stories, sitting around the table drinking apple cider, and are having a good time when Bruno realizes that he is out of cigarettes. There is no paper to roll the tobacco in, so we decide to use some newspaper.

Well, we should have known better.

I carefully light the printed newspaper cigarette after rolling the tobacco in the inky paper, and it suddenly bursts into combustible flames. As an automatic reaction, I drop the fast-burning cigarette on the already toxic coat before it can burn my fingers right off, and instantly, the almost dry coat lights on fire. We begin screaming, not realizing how flammable the coat is.

Bruno becomes our hero as he grabs a nearby pail of water on the counter used for cleaning and extinguishes the orange and yellow flames by immediately pouring the cool water on them.

We decide the coats need to be thrown away so no one will ever again have to encounter such a horrible stench, and since the rain has died down considerably, we decide to take the coats out to the trash before the entire house becomes infected with burnt skunk.

We soon realize, after placing the coats in the trash, there is a possibility they will stink up the entire neighborhood, so we take them to the backyard, dig a four-foot-deep narrow hole, and happily place the coats in. Bill makes sure to cover them with dark wet dirt.

"Good riddance!" We all exclaim with laughter knowing that this memory will go down in our history as one to remember.

Along with the coat story, I must rightly inform you of why we were required to come home early from dancing.

We went dancing in Meaderville, which is up above Finn Town. Meaderville is where the Italians live. Bill wanted to go dancing and gambling, and Meaderville has gambling. Bill is eighteen now and likes to come with us on dates. Well, Bill had a little too much playful fun and unintentionally got into a fight before we came home.

Warren and Bruno tried to help Bill, and the result was that we got thrown out of the dance hall without much damage.

So, there are many reasons this night will be remembered.

I will miss Bill when he leaves to go to fight with the Marines.

CHAPTER 60

December 1944

I haven't talked to, or seen, Bruno for a couple weeks—until today, and he was not too happy with me. He was here in Butte a couple of weeks ago visiting with me and found out I was going out with a guy named Joe.

Joe had been stationed here for about a month, and when I was out one night with my friends, he noticed me and asked, "Do you want to go to the movies tomorrow night."

I say to him, "Sure."

So, we went to the movies a few times during the week. I mean, it has been a whole year, and Bruno has not mentioned even once whether he is going to marry me, and I haven't seen or heard from him for two weeks now because of Joe.

Does he really think I am going to just sit around and wait for him when he has given me no reason to wait. I don't think so!

BRUNO is here, and it is the weekend. Bruno is staying with us, and we are now dancing and gambling in Meaderville. We get done dancing when who suddenly appears?

Of course, Joe.

Joe naturally puts his arm around me, and asks, "When are you going to go marry me?"

Before I can answer or have any words at all come to the tip of my tongue, Bruno sharply asks Joe, "Who are you?"

"I am Joe, and I am from South Dakota. I live on a wheat farm, and I am going to marry this beautiful, amazing, sexy woman."

Joe points to me, and I am immediately dumbfounded.

Joe had mentioned this the other night, but I thought he was just teasing. I was having fun with him, but I don't want to go live in South Dakota.

Bruno angrily grabs my arm and quickly pulls me outside.

"Do you want to marry that guy?"

"What if I do? It is not like this is the first time anyone has asked me to marry them. And you never even speak of it, so what do you think, I am just going to sit around waiting for you to ask me? I don't think so!"

I mean, I really didn't want to marry this guy, but I am trying to make Bruno jealous, because he hasn't asked me. Bruno is so fire burning mad, he quickly gets in his car, angrily slams the car door, and speedily drives off.

IT has been more than a week ago that this escapade happened, and here is Bruno now knocking at my door again. Until today, I didn't know where he drove off too.

He tells me today after I open the door and ask, "Well, where have you been?"

"I drove to Elliston, and I was so fiery mad, I stupidly drove into a nearby mountain and instantly wrecked my car."

I suddenly notice the car and can see that it is pretty badly beat up. I must say, I am glad that he got mad.

"Are you still seeing that guy?"

"I only saw him a few times, and there is no way I am going to South Dakota."

"You better make up your mind soon though, because I am not going to wait around forever."

He stayed all weekend, and we haven't spoken much to each other. I am not giving in. I am a good woman, and there are plenty of available men that want me to be their wife.

CHAPTER 61

Mart Gets Married
(February 27, 1945)

WE received another letter from Mart.

Dear Family,

Well, I had quite the time in Hawaii.

There are a couple stories I need to share.

The islands sure are beautiful; even more so than I imagined. Coming from Alaska and going to the islands was quite the change in weather. I thought the heat was going to kill me until my body got adjusted.

We stayed in a nice place there—the Royal Hawaiian. It was on the beach, and it was only 25 cents a night. All I had to do was buy some sheets and keep my room clean. What a beautiful, beautiful place it is.

The Hawaii natives are so friendly too. There were thousands and thousands of troops there, so there wasn't much time to find a girl. I kept thinking about Doris anyways. We were writing often.

At one time, I was in a fog bank hiding along the Jap coast and here was a Japanese cruiser laying there. She spotted us, and she shot about three big shells at us. We happened to escape from that. We got away and went to Honolulu.

From there, we went to the Gouda Chanel and that is where the Japs were really bombing. At one time, there were ninety Japanese torpedo planes coming down the slot there, just sinking everything that was in their way. There was more than ten of our transports blown up and sent to the bottom of the ocean. They called it Gouda Chanel and Toerage Iron Babe Bottom, because the bay was just lined and lined with ships.

One night, while I was there, I was asked to go to the beach and take a Higgins boat and pick up the payroll. The payroll for the ship was $80,000. So, brave me, I took this boat and a couple of gunners with me over on the beach. I pick up the payroll, and they put a set of handcuffs on me and handcuff me to the satchel of money.

I got back down the beach and looked for my ship, and my ship was gone. They had a hurry up call, and she left for three days, and there I was sitting in a foxhole with the Marines for three days with that satchel of money handcuffed on my wrist.

Well, I'll tell you, if that wasn't a thing to behold now sitting in the bottom of the foxholes in a hatful of water and mud. And those land crabs would crawl all over me at night. Them suckers were about eight or ten inches across. They had big, long arms for crabs, and they take a nip out of you, and they get a hold of you real good.

All the while, I was getting nipped by land crabs, there was a Jap sitting about 150 feet on the beach inside the fog and trees calling us all kind of names. He called Roosevelt all kinds of names. I won't mention the kinds of names, but all night long you could hear him.

Occasionally, one of them Japs would come out of the bush, thinking they were going to make a name for themselves making Hairy Carrie or whatever they called it. Bansi, that is what they call it—Bansi.

They charged, and those Marines would blow them to bits. The Marines have great big guns called BAR's, and they would just cut everything in half. Anyhow, I stayed there for three days. The ship came back and picked me up. I took the money to the ship, we distributed it, and had to go back for two days more.

While in Hawaii, a pilot asked me if I wanted to take a ride with him in his P38. Those planes are fast.

I said, "Sure."

So, he put me in the jump seat behind him and off we went.

That plane just churned my insides up one side and down the other, and when we got up in the air, he tested his guns. When he fired those cannons, I thought we'd hit a brick wall the way we'd stop in the mid-air like that. Well, we really didn't stop, but it felt like it.

He brought me back down, and I am lucky I didn't throw my insides up. Well, that is the last spider plane I will accept to go up in. Haha.

We were soon transferred to the Solomon Islands. The Marines were having a tough time of it there. There were just a few destroyers and a couple of battleships. So many ships are still sunk in Pearl Harbor. None have been raised up yet. We had to dodge all the time, island to island, refueling wherever we could get it.

Finally, they took pity on us, and we went on our way to Australia. We spent two weeks in Australia. It was like seeing the world again. What a beautiful place and beautiful people. You never saw, you never talked to, or had anything to do with such wonderful people in all your life.

New Zealand was right across the straits from Australia, and we were over there for a short while, but those people were pretty uppity, they didn't like servicemen. But we had a good time in Australia.

From there, we went back to the Solomon Islands.

Our ship was a destroyer, and it packed 85 mines. Those mines looked like porcupine quills sticking out of them. When you go down the deck and take a hammer and ping, ping, ping; those mines make music. Of course, they wouldn't go off unless they were in the water.

I have news. I married a girl. We were married in San Francisco, California. Her name is Doris Diller. Of course, you all know her. Well, now it is Doris Miller. She sure looked pretty in white. I think I fell in love with Doris the first time we met so many years ago. I am happy, and I hope you all are too.

I hope to see you all soon as the war seems to be dying.

Mart

CHAPTER 62

Do I Stay, Or Do I Go? It's Up To You (March 1945)

IT is March 14, 1945, and today is my wedding day. While Bruno was deciding what he wanted concerning me, I was meeting this boy from New York at the Train Depot on Wyoming Street. He is from England, but he is stationed in New York.

My friend and I have been visiting the train depot the past four weeks—watching and waiting for the soldiers to get off the train. Most of them had a three-hour wait until the train started again, so we were able to meet quite a few soldiers.

I met this soldier named Tom, and we started to visit with one another. He liked me—I could tell, and I have to say, he was interesting.

HE says to me, "Here is my address, would you write to me?"

He gives me his address, and I say, "Sure."

"How long are you in Butte for?"

Tom is much closer to my own age than Bruno is.

THE STORYBOOK ADVENTURES OF MARY MILLER 317

"I am on leave for a week."

"Where are you staying?"

"I am not sure."

I knew Bruno would be in town this weekend, and it was just Tuesday, so I thought I would ask Tom if he wanted to stay with us.

I invite Tom saying, "Do you want to stay with us for that week, I could show you around town."

He eagerly says, "I would love that!"

I found out on the way to Silver Bow Homes that Tom was stationed in New York.

I know that Bruno is coming this weekend, and that is why I am doing what I am doing. I mean, he still has not asked me to marry him, and it has been a whole year and a half since we have been together.

The only reason he is not marrying me, is because he still wants to play the field. I know he is seeing some other women in Helena and Elliston. He thinks he can get what he needs from them and then come back to me—his sweet, innocent girl in Butte.

I'll show him.

I am sure that God doesn't mind if I do this act of deceit, because how else will I get Bruno to commit. He thinks he has me in his back pocket while he goes off with those other easy women. I am going to show him that he does not have me securely in his pocket.

Mom is happy to have Tom staying with us. Tom and I have been having fun the last few days. We have walked around town, and he took me to The Gardens. We even went dancing one night. I have enjoyed my time with Tom, and if he lived here in Butte, I imagine, he would be more of a real possible competition for Bruno, but I don't want to leave Butte. I'm only sixteen after all.

It is Saturday, and Bruno is just showing up. He is not excited to see Tom.

"Who is this guy?"

"This is Tom. We met on Tuesday at the train depot."

"Well, I am here now, so he can go stay somewhere else."

"He is not going to stay somewhere else, he is staying right here, in this apartment, and if you don't like it, you can go back to Helena."

∞

BRUNO is staying and not going back to Helena. I think even Bruno can recognize that Tom is handsome and would be quite the catch for me, especially, since he is closer to my age.

Bruno and Tom have been here at the apartment all day, and now we are all going to the movies.

The Movie is "Casablanca." I think an appropriate one for tonight.

We are at the movies, and Bruno is on one side of me, and Tom is on the other side. They are both glaring at each other and have been acting this way during the entire movie. I am not worried about a thing though. I am just watching and enjoying the movie.

What a great movie. I am sure every time I see this movie from now on until I die, I will remember this monumental night.

∞

THE movie is over, and we are now home. We walked home in complete and utter silence. After we arrive home, and before we go into the house, Bruno takes my arm and leads me away from Tom until we are further outside.

Tom comes after us, asking me, "Is everything all right Mary?"

I say, "Sure." And wave my hand for him to go inside.

Bruno says to me, "What are you doing with that guy?"

"It is none of your business. It is not like you own me. You think you can come here and date me while you date all those other women, and I am still going to be here waiting. Well, Bruno Dominick Cipriano Roggia, I am not."

"I can get any woman I want. I had women all over the world, wherever we docked there would be some woman."

Then he says, "I always got what I wanted too."

He is right, I remember him telling me a few stories about the women he could have married. He told me that when he was in Norway, the women were all light colored with light hair, and he was dark, and he always had the time of his life there. He said he and the guys would dance all the time in those countries, and the girls would bring the guy's home to the parents and many of the parents wanted their daughters to be taken home to other countries.

He was engaged to a girl in North Fork, Virginia before he met me—when he was docked there. He knew her for about three months. He told me that the guys from the boat took silver from the ships and gave it to this gal's father to hold for them.

He told the father that he would come back and marry his daughter when he was settled, but until then, if he could send the silver when he called for it. The father agreed.

He was never planning on marrying his daughter, he just needed somewhere to put the silver. Naturally, the father never did give the silver back when Bruno sent for it.

He was also engaged to a gal in Italy.

But now he is telling me about one I never knew about.

"You know Mary, in Argentina, we were loading wheat onto our ship, and we were there a couple months. This one farmer had large fields of wheat, and the farmer wanted me to marry his daughter, but I just couldn't, because I wasn't ready."

I say to him with anger and jealousy, "Well, you could have had your life set and lived high on the hog on a wheat farm, and here I am worth nothing. Why would you choose to marry me, I guess?"

Finally, Bruno says, "I am tired of waiting. The reason I guess I never got married is because it never seemed right. But now it seems right. Now, I am ready. I suppose I never really got what I wanted, because I never had you. And you are worth something. You might not have money, but that is not why I love you. You are not like all the women I have been with. You are special in a way I just can't explain or understand, and I guess I was just afraid to do it. I mean, I was afraid to ask you to marry me, but I want you to be mine and no one else's."

I cannot believe what I am hearing. I must pinch my side just to make sure I am not dreaming.

"You probably just want to marry me, so you can get your citizenship papers and live in the States."

"Mary, I would not want to live in the States if I could not have you as my wife. You are the only one for me. I have traveled around the world, and not once did I feel about anyone the way I feel about you. Not once did anyone stir my heart strings the way you drive mine crazy. You are stubborn as an old mule, but you are as nice, kind, and beautiful as an angel with golden wings and a bright halo."

I can't stop the wide smile that I can feel quickly spread across my thin lips.

In this tender, romantic moment, Tom comes out of the door and says, "I want to marry you, Mary."

Tom must have been listening to the whole conversation, when suddenly, Bruno jumps at Tom and starts to throw a punch, but I intervene and get in between them.

I turn to Tom and say, "Tom, please, go inside."

Tom goes inside, and Bruno turns me towards him as he grabs my hands and says, "You marry me, or I go back to Italy."

Then he explains, "Do you want to know what Caramia means."

I really wanted to know, and I was so excited that he was finally going to tell me.

I nod my head.

"It means, My Love. I have never called anyone that name, but you. I might have been around the world a few times, and I might have had many chances at love, but you are my only Caramia. You are my only love."

Okay, so how could I have written my love story any better than that? How could I say no when that is all I have ever hoped for?

I lean into him as he leans into me, and my lips meet against his, and never have we had a kiss so sweet. I feel him wrap his arms tightly around me as he squeezes me closer to him. I can feel his thumping heart beating directly next to my fluttering heart, and I bring my arms around his thick neck as my fingers find his dark, thick hair.

This frozen moment in time seems to be lasting forever, even though in reality it is just a few precious unforgettable moments. A few sweet moments, I shall never forget.

"Well," I say as I pull slightly away while looking up into his dark, brown eyes, "Instead of spending all that money to go back to Italy, you might as well just stay here."

He smiles, and then we kiss again. A beautiful, sweet, magical, haunting kiss.

CHAPTER 63

The Big Day
(March 14, 1945)

BACK to the big day.

I know today is not going to be an extremely elaborate affair, but one thing I have learned about my life is that it is simple. I like it that way. I don't need riches or fancy things to be happy. I am sure it is nice to have a few things in life, but I am happy right now, and I have nothing. So, I know you can be happy with nothing.

Bruno and I are going to the department store to pick out my wedding suit. I am not getting a white wedding dress because it is short notice and too expensive. Bruno is going to buy my suit though. Bruno is driving.

He wanted to go to Salt Lake for a honeymoon, but I don't know what to expect, so I am sort of afraid to leave my mom. I might need her after this day is over. Bruno won't be staying long—he is getting called out to duty which is why we must get married today. He wants to make sure, while he is gone, that I don't change my mind.

There are many suits to pick from.

Bruno asks, "Which one do you want?"

"This one," I tell him happily.

The magnificent suit is a light medium blue suit. The light, free flowing blouse is a dusty rose color and there is rose-colored, ankle strapped high heels to go with it. I have never had such a striking outfit.

Bruno says, "You will look beautiful in that."

I can't believe I am getting that outfit. I still feel like I am dreaming.

Bruno says, "Let's go get the ring."

We walk a little down Park Street to the jewelry store. I knew that I could not spend so much money, so when Bruno told me to pick one out, I tried to be reasonable.

"This one," I say.

The ring is so glorious and admirable. I still cannot believe I will have such an impressive piece of jewelry. It is worth a whole $35.00.

We are now at the furniture store. Bruno is picking out a bed, and I have never thought about having such a bed, much less sleeping in one so nice. He pays cash for it. A hundred-dollar bill. I never knew he had so much money. He even bought sheets, some pillows, and a soft, but firm mattress.

He tells the sales associate, "Send it today to our address."

Then Bruno gives the man my address.

We are now leaving the store and are going to pick up Mom and Kay. Mom must sign the papers for the marriage, since I am only sixteen. I am almost seventeen, but you need to be eighteen to get married without having your parent sign the papers.

We are now at the courthouse, and we forgot to get a corsage. We are waiting for the judge in a little 25X25 foot room with a few chairs in it. The judge is walking in and the first thing I notice is that he is blind. A little dog came in with him. I guess the dog might be to help him get around.

Of course, the judge is blind—just another interesting note to add to my story.

Ha ha!

The Judge gives Mom the paper she needs to sign, so I can get married. It is like she is giving me away. I guess she really is.

The judge then asks, "Do you have a corsage?"

Bruno and I look at each other speechless as to what is happening, and we both say, "No."

The judge then reaches into a cabinet by the wall and pulls out a corsage. It is not a real one, but it looks like it will match the outfit.

The judge begins the normal speech we all get when there is a wedding.

"Do you take this person to be your lawful wedded spouse to love and to hold through sickness and health until you both shall live?"

I sit here thinking as Bruno is saying, "I do." What a big step I am taking, and I am still so young. My whole life is ahead of me, and what kind of life will that be? I hope it is a good one. I hope I will find happiness and joy as I live this life that I am only given once to live. Which makes me wonder, is this all there is? Will I always be with this man, and what about when we die? I don't want to have it end when we die. I want to be with Bruno forever.

"God, how do I have that happen," I ask silently in my imaginative brain. "How can Bruno and I be together forever?"

I will have to find out the answer to that question later, because the judge is telling me it is my turn to say, I do.

After I say, "I do," Bruno slides the ring onto my finger, and the judge says, "You may kiss the bride."

This is the part I like the most.

Bruno carefully and lovingly grabs firmly a hold of my small hands as he happily leans into me, and we finally seal our relationship, and so far, experiences up with a magical kiss.

After we lovingly kiss, the judge says, "Go next door, and get a picture taken."

We instantly follow the judge's directions, and when we arrive next door, the photographer tells us to sit down as he gives us beautiful rainbow-colored flowers. They are exceptionally beautiful and perfect as I remember all the promises Bruno and I had just minutes before made to one another. Roses. One of my favorites.

AFTER the wedding, we go to a fancy restaurant called, Howard's Restaurant, which is located on the flats. It is supper time, and we order spaghetti and chicken. So good. I don't often eat out, so this dinner is a special treat in itself.

After we drop everyone off to the house, I say to Bruno, "We should go to the movies."

I could tell he wants to do something else, but I must say, I am scared.

We watch the show three times before Bruno tries to get me out of the show to go home, but I do not want to go home.

After the third time Bruno says frustrated, "We are going home!"

I say, "Well, I guess we can go home now."

After we arrive home, I notice that everyone has left the apartment. I thought that maybe, I would have my own home when I got married, but with Bruno going to be gone for a few months, we thought it would make sense for me to stay with Mom.

We walk slowly through the house, and I tell Bruno to wait in the living room until I am ready. Bruno had previously bought me some sexy, nighty clothes when we were at the department store and had them in on the bed in a nice, fancy box waiting for me to put them on.

I go into our bedroom and attempt to put them on when I realize the holes in the outfit are all sewed together. O, I am sure this was Kay's malicious doing.

So, now, I have nothing to wear but what I have on.

Through the door, I tell Bruno what has happened, but he does not seem to care, and I open the door as he enters the bedroom.

"I know my way around a women's body," he says with confidence as he gently picks me up and carries me to the new, comfortable, green sheeted double bed.

As he lays me on top of the bed, we hear a crunch. I quickly get off the bed and take the top green emerald cover off and can see that underneath it is a bed full of cracker crumbs, rocks, and soft sand.

"Kay again," I say out loud. "I can just kill her."

For some strange reason though, I just start to laugh uncontrollably.

Bruno asks curiously, "What is so funny?"

We look at each other, then he begins laughing too.

Well, that broke the ice, and everything just went natural after that.

A wonderful night, and a wonderful life.

Marriage of Mary Miller to Bruno Roggia

CONCLUSION

THE reason I came to this family is to teach my posterity how to continue building on top of a sure foundation that is built from generations of courageous ancestors learning and growing to be the best they know how to be.

No matter what circumstances we are placed in—in this life, it's our spirit, it's who we are on the inside that determines how we end up living and who we eventually turn out to be. We all have choices to make, and we are responsible for those choices. We are the makers of our own destinies.

I know why I came to this family. By my age, I hope I have it figured out. I have two children, 10 grandchildren and 29 great-grandchildren, and because I've brought them into this world and showed them the way, they know and love God. That's the most important role I could ever play—helping my posterity love God.

You could say, I lived happily ever after, and instead of being a dress designer, I was a house and yard designer. Bruno and I remodeled many homes and yards.

Bruno was a good husband and a good father—the best he knew how to be. He worked hard and provided for us.

I don't regret anything in my life. In fact, I think I have lived a wonderful, full life. I can't complain. I raised a wonderful daughter, who is a strong confident woman, and I have a successful son. I have grandchildren who love the Lord, so who could ask for more.

AFTERWORD

Mary Roggia's Thoughts To Her
Children—Rick and Linda

YOU are both good kids. I never had any trouble with you like parents do now. You never had your own car to run around in, never had all that money to spend like kids do now, and you were both supervised closely. I know that you complained about our house rules when you were younger, but I hope now you see now that we did it for your own good. Your dad and I were learning too.

As the years go by, there's more bad influences around your kids and grandkids, they are going to have quite a struggle because you can't keep a tight little circle around them.

They're going to get out and mingle, and there will be other influences in their life that you won't want them to be around, but you will be able to help them because of your life experiences. Most the time, you will have to wait until they come to you for advice.

You will see as you and your kids get older and live life that the problems you had and have with them might be like the ones, we had with you. You will then understand why your father was so tough with you and why he made you do certain things. You will understand why he wanted you to study, because you will have taken the same actions, or maybe, take different actions because you learned a better way.

It's a tough job raising kids, that is all I can say. When they are small, they are innocent, and as they grow you must allow them to live in this, sometimes, cruel world.

You worry about them when they are on their own and when they get married. When they get married, you worry twice as much. You wonder and hope they are getting along with their spouse and whether this one or that one is happy. You can't butt into their business or ask them what is going on because they turn around and say, "It is none of your business."

Then along comes the grandkids, and you figure you don't have to worry about them, because they have parents, but you worry about them the same—probably more so than your own kids. You hope they are growing up alright, and you worry about whether they are getting along with their parents. You see the parents do things you wish they wouldn't concerning them, but you can't say anything.

You think I am talking silly, but just wait.

I hope you see that being a parent is not easy. You might say to yourself when you are my age, "How did I get through it all?"

As your life comes closer to its end, hopefully you will see that your posterity came out well-adjusted, then you will say, "I did a pretty good job."

But your kids aren't going to think that way until they have a family of their own—just a mean old mama and daddy. You just wait. Ha Ha! Then, you'll give me a pat on the back and say, "Mom, you weren't so bad after all."

Just a little bit of knowledge from your old mother.

LESSONS LEARNED

To All My Grandchildren

I learned from my ancestors that no matter how bad off you think you are, you're not that bad off. There is always someone worse off than you. We were raised to help and be generous with other people.

I learned how to be tough, struggle through, and make a go of life, no matter how hard it is. Take it from me—you must be tough, and struggle through it.

I learned to have a strong mind. My mom taught me by example. If she could do it, I could do anything. Don't let anything get you down. Remember that tomorrow is a new day, and you can make it a better one than the previous day.

I learned to be honest. When you are honest, life will be honest with you.

I learned that reading ignites your memory and keeps your brain active. Remember to read. Reading is an activity I enjoyed throughout my life. You can have all the education in the world, but if you don't sit down and read a book once a while, you'll never learn anything. I love reading about history and autobiographies and a nice love story occasionally; mostly, a good love story. Ha, Ha.

I learned to cultivate a flower garden. Working in the garden, standing at the window and watching my flowers grow has brought such joy in my life. I recommend you grow something.

My advice for my granddaughter's and great-granddaughter's is ...

1. Be morally clean. Don't let a man sweet talk you into sex, you'll regret it. It never is worth it if you give in. If you can wait, it will be the sweetest thing in the world; otherwise, you will be sorry that you gave something precious away to someone who isn't so precious.

2. Get an education or develop a trade. You will want to have some sort of independence after you are married.

3. Let men think it is their idea. I think women are 99% smarter than men, but just don't let them think so. Let them think that every idea you had is theirs. Take it from me—Bruno had it made. If I wanted something, I would plant the idea in Bruno's mind, and slow, but sure, it was his idea eventually, and he would say, "Maybe, we better do this. I think it's a good idea." In everything let them think it's their idea.

4. Be the parent. I never used any discipline with the kids. I don't remember ever spanking. Bruno would use the discipline, but he never hit anyone. He used his voice with authority, and when he said something—that was law. I don't believe in kids telling parents what to do, that is the worst thing of all. If you can't be strong enough to stand up to your kids and tell them that you're the boss, then it's too late.

5. Look nice. I have always kept myself looking nice. It doesn't matter what other people think, only what you think about yourself. People say, why do you bother to get your hair done, why do you bother with the clothes, or why do you take so much time in keeping yourself up—you don't have to impress anybody?

I think if you are going to impress anybody, it should be yourself. You must have pride in yourself. If you don't have pride in yourself, no one else is going to.

Look nice, instead of looking like everyone else. Try to be an individual, and don't follow the pattern of everyone else. Always be neat, clean, and look your best—wherever you go. Don't look like a scrounge and follow the crowd. Look nice and stand out. You will feel good about yourself if you do.

6. Read the Bible. I hope you carry on the generations of my ancestors that had a Bible, and I hope you read it and use something out of it every day to live by. It will show you what to do if you have any problems. Open it up, read it, and it'll tell you the truth and help you find the answers to your troubles.

   You're going to need the scriptures with all the things happening in the world. Wherever you go, whatever you do, there will be people that will make fun of you because you do read the good book. Don't worry about them—read it anyways and believe what you read. People might mock you, but if you stick to it, you'll come out okay. The scriptures guide us to the Lord.

7. Speak your mind when prompted. I tried not to be the meddling mother-in-law, but sometimes it's hard not to say something. If there is something you want to say to your mother-in-law, say it, and if not, don't. I never wanted to be one of those mothers-in-law that had her nose into everybody's business all the time. I wouldn't want anyone do that to me.

   I never had a mother-in-law that lived in this country. The one I had was nice to me. I wish she could have been around more and lived closer, because I could have gotten to know her, and maybe, we would have gotten along good. Who knows, maybe, we wouldn't have either. When we went to Italy my mother-in-law treated me better than she did Bruno. Too bad she and Bruno's sisters were so far away, we could have had another family, because they treated me like one. Even though I couldn't understand them, I thought of them like family.

8. Record your history. I'm recording my history, because I want my generations to learn something from my experiences. If anything I say or have done in my life can help them make good choices, than everything I have gone through was worth it. My purpose on earth would be fulfilled.

9. Let your family know you love them. I want my family to know that I love them, and when I leave this earth, I will be rooting for them on the other side. The reason I came here was to teach, and I feel confident that I did.

MARY MILLER'S ADVENTURES
LEAD HER TO HER OWN STORY BOOK ENDING
Underneath my bed is a place I hide often when I'm in trouble ...
Oh No! I'm dying. God is Punishing me...

The Halloween Prank
"It's time Becky, are you ready?" I ask her.
"Mary, I am sorry. I don't think I am going to do it."
"Why not," I ask disappointed and a little angry.
"What if we get caught?"
"O, we won't get caught, you, sissy. No
one is at the school this late."
"Sorry, Mary, I'm just not going to help you. I
will watch you from a distance though."
"No matter," I say. "I'm not a sissy and won't back out of
my word, even if my word is to myself. It is important, I
think, to keep the promises you make to yourself."

The Fight
I am so fed up and have had enough of her making fun
of me about the way I dress, and about how poor I am,
so I stand up and I say with boldness in my voice to Miss
Prissy, "I dare you to say that again to me Miss Prissy."
"Mary, Mary quite contrary dresses like a canary.
Halloween is not today Mary, it is in a couple of
weeks, but I see you dressed up for it today."
Then she adds, "And Mary has to sell popcorn at
Christmas because she is so poor and dirty."
Well, I must say I am surprised she said it again
and then went and added something to it.
I get right up in her face, and I say to her, "You might be
rich Miss Prissy, but I know I can beat you in a fight.

The Kiss

I don't know how long we have been kissing, but I feel lost
to the real world, and find that I am enjoying my present
predicament. I find myself easily kissing him back with just
as much determination and force. My able hands seem to
find their way up to and then over his wide shoulders. My
wanting fingers slowly find their way through his thick,
black, wavy hair. As he pulls me deeper into his boxcar, at
this moment, I realize that Bruno might be some nut wanting
to take advantage of me. I am a lady after all, and I can't go
around letting strange men, much less a thirty-year-old Italian
prisoner of war, go on kissing me in such a passionate way.

As soon as I can catch a breadth, I start screaming,
"Help! Help! Help! This crazy man has me."

THE STORYBOOK ADVENTURES OF MARY MILLER
MONTANA WOMEN
TRUE FAITH TRUE DEVOTION
ONE GENERATION AT A TIME

BASED ON THE TRUE EVENTS OF MARY JANETTE MILLER'S LIFE

Genre: Non-Fiction Romance Coming of Age Novel, Based on a True Story.

This manuscript is a True Story Novel based on the life of my grand-mother growing up in Butte, Montana in the early 1900's. This story covers WWI, WWII, the struggles and joys of growing up in the building of a famous city in the United States, the Great Depression, and lessons about love conquering all.

This book is unique in that it involves true history, true love, and overcoming challenges. It is a true story written in novel form. It engages the reader, because it brings them into a world full of fantasy and real-life challenges. It is a story comparable to Anne of Green Gables, except it is based on the real-life story of a real American young girl who defeated all the challenges she faced.

Name: Charity Lovshin.

Email: Charitykohler@gmail.com

Printed in the United States
by Baker & Taylor Publisher Services